CHARTER SCHOOLS, RACE, AND URBAN SPACE

Charter schools have been promoted as an equitable and innovative solution to the problems plaguing urban schools. Advocates claim that charter schools benefit working-class students of color by offering them access to a "portfolio" of school choices. In *Charter Schools, Race, and Urban Space*, Kristen Buras presents a very different account. Her case study of New Orleans—where veteran teachers were fired en masse and the nation's first all-charter school district was developed— shows that such reform is less about the needs of racially oppressed communities and more about the production of an urban space economy in which white entrepreneurs capitalize on black children and neighborhoods.

In this revealing book, Buras draws on critical theories of race, political economy, and space, as well as a decade of research on the ground to expose the criminal dispossession of black teachers and students who have contributed to New Orleans' culture and history. Mapping federal, state, and local policy networks, she shows how the city's landscape has been reshaped by a strategic venture to privatize public education. She likewise chronicles grassroots efforts to defend historic schools and neighborhoods against this assault, revealing a commitment to equity and place and articulating a vision of change that is sure to inspire heated debate among communities nationwide.

Kristen L. Buras is an associate professor in the Department of Educational Policy Studies at Georgia State University. She is the author of *Rightist Multiculturalism* and coeditor of *The Subaltern Speak*. She is also cofounder and director of Urban South Grassroots Research Collective for Public Education.

CHARTER SCHOOLS, RACE, AND URBAN SPACE

Where the Market Meets Grassroots Resistance

Kristen L. Buras

Routledge
Taylor & Francis Group

NEW YORK AND LONDON

First published 2015
by Routledge
711 Third Avenue, New York, NY 10017

and by Routledge
2 Park Square, Milton Park, Abingdon, Oxon, OX14 4RN

Routledge is an imprint of the Taylor & Francis Group, an informa business

© 2015 Taylor & Francis

Library of Congress Cataloging-in-Publication Data

Buras, Kristen L.
Charter schools, race, and urban space: where the market meets grassroots
    resistance / Kristen L. Buras.
        pages cm. — (The critical educator)
    Includes bibliographical references and index.
    1. Charter schools—Louisiana—New Orleans.   2. Public schools—
Louisiana—New Orleans.   3. Urban schools—Louisiana—New Orleans.
4. Education and state—Louisiana—New Orleans.   5. Business and
education—Louisiana—New Orleans.   6. Education—Louisiana—
New Orleans—Citizen participation.   7. Community and school—
Louisiana—New Orleans.   8. Racism in education—Louisiana—New
Orleans.   9. Educational change—Louisiana—New Orleans.   I. Title.
    LB2806.36.B86 2014
    371.0509763'35—dc23
    2013048092

ISBN: 978-0-415-66050-1 (hbk)
ISBN: 978-0-415-81462-1 (pbk)
ISBN: 978-0-203-06700-0 (ebk)

Typeset in Bembo
by Apex CoVantage, LLC

DEDICATION

for Ian and the children of New Orleans:
may your generation find justice
and honor the elders who struggled to defend
the sacred ground you stand on

for the veteran teachers of New Orleans:
they may try to take your position
but they will never take your place

for the members of Urban South Grassroots Research Collective:
with respect and love
so what has been built and shared
will never be forgotten, lost, or stolen

for friends and allies:
who value truth over promises
recognize the difference
and wade through the muddy waters
with us

for our city:
our feet can't fail us now

CONTENTS

FIGURES

Figures

Tables

Boxes

CREDITS

Chapter 2 is adapted from "Race, charter schools, and conscious capitalism: On the spatial politics of whiteness as property (and the unconscionable assault on black New Orleans)," Kristen L. Buras, *Harvard Educational Review, 81*(2), 2011, reprinted by permission of Harvard Education Publishing Group.

Chapter 3 is adapted from "'We're not going nowhere': Race, urban space, and the struggle for King Elementary School in New Orleans," Kristen L. Buras, *Critical Studies in Education, 54*(1), 2013, reprinted by permission of Taylor & Francis.

Chapter 4 is adapted from "'We have to tell our story': Neo-Griots, racial resistance, and schooling in the other South," Kristen L. Buras, *Race Ethnicity and Education, 12*(4), 2009, reprinted by permission of Taylor & Francis.

Chapter 6 is adapted from "New Orleans education reform: A guide for cities or a warning for communities (Grassroots lessons learned, 2005–2012)," Kristen L. Buras and Urban South Grassroots Research Collective, *Berkeley Review of Education, 4*(1), 2013, reprinted by permission of the University of California, Berkeley.

Figure 4.1: Memorial arch and Figure 4.2: Protest against desegregation of Nicholls High School are reprinted by permission of the Orleans Parish School Board Collection, Francis T. Nicholls High School Series, Louisiana and Special Collections Department, Earl K. Long Library, University of New Orleans.

Figures 5.1 and 5.3 are reprinted by permission of Cherice Harrison-Nelson.

Figure 5.2: New Orleans brass band is reprinted by permission of artist Charles E. Siler.

ABBREVIATIONS

ACSA—Algiers Charter School Association
AFT—American Federation of Teachers
ARK—Absolute Return for Kids
BESE—Board of Elementary and Secondary Education
BNOB—Bring New Orleans Back commission
CEE-Trust—Cities for Education Entrepreneurship Trust
CMO—Charter Management Organization
DCC—[Frederick] Douglass Community Coalition
FEMA—Federal Emergency Management Agency
FIN—Future Is Now charter management organization
JJPL—Juvenile Justice Project of Louisiana
KIPP—Knowledge Is Power Program
LAPCS—Louisiana Association of Public Charter Schools
LFT—Louisiana Federation of Teachers
L9SDG—Lower 9 School Development Group
NAACP—National Association for the Advancement of Colored People
NEA—National Education Association
NLNS—New Leaders for New Schools
NOPS—New Orleans Public Schools
NSNO—New Schools for New Orleans
NTR—New Teachers' Roundtable
OPSB—Orleans Parish School Board
RSD—Recovery School District
SAC—Students at the Center
SCLS—Southern Christian Leadership Conference

SFMP—School Facilities Master Plan
SOS-NOLA—Save Our Schools-New Orleans, Louisiana
SPS—School Performance Score
TF—Teach First
TFA—Teach for America
TNTP—The New Teacher Project
USGRC—Urban South Grassroots Research Collective
UTNO—United Teachers of New Orleans

1

BLACK EDUCATION IN THE SOUTH

Critical Race Reflections on the Historic Policy Landscape

Scholars' inattention to the nexus of race and place, and their omission of the South, despite its centrality in African American people's experiences, has led to a truncated understanding of Black academic achievement throughout the United States.
— Jerome Morris and Carla Monroe, writing on "Why Study the U.S. South?" in *Educational Researcher* (2009, p. 31)

You don't know American history until you know Louisiana history.
— Keith Plessy, New Orleans resident and descendent of Homer Plessy, who challenged segregation in the landmark Supreme Court case *Plessy v. Ferguson* (Reckdahl, 2009, para. 21)

Railroad tracks run along Press Street in the Upper 9th Ward of New Orleans. Where Press intersects with Royal Street, an old warehouse with graffiti sits on one side of the track. Overgrown patches of grass line the other side. To the everyday observer, it appears to be a street corner forgotten long ago. Yet this is the place where Homer Plessy, an Afro-Creole citizen of New Orleans, was arrested on June 7, 1892, for refusing to vacate his seat in a "whites only" railcar (Michna, 2009).

Plessy protested Louisiana's Separate Car Act of 1890 as part of a civil rights campaign by the Citizens' Committee, a group organized by Afro-Creoles to challenge racial segregation. In *Plessy v. Ferguson*, the landmark Supreme Court case that followed in 1896, "separate but equal" became legal doctrine (Medley, 2003). In reparation, one would expect local and state officials to memorialize the place where Plessy resisted white supremacy. Any attempt to do this, however, would be left to teachers, students, community members, and ancestors—a reminder of the unequal dynamics of race and how they define struggles over urban space.

On June 7, 2005, more than 100 years after Plessy's courageous actions, members of the Frederick Douglass Community Coalition (named after Douglass High School just a few blocks away) gathered at Press and Royal for the third annual Homer Plessy Day. Catherine Michna (2009) explains: "The attendees at Plessy Day 2005 were mostly members of an alliance of educators, community organizers, artists, and students who had been working for the past seven years to empower Ninth Ward neighborhoods and schools through practices of collective storytelling" (p. 532). It was the Douglass Community Coalition that fought to have Plessy Day recognized as a state holiday. The coalition also turned to two of its member organizations, the Crescent City Peace Alliance and Students at the Center, to develop plans for Plessy Park. Students at the Center, a writing and digital media program cofounded by veteran teachers and students and partly housed at Douglass High School, worked with a local artist to envision the park "as an interactive, changing memorial that would have paired students' stories about their schools and neighborhoods with stories about historic local civil rights struggles" (p. 537). More specifically, they imagined a railroad track with stops along the way for turning points in New Orleans' civil rights history, alongside student narratives that "provoked visitors to think critically about the way in which that historical moment continues to resonate" in the city (p. 538). Additionally, Plessy Park was envisioned as a space where students could perform, read poetry, and organize the community around racial and educational justice projects. Then Hurricane Katrina came.

New Orleans was struck on August 29, 2005. Waters had barely receded, but top-down plans were being made already for the city's students, public schools, and neighborhoods without consulting grassroots constituencies, such as the Douglass Community Coalition. With black working-class communities displaced, policymakers acted with shocking speed and precision to remake the landscape of New Orleans. At the local, state, and national levels, policymakers and entrepreneurs determined New Orleans would be the nation's first charter school district. To date, there is no other city with a higher proportion of privately managed charter schools or a more comprehensive program of human capital development, including alternative teacher recruitment. The collective bargaining agreement of the teacher union was nullified when the state-run Recovery School District (RSD) took control of the vast majority of public schools in New Orleans. Black veteran teachers were fired en masse while white recruits with Teach for America (TFA) were sought aggressively to replace them. Nearly a decade later, 85 percent of the city's public school students attended charter schools. New Orleans quickly became the premier site for market-based urban education reform. It is due time to assess this experiment honestly and from the bottom-up rather than the top-down. This is the purpose of this book.

In *Charter Schools, Race, and Urban Space,* I reveal a strategic and racially exclusive set of education policies centered on New Orleans. I draw on almost ten years of qualitative research and critical theories of race, political economy, and space to analyze the policy ecology and networks surrounding reforms. I show that New

Orleans charter schools are less about the needs of racially oppressed communities and more about the *Reconstruction* of a newly governed South—one in which white entrepreneurs (and black allies) capitalize on black schools and neighborhoods by obtaining public monies to build and manage charter schools.[1] Equally important, I document grassroots resistance to this southern strategy, sending a powerful message to communities nationally that New Orleans is not a blueprint for democratic and equitable transformation of urban public schools.

Since 2005, a host of reports have been issued that present New Orleans as a model to be followed by cities across the nation:

- *Born on the Bayou: A New Model for American Education* by Third Way (Osborne, 2012);
- *The Louisiana Recovery School District: Lessons for the Buckeye State* by the Thomas B. Fordham Institute (Smith, 2012; for a critique, see Buras, 2012);
- *Creating Opportunity Schools: A Bold Plan to Transform Indianapolis Public Schools* by the Mind Trust (2011);
- *Portfolio School Districts for Big Cities: An Interim Report* by the Center on Reinventing Public Education (Hill et al., 2009);
- *After Katrina: Rebuilding Opportunity and Equity into the New New Orleans* by the Urban Institute (Hill & Hannaway, 2006); and
- *From Tragedy to Triumph: Principled Solutions for Rebuilding Lives and Communities* by the Heritage Foundation (Meese, Butler, & Holmes, 2005).

Additionally, there has been much discussion in the media about the "success" of the New Orleans model. Illustrations are too numerous to compile here; major news outlets from *Time Magazine* (Isaacson, 2007) and the *New York Times* (Tough, 2008) to the *Wall Street Journal* (Kaminski, 2011) and the *Washington Post* (Armao, 2012) have highlighted New Orleans as a site of innovation, a source of inspiration, and a model for replication.

The evidence does not support such exuberance. Just the opposite: New Orleans reveals how destructive the culture of the market is to children of color and the neighborhood public schools they traditionally have attended. It is important for me to state something upfront—loudly and clearly. *The critique presented in this book of market-based school reform does not imply the preexisting system in New Orleans was ideal.* This certainly was not the case due to white supremacy and state neglect of black public schools. I underscore this point because "reformers" have discursively positioned critics of market-based intervention as "defenders of the status quo." This makes for good propaganda, but does little to illuminate the root causes of the problems faced by urban public schools and what is required to truly enable the teachers and students in them to thrive. Most alarmingly, "reformers" have co-opted the language of the civil rights movement to legitimize for-profit ventures in the public schools of racially oppressed communities (Buras, 2008; Scott, 2013). Neerav Kingsland, CEO of New Schools for New Orleans, a local charter school incubator bankrolled by the Broad, Gates, and Fisher Foundations and the federal government, proclaimed: "This transformation of the New Orleans educational system may turn out to be the most significant national development in education since desegregation" (Gabor, 2013, para. 4). Wendy Kopp, founder and president of Teach for America, an edu-business that provides temporary and uncertified teachers for impoverished urban and rural public schools, wrote a book entitled *One Day, All Children* (2001). TFA's alumni magazine is likewise entitled *One Day*. This language invokes the words of Martin Luther King's well-known "I Have a Dream" speech, in which he proclaimed at the 1963 March on Washington:

> I have a dream that one day on the red hills of Georgia sons of former slaves and sons of former slave-owners will be able to sit down together at the table of brotherhood.
> I have a dream that one day even the state of Mississippi, a state sweltering with the heat of injustice, sweltering with the heat of oppression, will be transformed into an oasis of freedom and justice. ...
> This will be the day when all of God's children will be able to sing with new meaning. "My country 'tis of thee, sweet land of liberty, of thee I sing."
> (King cited in Washington, 1992, pp. 104–105)

The civil rights rhetoric of education CEOs should prompt us to ask: Are privately managed charter schools in New Orleans *really* an oasis of freedom and justice?

Education entrepreneurs, such as Kingsland and Kopp, would have us believe that charter school development in New Orleans represents third-wave civil rights activism or what may be called *Brown III. Brown v. Board of Education*, also known as *Brown I*, struck down *Plessy* in 1954, rendering "separate but equal" schools unconstitutional. *Brown II* sought to remediate the legacy of "separate but equal" through court-ordered desegregation; federal desegregation mandates were to be implemented "with all deliberate speed." *Brown II* met massive resistance as white parents withdrew their children from public schools and state policymakers invented schemes to deter desegregation. Interestingly, while *Brown II* met massive white resistance, *Brown III*, school choice through charter schools, confronts growing black resistance. In New Orleans and other cities, increasing numbers of veteran teachers, students, and parents are coming to recognize that "freedom of choice" is not freedom at all. In the hands of mostly white entrepreneurs and philanthropists, charter school development has compounded the injustices perpetrated as a result of *Brown II*. Only this time, black veteran teachers are replaced by TFA recruits, most of them white and inexperienced, while public schools attended by black students are either closed or taken over by white charter school operators. There is a long history of white control over black education (Scott, 2009; Watkins, 2001); unfortunately, we have entered a new era of this. Black communities stand to lose a great deal once again. As I show in upcoming chapters, underfunded all-black public schools in New Orleans, despite their struggles, were sources of community cultural wealth (Yosso, 2006) and heritage knowledge (King, 2009). Like many black schools throughout the South, these schools anchored and sustained neighborhoods (Horsford, 2011; Morris, 1999; Walker, 1996).

Let us get back to Plessy for a moment. In 2009—four years after the storm in New Orleans—Crescent City Peace Alliance and ancestors of Homer Plessy and Judge John Howard Ferguson (who ruled against Plessy in Orleans Parish Criminal Court, with his decision upheld by the Supreme Court) installed a plaque at the former site of Press Street Railroad Yards to honor Plessy's legacy (Reckdahl, 2009). Keith Plessy, whose great-grandfather was Plessy's first cousin, learned as a child about his relationship to the case from teachers at Valena C. Jones Elementary School. Phoebe Ferguson, whose great-great grandfather was Judge Ferguson, joined with Keith Plessy to establish the Plessy and Ferguson Foundation. Keith Weldon Medley, a local historian who wrote a groundbreaking book on *Plessy* (Medley, 2003), and Brenda Square, a local archivist, also acted as cofounders. Through the foundation, they aim to educate community members about civil rights issues, preserve and expand public awareness of historic spaces, and develop outreach initiatives to promote racial justice (Plessy and Ferguson Foundation, 2013). There is a striking difference between the educational vision and motivations of indigenous community groups, such as the Douglass Community Coalition and Plessy and Ferguson Foundation, and the policymakers and entrepreneurs who seek to reconstruct New Orleans and its public schools based on competitive market principles.

FIGURE 1.1 Homer Plessy memorial plaque in Upper 9th Ward

In chapter 4, I chronicle the history of Douglass High School and community resistance to its closure by the state-run RSD and master planners. As I will show, rather than building on successful and indigenous models at Douglass, such as Students at the Center, officials shut down the school and gave the building to the Knowledge Is Power Program (KIPP). KIPP is a national charter management organization (CMO) with a highly regimented program of study focused on compliance, not culturally relevant curriculum. This was devastating to community members who had worked for years to improve the school without any support. Unfortunately, what transpired at Douglass would prove to be a pervasive pattern of decision making under the emerging "model" in New Orleans.

Beginnings of the Charter School Market in New Orleans

To understand what has transpired in New Orleans over the past decade, it is important to recollect the exclusionary processes set in motion early on. The formation of the Algiers Charter School Association (ACSA) in early 2006 foreshadowed tensions surrounding charter school development in New Orleans. On the West Bank of the Mississippi River in Algiers (across the river from the city), public schools were largely spared storm damage. Brian Riedlinger, director of the School Leadership Center under Baptist Community Ministries, the largest private foundation in Louisiana, and advisor to the education committee of the Bring New Orleans Back Commission, which advocated the charter school model for New Orleans, led the ACSA in taking over 13 public schools. "Nearly overnight, the school board established the Algiers Charter district and the state legislature virtually eliminated the central office" (Mirón, 2008, p. 244). Each school was given its own operating budget and the ability to hire and fire teachers. In fact, the ACSA dismissed 400 veteran teachers. The People's Hurricane Relief Fund filed a lawsuit challenging the legitimacy of the ACSA and also charged it had failed to enroll students due to school admissions requirements (Mirón, 2008). Conflicts over school governance were intense and "the first public meeting of the newly created [ACSA] had to be guarded by armed National Guardsmen" (Cowen Institute, 2009, p. 10).

One of the first charter school proposals was submitted in late 2005 by Lusher, a preexisting K–8 public school in the wealthy uptown Garden District. Before the storm, Lusher wanted to expand; thus its board seized the moment and "appealed for permission to open a second campus, extend their school through 12th grade, and prioritize enrollment for the children of faculty members at nearby Tulane University" (Dingerson, 2008, p. 21). With no public hearing, Orleans Parish School Board not only permitted expansion, but "agreed to hand over the historic Alcee Fortier High School building to accommodate their added grades." Formerly an open-access public school attended by working-class black students, Fortier suddenly received $14 million from the state and an additional $1.5 million from Tulane to fully transform the physical space. The newly renovated school came with newly renovated admissions policies; it now would be selective and many former students were prohibited from attending based on academic records (Dingerson, 2008). In sum, Fortier was taken from a racially marginalized group of students and reconstructed with plaster, paint, and new education policies. In the process, Principal Kathy Riedlinger became the highest paid principal in New Orleans, making $203,559 (Thevenot, 2009) for running one of only a handful of charter schools in New Orleans that is majority white and disproportionately upper-income (Cowen Institute, 2010; New Orleans Parent Organizing Network, 2009).

Prior to August 2005, Thurgood Marshall was one of the top public middle schools in New Orleans. The school suffered minimal storm damage, but remained closed after the state-run RSD assumed control. Millions were spent on renovations, and the school was set to reopen for the 2007–2008 school year. The first day of school stunned the community:

> Parents brought their children to the newly renovated Marshall building only to find that two charter schools (Langston Hughes and P. A. Capdau) were in the building. The Marshall students were to be bused to modular buildings in the Lower Ninth Ward on the site of the damaged and abandoned Holy Cross Catholic High School. ... There was no one from RSD to explain to parents and students why they were being moved or why their school was being occupied by two charter schools. The only explanation ... received through the principal was that the charter schools' buildings were not ready.
>
> (Sanders, 2009, p. 2)

The conditions at Holy Cross were terrible and the principal was assigned a teaching staff by the RSD, with 100 percent first-year teachers from teachNOLA (an alternative teacher recruitment initiative) and TFA; within two months, 70 percent had quit. In May 2008, then RSD superintendent Paul Vallas agreed Marshall would return to its original site, but the next school year, it was given access to the third floor only. Capdau, a school in the Capital One-University of New Orleans (UNO) charter network, continued to occupy the first and second floors. But that was not all. In December 2008, UNO was granted a charter for Thurgood Marshall High School, meaning it had not only made itself at (someone else's) home but likewise appropriated (someone else's) Marshall's name and all of the positive markers associated with it. In March 2009, Marshall's principal met with Vallas and learned the school would be closed—not the school building, which charter schools occupied, but Marshall itself. Vallas promised he would meet with parents and teachers to explain the reasons, but the meeting never occurred (Sanders, 2009). In sum, Marshall was treated as a building rather than a community with a history, next displaced, and ultimately replaced by an intruder turned imposter. While the Capital One-UNO charter network secured a place for one of its schools and Langston Hughes secured a temporary site prior to its move to a newly constructed building, the well-established Marshall Middle School was closed. Raynard Sanders (2009), a former New Orleans public school principal and public education advocate, writes:

> One would think that given [RSD's] mission to improve schools, it would at least make every effort to replicate the academic achievement that occurred at Marshall before [August 2005]. Instead, the RSD has made a very concerted effort to destroy the school and give the building to a charter operator, who has not demonstrated success.... [This state of affairs] calls into question the stated reason for the state takeover, allegedly to improve academic achievement.
>
> (p. 5)

Time and again in New Orleans, charters would be given funding and facilities in what amounts to an educational land grab premised on historical erasure and the racial–spatial redistribution of resources.

Langston Hughes Academy, which at one time occupied Marshall, is a charter school originally run by the nonprofit NOLA 180—a CMO partnered with New Schools for New Orleans, teachNOLA, TFA, and Echoing Green, an organization that provides support for social entrepreneurs. Among the first to get funding under the School Facilities Master Plan, Hughes received $30 million (RSD & NOPS, 2008, p. 1). Not long after opening at its new site, the school's business manager was investigated by the FBI and pled guilty to stealing $675,000 from an annual budget of about $6 million by withdrawing cash from accounts and writing checks to herself (Carr, 2010; *Times-Picayune*, 2010). Despite the fact that charter school autonomy is premised on heightened accountability, Vallas promised only "sniff tests" at charter schools in collaboration with the Louisiana Association of Public Charter Schools (Carr, 2009). A parent organizer with SOSNOLA (Save Our Schools–NOLA), a public education advocacy group, reflected:

> If the argument against the central office is that there's corruption, there's mismanagement ... if these are the problems, then you don't just hand over the reins to someone else. ... Simply changing who's in charge won't ensure that every child is educated. Our system is broken, so we must fix the system and we should start by improving public transparency.
>
> (Interview, 2009)

Charter school development in New Orleans has not done this. Instead, "reformers" covet and control the city's schools with scant public input or oversight.

From these examples, a number of patterns can be delineated in New Orleans—ones that will be documented more thoroughly in the chapters to come. First, charter schools have taken over or replaced traditional public schools, with little input from community members. Second, CMOs and education entrepreneurs have acquired immense decision-making power as well as power over local, state, and federal education funds. Third, charter schools often engage in selective admission and retention of students. Fourth, veteran teachers have been fired while human capital edu-businesses such as TFA provide new and transient recruits. Fifth, entrepreneurial leaders in the system are generously paid. Sixth, privately managed charter schools have access to upgraded facilities at public expense. Seventh, unregulated charter school autonomy allows corruption to go unchecked and "reformers" to prosper in the process. Eighth, charter school development is not necessarily driven by performance or evidence, as traditional but promising public schools are closed to make room for unproven start-ups. Ninth, there is a racial dynamic to all of this, as mostly white entrepreneurs and recruits attempt to impose "reform" and capitalize on black working-class communities. Tenth, charter school development has generated lawsuits and community resistance. Last but not least, this reconstruction of public education has the support of most local, state, and federal policymakers despite its anti-democratic tendencies.

These dynamics are disturbing (or should be). If New Orleans is viewed as a national model, this suggests that more serious consideration should be given to the South as a site of research on education reform. In fact, it may be argued that black education writ large cannot be understood adequately without examining the reconstruction of public education in the South. While the dynamics noted above are present in cities across the nation—Chicago, Detroit, New York City, and elsewhere (Lipman, 2011; Ravitch, 2013; Stovall, 2013)—they are most robust

FIGURE 1.2 Charter school advertisements on New Orleans' streets

in New Orleans. This may not be coincidental. Few cities or regions in the country have a higher proportion of black students than the South, especially New Orleans. In this regard, New Orleans represents a crucial site for defending and improving black education nationally. New Orleans is the proving ground, where the *powers that be* will see how far they can advance privatization, and precisely how, before taking their project to scale in other places and spaces, especially in urban communities of color.

Race and the Urban Space Economy of New Orleans: Toward a Theory of the South's Public Education Market

In their thought-provoking essay in *Educational Researcher*, Jerome Morris and Carla Monroe (2009) examined the question, "Why study the South?" Despite the attention given to disparities between black and white students, they write:

> Not much scholarship ... focuses explicitly on the U.S. South—historically considered the reservoir of African American culture in the nation as well as the place where most Black people reside—as a significant place to study in developing an understanding of the issue [racial disparities].
>
> (p. 21)

"Knowledge of African American schooling in the South," stress Morris and Monroe, "is primarily historical in nature" (p. 21). The failure to appreciate the South as a critical site for the contemporary investigation of black education, including racial, cultural, political, and economic dynamics, has serious consequences. Ultimately, they argue, the absence of this scholarship "has facilitated an uneven understanding of Black academic performance throughout the United States" (p. 21).

Morris and Monroe (2009) note that the majority of the nation's black population has always resided in the South. As late as 1910, about 90 percent of black people in the United States still lived in southern states, and more than 50 percent remained there even after the Great Black Migration of the early 20th century. Between 1990 and 2000, 3.6 million black people moved to the U.S. South— the largest internal migration of blacks since the early 20th century. Moreover, although black people constitute approximately 13 percent of the total U.S. population, just ten southern states are home to 47 percent of the nation's black population. As a result, they conclude, "southern experiences continue to frame Black life" within and beyond the region (p. 23).

Understanding the race–place nexus, or the ways that race and regional place contribute to the uneven *geography of opportunity* for African Americans (Briggs, 2005; Morris & Monroe, 2009; Tate, 2008) and other racially marginalized groups, including Native, Latino/a, and Asian peoples is central (Buendía, Ares, Juarez, & Peercy, 2004; Grande, 2004; Ng-A-Fook, 2007; Tang, 2011; Truitt, 2012). Writing about race and the politics of place, Katherine McKittrick and Clyde Woods

(2007) explain that "physical geographies are bound up in, rather than simply a backdrop to, social and environmental processes." That is, "the environment is racialized by contemporary demographic patterns as shaped by historic precedents" (p. 3). Take, for example, homes, schools, and the racial geography of New Orleans.

Most of New Orleans is below sea level, but there are elevation differences that have shaped settlement along racial lines. For centuries, artificial levees and canals were built for flood protection, often by enslaved Africans. The Mississippi River, however, also produced a *natural levee* along its banks. It may surprise many to learn "the crest of the natural levee is about ten to fifteen feet above sea level." By contrast, the backswamp was "the low, perennially flooded area" (Lewis, 2003, p. 27). In the early 1800s, whites settled upstream (Uptown) along the natural levee. Less affluent Creoles of African, French, and Spanish descent as well as poor Irish and German (and later, Italian) immigrants settled downstream (Downtown)—many in the Ninth Ward, an area "of little importance to the city's decision-makers" (pp. 44–45). The legacy of segregation explains why street names change as streets cross Canal Street, a dividing line between the largely white Uptown area and the largely black Downtown area (p. 46). In time, white elites moved farther Uptown into the neighborhood currently known as the Garden District (where Lusher School is located) and a grand thoroughfare, now called St. Charles Avenue, was constructed (pp. 47–49). In sum:

> With whites occupying the highest and best part of the natural levee ... blacks were pushed into the demi-land on the inland margin of the natural levee, where drainage was bad, foundation material precarious, streets atrociously unmaintained, mosquitos endemic, and flooding a recurrent hazard. ... By the mid-twentieth century, the backswamp black belt had grown so crowded that ... it [was] beginning to merge into something that looked like ... [a] superghetto.
>
> (p. 52)

Additionally, the Orleans Parish Levee District had been lax in providing flood protection Downtown, where income and race translated into weak political influence (p. 63). Fast forward to August 2005 and it becomes evident why uptown homes in New Orleans suffered substantially less damage, while downtown areas such as the Lower 9th Ward received a deluge of water that destroyed homes and schools. Historic patterns of segregation and unequal racial power have shaped differential access to land, which, in turn, renders black property and life more vulnerable. This is the uneven geography of opportunity (see Figure 1.3). In chapter 3, the lived consequences of this are made clear when I discuss the immense struggle to rebuild schools in the Lower 9th Ward in the wake of the storm, charter school development, and elite plans for a "new" New Orleans (read: whiter and wealthier).

David Harvey (1973) discusses what he calls the *urban space economy*. Through this concept, he emphasizes that the city is a built environment. There is nothing

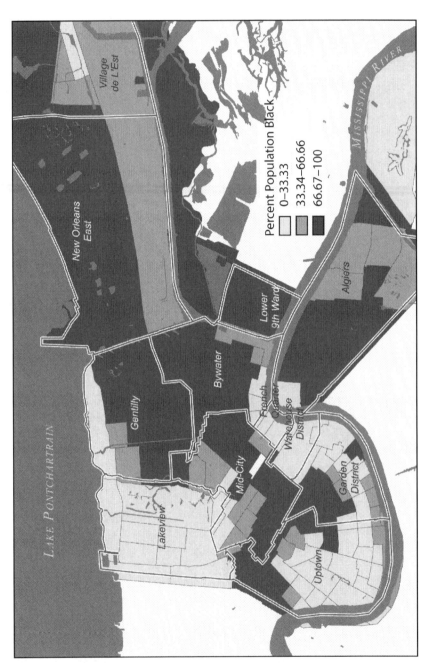

Percent Population Black
☐ 0–33.33
▨ 33.34–66.66
■ 66.67–100

LAKE PONTCHARTRAIN

Village
de L'Est

New Orleans
East

Lakeview

Gentilly

Bywater

Lower
9th Ward

Mid-City

French
Quarter

Warehouse
District

Garden
District

Uptown

Algiers

MISSISSIPPI RIVER

FIGURE 1.3 Map of racial geography of New Orleans

natural about its organization. Rather its contours are shaped by the interests of powerful groups. He argues that the city embodies the conditions and spatial ordering necessary for capital accumulation, or economic profiteering, to proceed. Consider for a moment the history of the market in New Orleans and the ways in which race and spatial order have enabled whites to advance their property interests; the city's geography has influenced possibilities for black resistance as well.

The institution of slavery is the most brutal example. Enslaved blacks in the South were treated as property and subjected to white ownership, exploitation on the plantation, and market exchanges beyond their control (Blassingame, 1977). Even after the abolition of slavery, state-sanctioned violence and segregation in labor markets, schools, and other private and public venues curtailed the choices available to African Americans and perpetuated racial, economic, and cultural subjugation (Anderson, 1988; Du Bois, 1935).

Historically, the racial structure and market in New Orleans were more complex than other southern cities. Many Maroons (escaped slaves who formed independent settlements in the backswamps) populated New Orleans (Bell, 1997; Hall, 1992). The city's geographic proximity to Haiti, where enslaved blacks liberated themselves from French colonial rule, also contributed to the presence of free blacks in New Orleans. New Orleans had one of the largest free black communities of color in the United States. This meant that some level of cultural and economic power—albeit, relative, constrained, and always under threat—was exercised by Afro-Creole professionals as well as tradesmen and women who created markets to meet community needs (Desdunes, 1911; Gehman, 1994). At the same time, a portion of enslaved blacks in antebellum New Orleans, unlike those on plantations in rural Louisiana, were skilled and unskilled laborers—carpenters, bricklayers, painters, blacksmiths, bakers, barbers, dock workers, seamstresses, nurses, and street vendors. While their labor power was largely controlled by white owners, their involvement in a range of occupations meant they experienced relatively more mobility and the chance to develop a richer social life in the city. In New Orleans, moreover, enslaved blacks were released from work on Sundays. Gathering in local black establishments and marketplaces to sell the products of their labor, generate income, and purchase needed goods, the day generally ended at Congo Square, a grassy tract of land bordering the city. In this place they reinvented the music and dance of Africa, ultimately developing rich cultural forms indigenous to New Orleans (Blassingame, 1973; Evans, 2011; Sublette, 2008). While for enjoyment, these cultural practices likewise fostered solidarity and resistance to white domination.

Demonstrating the hyper-exploitative and racially inflected tendencies of the market, black cultural forms ultimately became the focus of white profiteering. The present-day economy of New Orleans largely revolves around cultural tourism in the French Quarter (Bring New Orleans Back Commission, 2006; Souther, 2006). Although the French Quarter is the place where white business leaders, local white consumers, and white visitors invest themselves, the entire "industry" is based on cultural forms produced in largely black spaces, whether in historic Congo Square or later in black working-class neighborhoods. Writing about the racial dynamics of the market in New Orleans, Souther (2006) explains:

> If tourist dollars enriched businessmen who could profit from the popularity of the French Quarter, only low wages went to most of the many African Americans who worked [there]. ... African American cultural contributions underlay most aspects of the tourist experience in New Orleans, but in the French Quarter, white promoters cast blacks merely as supporting actors who furnished services and amusement to a tourist-oriented tableau. ... Although much of the city's peculiar charm sprang from Afro-Caribbean roots, blacks were seldom beneficiaries of their own contributions. ... Tourism ... rested to a great extent on white exploitation of African Americans.
>
> (p. 28)

It should be clear by now that such exploitation has a long history (see also Hall, 1992).

The cultural and economic exploitation of African Americans within markets has an educational correlate. Under current reforms in New Orleans, the public schools attended by African American schoolchildren have been commodified by white entrepreneurs (and black allies), who care less about improving the life

FIGURE 1.4 New Orleans' French Quarter on Mississippi River

chances of black youth than about capitalizing on schools, obtaining contracts, and lining their pockets with public and private monies. In light of the preceding history, there is little reason to believe that black communities will fare well in an educational market or that it is intended to advance their interests. For education entrepreneurs, as I will show, black children and black schools are the market.

Charter school proponents say that educational markets are neutral, driven by informed consumer choice and mediated by individuals acting in self-interested ways that ultimately produce wider social good. Ineffective, inefficient, and inequitable schools will be disciplined by the "invisible hand," which ensures that substandard products and services do not survive. This rendering of market dynamics, however, is ahistorical, place-less, and ignores how economic transactions occur in racially structured landscapes. Historian Robin D. G. Kelley (1997) challenges the myth of the color-blind market and emphasizes the role of the state in upholding whites' property rights:

> Calls for color blindness and laissez-faire economic strategies also camouflage the critical role the state has played in reproducing inequality and creating an *uneven* playing field. Tax laws and social welfare, retirement, and housing policies have impaired the ability of African Americans to accumulate assets while facilitating white access to wealth.
>
> (p. 92)

The market exists in living color, often perpetuating an uneven geography of opportunity through state policy.

Think back to the illustrations that I provided about early charter school development in New Orleans. Without community input, public schools in New Orleans' Algiers neighborhood were subjected to the control of the ACSA; hundreds of veteran teachers were fired despite decades of service. Fortier High School, once attended by black working-class students, suddenly acquired millions for renovations that benefitted a small number of carefully selected, mostly white students allowed to attend. Marshall, a successful middle school, was physically removed from its own campus to make room for privately operated charter schools and was ultimately closed despite its record of success with black students. Hughes also received support from master planners, only to have its business manager steal financial resources that rightfully belonged to students. Charter school and human capital development, which make white entrepreneurs the beneficiaries of public resources intended for black students and teachers, represents "reforms" that foster *accumulation by dispossession*. David Harvey (2006) describes this as a process in which assets previously belonging to one group are put in circulation as capital for another group. Doing so has required that "sectors formerly regulated by the state … are turned over to the private sphere or deregulated" (p. 25). In New Orleans, public schools have been turned over to white entrepreneurs at the expense of black students, teachers, families, and neighborhoods.

From the standpoint of critical race theory, a tradition that recognizes racism as endemic, we might question how *whiteness as a form of property* functions in the context of New Orleans, especially in relation to public schools. Cheryl Harris (1995) reminds us that "American law has recognized a property interest in whiteness" (p. 277). By this she means that:

> ...property as conceived in the founding era included not only external objects and people's relationships to them, but also all of those human rights, liberties, powers, and immunities that are important for human well-being. ...White identity conferred tangible and economically valuable benefits, and it was jealously guarded as a valued possession.
>
> (pp. 279–280)

Among the property rights of whiteness were and are "the right to use and enjoyment" and "the absolute right to exclude." Simply put, the right to use and enjoyment refers to those benefits secured as a result of one's ability to stake a claim to whiteness. If one possesses "it," one can access and accumulate an array of social goods. Moreover, whiteness translates into the absolute right to exclude or to dispossess others of such benefits and privileges. These racialized and racist processes are all too apparent in New Orleans, where *who* possesses the right to housing and education, authority over school governance, or a place in the historical and cultural landscape is becoming increasingly clear. As this book reveals, white identity and power have been used to secure the accumulative interests of entrepreneurs and policymakers, while black identity has translated into unspeakable levels of racial and economic dispossession.

Remember the struggle to recognize Plessy's legacy racially and spatially. For a long time, the significance of the railroad at Press and Royal was "hidden" from view. Equally troubling, those who struggled to educate the community about the history of this place were themselves displaced from Douglass High School by a charter school operator that took over the building without regard for the efforts and successes that occurred there. I am reminded of the words of McKittrick and Woods (2007) when they discuss black geographies and how the "unknowable" figures in the production of race and space. With New Orleans and Hurricane Katrina in mind, they write about "the oceanic remnants of the middle passage and transatlantic slave trade" and emphasize "the Atlantic Ocean as a geographic region that can also represent the political histories of the disappeared" (p. 4). They continue:

> The materiality of a body of water prompts a geographic narrative that may not be readily visible on maps or nautical charts. This tension between the mapped and the unknown, reconfigures knowledge, suggesting that place, experiences, histories, and people that "no one knows" do exist, *within our present geographic order.*
>
> (p. 4; italics in original)

This book prioritizes the vantage point of racially oppressed communities in New Orleans, unearthing a history of attempted erasure and grassroots resistance through a critical analysis of charter school development and the city's historic landscape.

New Orleans has been described as "one of America's most African cities" (Robertson & King, 2007). This certainly makes it a crucial place for studying black education. Simultaneously, as a city in the Deep South, New Orleans is a place where white supremacy has reigned in some of its harshest forms and where a racial marketplace existed long before the emergence of charter schools in recent years. I want to turn now to a brief history of public education in New Orleans, which provides context for my analysis of charter school development in the remaining chapters of this book.

A Brief History of Public Education in New Orleans

For most of their history, public schools in New Orleans were not intended to support children of color or their black teachers but were instead considered the property of southern whites. The history of slavery, legalized segregation, ongoing racism, and white flight from the city has translated into strategic state neglect and disinvestment in African American education (Buras, 2007; DeVore & Logsdon, 1991). This neglect, however, did not go unchallenged, as African Americans created educational spaces of their own and fought for support of black public schools.

In the mid-1840s, a state constitutional convention called for the free public education of white children in Louisiana. Some of the early public schools in New Orleans were built through the funds of John McDonogh, a wealthy landowner and slaveholder who died in 1850 and willed half his estate "for the establishment and support of Free Schools…wherein the poor, (and the poor only) of both sexes and all classes and castes of color, shall have admittance, free of expense" (McDonogh in DeVore & Logsdon, 1991, p. 34; Ciravolo, 2002). Many of the schools were named after McDonogh—so many, in fact, that they were numbered (e.g., McDonogh No. 5, McDonogh No. 32). Only a small number of new public schools, however, were built for black students from the McDonogh School Fund (Ciravolo, 2002). McDonogh's legacy is a reminder that white philanthropy in public education, both past and present, is intertwined with white supremacy (see also Watkins, 2001). Before the Civil War, which began in 1861, white policy-makers in New Orleans did not invest in black schools. The education of enslaved blacks was prohibited by state policy and free blacks, most of them Afro-Creole, had to organize their own schools.

During Reconstruction, blacks fought for the integration of public schools, only to meet white resistance. In late 1874, the New Orleans chapter of the White League encouraged white students "to boycott schools to which blacks had been admitted and to remove them forcibly from their classrooms" (Blassingame,

FIGURE 1.5 John McDonogh statue in Lafayette Square

1973, p. 117). As a result, hundreds of white boys expelled black students "while armed Negro parents began marching to the schools to protect their children" and "fought pitched battles," leading the board to temporarily close the schools (p. 117). Nonetheless, blacks pursued education with unfaltering commitment. *The Louisianian* noted in 1875, "The diligent observance of scholastic duties, and excellence and ability in recitation and deportment of the indubitably colored boys and girls have done much to disarm the foolish opposition to their atten-dance" (p. 119). At the Mason School, for instance, three black boys were at the top of their class. Some of these students would go on to study at one of three black colleges established in New Orleans during Reconstruction—Straight, Leland, and New Orleans universities. Although Straight (later merged with New Orleans University to form Dillard University) was the most influential, together these colleges produced the majority of black teachers, lawyers, and physicians in New Orleans from 1869 to 1930 (Blassingame, 1973).

In the shadow of the Civil War, the Freedmen's Bureau was created to assist recently emancipated blacks in obtaining access to land and organizing schools. Even the freedmen's schools established during Reconstruction ultimately suffered from state disinvestment and abandonment. W. E. B. Du Bois (1935) critiqued the lack of appropriations for the bureau and the veto of the Freedmen's Bureau Bill (which would have extended the life of the agency) by President Andrew Johnson in 1866. This had a devastating effect in New Orleans, where tuition was implemented and student enrollment declined "from 5,330 in December 1865 to 1,359 in Febru-ary 1866" (Blassingame, 1973, p. 111). This was unfortunate. Mortimer A. Warren, superintendent of Freedmen's Bureau schools in New Orleans, noted as early as 1865:

> I have never witnessed such progress among white children … as I daily see in the [black] schools under my charge. … A thirst for knowledge has been kindled in young and old which will not soon die out. It is talked of at home, it is preached from the pulpit, it is advocated at the rostrum.
>
> (Blassingame, 1973, p. 110)

Regardless, many northern whites did not support the use of public funds for black education. Most southern whites attacked the bureau because it was a bar-rier to reestablishing the structure of racial power that prevailed before the war (Foner & Mahoney, 1995). Money was better spent on white infrastructure and its restoration than on forty acres, a mule, and a school for African Americans.[2]

With weakening federal commitment to Reconstruction, the Ku Klux Klan's terrorism and attacks on the recently acknowledged rights of African Americans advanced. Newly freed blacks were subjected to white violence that destroyed churches and schools, the infrastructure of the black community. As mentioned earlier, in 1896, the Supreme Court's decision in *Plessy v. Ferguson* solidified the legal apparatus of segregation (Foner, 1990; Tourgée, 1879). Despite historic mobi-lizations for educational equity by African Americans, a segregated and unequal system of public education took root. In New Orleans, black public schools were few in number and located in poor facilities; they were grossly underfunded; black teachers were unequally paid in comparison to white teachers; and school days were often part-time due to overcrowding (DeVore & Logsdon, 1991).

In 1900, the New Orleans school board decided to limit public education for blacks to the first five grades. From 1900 to 1945, the city sought to improve its white schools while black schools suffered from ongoing state neglect. Thus the funding of African American schools largely fell to black community organizations within neighborhoods, alongside ongoing contestation, petitions, and reports that documented resource inequities. During the first decade of the 1900s, the average amount spent on building black public schools in New Orleans was $21,500; for white public schools, it was $42,500. To make matters worse, during the early 1900s, the construction of nearly every black school in the city was met with white resistance and violence. When plans were issued to build the Joseph Craig School for blacks in the 1920s, school board president James Fortier sided with white protesters, some of whom said they did not want a "Negro school" in the neighborhood. Fortier declared he was "unwilling to do anything that would affect the white man's supremacy" (DeVore & Logsdon, 1991, p. 201). New Orleans' black community mobilized and reminded the board of its decade-long effort to obtain a new school building. Craig opened and blacks remained there, but only until they were transferred to a new building elsewhere. A school superintendent's report in 1920–21 revealed that fewer than 20 of the city's 86 public schools served black students. As for secondary education, the city's first black public high school, McDonogh No. 35, was not established until 1917 and was largely the result of African American demands (DeVore & Logsdon, 1991; Buras, 2007). To be clear, the resources that existed in all-black schools prior to desegregation resulted from the cultural capital and demands of African American teachers, parents, and community members (Morris, 1999; Walker, 1996; White, 2002).

Beginning in 1916, Louisiana decided to supervise public education for blacks through the newly established Division of Negro Education (DNE), a shift from post-Reconstruction policy premised on opposition to or abandonment of black schools. The DNE's mission was shaped in large part by John D. Rockefeller's General Education Board, a group of northern white philanthropists that advocated elementary, agricultural, and industrial education for southern blacks (Chujo, 1999). Chujo (1999) explains: "Although its purpose in general was to develop 'education within the United States of America without distinction of race, sex, or creed,' the Board pursued a specific goal: The production of docile black laborers by means of mass education" (pp. 300–301). Rockefeller founded the Board in 1902 and by 1921 he had invested approximately $130 million in its campaign to restructure southern schools along industrial lines (Chujo, 1999; Watkins, 2001).

Louisiana's DNE was established with Board support in 1916. Leo M. Favrot, a Tulane University graduate and former Louisiana public school teacher, was appointed head of the Division and made clear:

> What we need is a type of school that stress [sic] the principles of sanitation and health, aim at cleaner homes in the negro quarters, that will exalt a better family life, that will point to habits of industry, thrift and economy, self-respect and decency, punctuality and regularity, and respectability.
>
> (Chujo, 1999, p. 308)

T. H. Harris, Louisiana state superintendent of public education, agreed and emphasized in particular the need for "as much vocational work as possible, especially gardening, farming, using hand tools to make the common, useful things about the home and farm, cooking, sewing, and waiting on guests" (Chujo, 1999, p. 308). This mission was closely tied to maintaining white supremacy and the region's sharecropping economy. Outside of rural Louisiana in New Orleans, where urban blacks often learned skilled trades, industrial education was useless (Blassingame, 1973).

The Board continued to fund Louisiana's DNE into the 1940s and it was not abolished until 1963. Throughout its history, however, many black leaders in Louisiana opposed its work. There is evidence as well that many black vocational teachers redefined the curriculum and taught "reading, 'riting, and reckoning" when beyond the view of state supervision (Chujo, 1999).

During this period in New Orleans, protests against segregated and unequal schooling continued. For example, in 1927, the city's Colored Educational Alliance petitioned the Orleans Parish School Board to increase funding for black public schools. This same year, 69 petitioners who had completed the eighth grade in one evening school demanded higher grades in their school. In 1938, the black chapter of the American Federation of Teachers in New Orleans was formed and fought for equalization of teacher salaries—a struggle discussed in chapter 5 on the city's black teachers. New Orleans' second black public high school, Booker T. Washington, did not open until 1942 and followed on the heels of the Grace Report (DeVore & Logsdon, 1991).

Headed by Alonzo G. Grace, the Citizens' Planning Committee for Public Education completed a relatively comprehensive study of New Orleans public schools during 1938–1939. The Orleans Parish School Board appropriated $10,000 for the study and an additional $11,000 came from local citizens. The Grace Report, officially entitled "Tomorrow's Citizens: A Study and Program for the Improvement of the New Orleans Public Schools," was issued in 1940 (Grace & Citizens' Planning Committee, 1940). It provided information on the school board and superintendent; school buildings; teacher training; programs for white and black children; and school finances.

Regarding elementary school buildings for black children—23 out of 25 were visited—the report stated: "Four of the buildings are fairly new but the others are quite poor, some of them serving merely as shelters in which children may be collected for a minimum of academic instruction" (Grace & Citizens' Planning Committee, 1940, p. 31). It was concluded that most required complete replacement. One-third of black elementary schools had enrollments exceeding 800 students and a total of 21,000 students attended with only 374 teachers and 23 principals (p. 112). The schools were provided only with "a minimum supply of educational materials and books" by the state and lacked supplementary materials such as "library books, visual equipment, globes, maps, radios, instruments, and some manual training and household art equipment" (p. 114). Only four schools had a separate room for a library and six reported no library books at all; only eight had an auditorium, none had a gymnasium, and the majority had playgrounds too small to accommodate students; and only seven had facilities to serve hot lunches. To the community's credit and despite state neglect:

> Although only eleven schools maintain school gardens, the work that has been done is most commendable. The cooperative work of the principal, teachers, children, and supervisors of school gardening to beautify the school grounds has stimulated similar activity in the neighborhood and in the homes of the children.
>
> (p. 115)

In terms of black public secondary schools, McDonogh No. 35 was the city's only senior high school, with two additional junior high schools in existence. At McDonogh No. 35, "practically every pupil studies two years of English, history, mathematics, science, music, art, and physical education," a program "founded on the belief that all pupils are preparing for college" (pp. 120–121). Only one-fourth of the school's graduates, however, were able to continue on.

On black teacher training, the Grace Report specified (as one illustration) that Valena C. Jones Normal School had 73 black teachers enrolled in April 1938; 78 percent came from McDonogh No. 35 High School. Jones' faculty experience ranged from 15 to 30 years. A two-year curriculum with 35 course offerings was taught, but the campus lacked "a library, laboratories, recreation rooms, gymnasium, auditorium, and other essential facilities for the adequate preparation of teachers" (Grace & Citizens' Planning Committee, 1940, p. 35). Of 42 graduates in 1936–1937, only 13 found teaching positions by May 1938. The report concluded many would have found positions "if class sizes in the elementary school were reduced" (p. 35). For those who taught in black high schools, the median length of classroom experience was 12 years, with female high school teachers at 17 years and female elementary principals at 22 years, revealing the central role of veteran teachers in sustaining black public schools in New Orleans (p. 142). Despite conditions, the report says of teachers:

> The data on training after employment show that degrees are secured at Xavier, Straight, New Orleans University, and Dillard. One hundred twenty of these teachers were in school during 1937–1938. At least one-half of the group [has] taken courses for credit within the last three years (1935–1938) in spite of depression and low salaries. ... The record of this continuous training is very remarkable especially since much of it has occurred during the depression days.
>
> (pp. 149–150)

Even in dire times, many teachers spent money on furthering their own education and the future of the students in their care.

The late 1930s and 1940s would see the development of the first black teacher union in New Orleans as well as struggles for salary equalization in the city and state (see chapter 5). The second era of Reconstruction came with *Brown v. Board of Education* in 1954, the Supreme Court case that overturned *Plessy* and deemed "separate but equal" unconstitutional in public education. As before, this led to massive resistance by local and state authorities as well as white citizens. By May 1960, Federal Judge Skelly Wright had yet to receive desegregation plans from the Orleans Parish School Board (OPSB). Thus he issued a proposal of his own that would desegregate one grade per year. Louisiana's governor and legislature passed a host of laws against desegregation, including a bill that authorized closing all the state's public schools to avoid desegregation and another prohibiting the provision of state funds to desegregated schools. A State Sovereignty Commission was formed as well and given substantial power. The federal court restrained the governor from interfering with public schools in New Orleans, declared state segregation acts unconstitutional, and ordered OPSB to follow Judge Wright's ruling. The state superintendent of education threatened that black teachers would lose their jobs and that black students would lose educational opportunities if desegregation proceeded. OPSB adopted the pupil placement plan, spurring the state governor to call a special legislative session, where laws would be passed to defy federal desegregation orders and a legislative committee would be appointed to run New Orleans public schools. Judge Wright intervened again and restrained the legislative committee from interfering with the operation of New Orleans public schools. The legislature next removed several members of the school board and fired the local school superintendent and board attorney. Notably, the legislature already had seized the funds of OPSB and forbade banks to lend money to the board. In mid-November, two all-white schools were set to be desegregated in New Orleans—William Frantz Elementary and McDonogh No. 19; white parents quickly withdrew their children. The legislature also authorized payment of Orleans Parish school employees, with the exception of those at Frantz and McDonogh No. 19 (Louisiana State Advisory Committee, 1961).

This history of race and education establishes one undeniable fact: white supremacy, not black deficiencies, accounts for the challenging conditions of black public schools in New Orleans. This is not a minor point—it is the crux of the matter. "Reformers" advocating charter school and human capital development in New Orleans responded to a perceived problem in August 2005. The "problem," they said, was inefficient local governance and unions protecting inept veteran teachers. The "solution" they instituted consisted of loosening local and state regulations, allowing privately managed charter schools to flourish, and creating a new pipeline of leadership into the city. Somehow, the problems generated by the history of white supremacy were to be resolved through market-based reforms. Interestingly, many of the strategies used to defend white supremacy in the 1960s—urgently calling a special legislative session, passing new and capricious legislation, using state power to disable the local school board politically and economically, attempting to remove the local school superintendent, threatening teachers' jobs and refusing to pay them, and closing the public schools—would be used once again in 2005. Only this time, the federal government would support state and local leaders in their actions. Notably, the takeover of New Orleans public schools in 2005 would be justified by civil rights rhetoric, even as white power defined a new era of Reconstruction. The state-run RSD and entrepreneurs had come to "save" black public schools from any further destruction, whether by nature or by nurture. As the next chapter shows, the reality is far less sanguine than portrayed by the "reformers."

The Book's Organization: Telling the Story of Charter School Reform in New Orleans

I charted the historic policy landscape in New Orleans, showing how white supremacy has shaped the city's geography, housing patterns, economy, and public schools. Likewise, I offered early illustrations of more general anti-democratic tendencies in the city's charter school movement, ones that cast doubt on claims that current policies are in the best interest of black students, teachers, and communities. Importantly, I provided a history of black educational struggle and resistance to white domination. Further, I introduced some of the theoretical concepts drawn from critical theories of race, political economy, and space to be used throughout the analysis: whiteness as property, accumulation by dispossession, and urban space economy. More will be said about these concepts as we move forward. Right now, I want to describe the research behind the book and the chapters to come.

Charter Schools, Race, and Urban Space is based on ten years of qualitative research in New Orleans, including document analysis, interviews with a broad range of stakeholders and organizations, observation of classrooms, schools, and public hearings, archival research, oral history, and spatial, geographic, and network analysis (for more on methodology, see the Appendix, with Table A.1). It is likewise based on tireless work with Urban South Grassroots Research Collective (USGRC) for Public Education, which I cofounded and direct (for more on USGRC, see chapter 6).

Chapter 2 examines educational policy formation in New Orleans and the racial, economic, and spatial dynamics shaping the city's reconstruction since 2005. Here I document the strategic assault on black communities by education entrepreneurs. Based on data collected from an array of stakeholders on the ground, I argue that policy actors at the federal, state, and local levels have contributed to a process of privatization and an inequitable racial-spatial redistribution of resources while acting under the banner of social entrepreneurship or "conscious capitalism." In short, I document the untold story behind how New Orleans came to be the "model" city for charter school reform, a story that raises serious questions about whose interests the reforms were meant to serve.

Chapters 3 and 4 are case studies that document how historic public schools have fared under charter school reform in New Orleans. Chapter 3 is based on oral history interviews with veteran teachers, administrators, and community members affiliated with Martin Luther King Elementary School in the Lower 9th Ward. Traversing time and space, I document the community's history of racial resistance and more recent struggles for education equity. I examine these struggles in the context of charter school reform and attempts to undermine the reconstruction of longstanding schools and neighborhoods and instead secure space for privately managed charter schools. Efforts to rebuild King Elementary in this reformed landscape reveal a distinct commitment to equity, culture, and a shared sense of place—the antithesis of the vacuous market-based policies that have guided reform in New Orleans. Such commitments have enabled and energized grassroots educational resistance to dispossession despite the power of venture philanthropy and exclusionary master plans.

In chapter 4, I focus on the struggle to defend Frederick Douglass High School, the historic secondary school in the Upper 9th Ward mentioned earlier. I draw on archival sources to situate the school within a history of white power and racial inequity, documenting massive resistance to *Brown,* white flight, and the transformation of Douglass (formerly Francis T. Nicholls) into an all-black public high school. Despite state abandonment, I show how teachers at Douglass built a curriculum rooted in the voices and histories of racially marginalized students by highlighting Students at the Center, the aforementioned writing and digital media program that envisioned Plessy Park. I draw on teacher interviews, student counterstories, and classroom and community observations to critically analyze implementation of market-based education reform. Most important, I show how community members came together to challenge the aspirations of policymakers to close their school and reinvent their neighborhood. Unfortunately, rather than supporting indigenous educational models at Douglass, master planners closed the school and the building was given to KIPP for Renaissance High School, not far, ironically, from a nascent riverfront development called "Reinventing the Crescent [City]."

Chapter 5 examines the role of Teach for America and human capital edubusiness in busting the teacher union and providing inexperienced white recruits from outside the community to teach, while black veteran teachers were fired. This chapter challenges the way in which black veteran teachers were singularly blamed for the shortcomings of New Orleans public schools in 2005 and counters with a history of black teacher associations in New Orleans to illuminate their contributions. I likewise discuss how veteran teachers' termination was deemed illegal by the Civil District Court for Orleans Parish, finding that state officials intentionally interfered with teachers' property rights. As a result, dramatic demographic shifts have occurred over the past decade as TFA provides recruits for the city's charter schools. This is discussed alongside testimony of veteran teachers who reveal firsthand what has transpired. To highlight implications, I document indigenous traditions developed by the city's veteran teachers and what stands to be lost if the culture of the community is replaced by the culture of the market. I argue the market disregards place-based consciousness and community knowledge in the education of black students and instead prioritizes racialized management principles and profit.

In chapter 6, I join members of Urban South Grassroots Research Collective in articulating "lessons learned" from the bottom up about charter school reform in New Orleans. This chapter is framed as a "Warning for Communities" nationally not to adopt the New Orleans model of urban school reform. More specifically, we respond to a *Guide for Cities* issued by the charter school incubator New Schools for New Orleans (NSNO). Through human capital and charter school development, the report asserts, New Orleans has become a national leader in school reform. NSNO's report was at the center of a forum hosted by Louisiana Senator Mary Landrieu in Washington, DC. In contradistinction, we discuss key lessons learned from the bottom-up in New Orleans, lessons we hope will be considered by communities nationally and globally. We conclude by charting the elite policy network in which NSNO plays a central part and reveal the accumulative interests of education entrepreneurs in New Orleans and other cities. Most crucially, we offer principles of educational reform rooted in a more democratic and critically conscious tradition.

The Education Market in New Orleans: Thinking Across Time, Space, and Race

Before turning to the next chapter, I want to acknowledge that charter schools have sometimes enabled racially oppressed communities to create culturally relevant spaces for self-determination and achievement. But these spaces are too few and far between and do not reflect the agenda of the wider charter school movement defined and controlled by market advocates. Lisa Delpit (2012) is correct when she says the "original idea of charter schools has been corrupted" by the "market model ... [Charter schools] were intended to develop models for working with the most challenging populations" (p. xv). Most of them no longer do in a competitive, profit-driven environment.

On August 5, 2006, one year after the storm, parents were invited to the New Orleans Arena where information was provided by schools planning to open in the city—many of them new charters with little performance data, but big promises (Ritea, 2006b). They spent "thousands of dollars in newspaper and radio ads," with one school expending $30,000 on its "outreach budget" to recruit students. The city newspaper urged, "Parents trying to maneuver the maze of public schools in post-Katrina New Orleans would do well to start with a new premise: Think of yourselves as consumers in a brand new marketplace" (Ritea, 2006a).

On October 14, 2010, five years after the "new marketplace" was instituted in New Orleans, the auditorium of McDonogh No. 35 High School was packed with hundreds of people. Students, teachers, principals, parents, and community members gathered for a public hearing before the Louisiana Board of Elementary and Secondary Education (BESE) about the RSD's control over public schools in New Orleans. Just a few weeks before, Louisiana state superintendent of education Paul Pastorek and RSD superintendent Paul Vallas (2010) had issued a set of recommendations addressing future governance of the city's public schools. If schools returned to local governance, OPSB would be expected to maintain the "autonomy" and "innovation" enabled by RSD governance of charter schools. In short, the plan imposed a host of rigid conditions on OPSB for reacquiring schools—all intended to ensure the educational market would persist despite substantial community opposition.

The BESE members, who were largely white, were seated on stage in the auditorium. Community members, mostly African American, meandered through the

FIGURE 1.6 Citizen with anti-RSD protest sign at BESE public hearing

crowd greeting one another and taking their seats. Some held posters expressing their views—"Discrimination is NOT innovation" and "Equal Education Access for ALL children"—referring to both the formal and informal selective admissions policies of many charter schools. Some wore t-shirts, with one reading "We are ready! Orleans Parish School Board," indicating a desire for public schools governed by locally elected officials. Stickers with slash marks through RSD (meaning "No more RSD") conveyed opposition to the state takeover. Stirring the humid southern air and the tension, others waved handheld fans printed with the message: "I support parents having a CHOICE in deciding the best school to educate their child" (Fieldnotes, 2010).

The hearing was called to order by Chas Roemer, BESE member and brother of Caroline Roemer Shirley, executive director of the Louisiana Association of Public Charter Schools. State and local officials were introduced and Louisiana Senator Mary Landrieu touted New Orleans as an educational model of "choice" and "opportunity." She characterized the experiment as a form of *coopetition* (a hybrid of cooperation and competition) where school officials, school management organizations, and communities "work together" to build an unprecedented marketplace of possibility. Red t-shirts worn by those associated with a few specific charter schools created bright clusters in the auditorium and reflected similar sentiments, reading "MY CHILD, MY SCHOOL, MY CHOICE" (Fieldnotes, 2010).

Despite the organized testimony of select charter school parents, most of the public testimony revolved around serious critiques of the educational market and its effects on community well-being. An African American woman presenting herself as a concerned citizen issued the following warning:

> I would like to go back to *Brown v. Board of Education* ... [which] simply said that separate was not equal. What I'm seeing now in this room as I listen to people talk today—we are more separated today than we have ever been. ... Our children have the right to be educated—be it charter, be it RSD, be it Orleans Parish. ... I'm listening to too many people talk about *my* school, *our* school, *their* school—all of the schools should be equal ... and it's not happening.
>
> (Fieldnotes, 2010)

One longtime volunteer in New Orleans public schools expressed her disgust over venture-driven reform enabled through top-down governance by outside leaders:

> I resent the fact that Paul Vallas came here from out of town. ... He said to the New Orleans residents: You cannot take care of your community or your schools. So we're bringing people from out of town to come here and charter your schools and run your schools. ...

> There are a lot of intelligent people here that are indigenous to this community. ... We all need to fight for local governance and input, so that we can properly educate our children and not let them be experiments.
>
> (Fieldnotes, 2010)

Another well-known community activist shared a damning critique of the legal assault on black schools:

> What we're talking about here tonight is a simple question of democracy. We want in Orleans Parish what every other parish has in this state and that's the right to control our own schools. High crimes and misdemeanors have been carried out against the people of New Orleans ... by the RSD and the people who run these charter operations. We don't believe that these schools have served the best interests of the majority of our African American students.
>
> (Fieldnotes, 2010)

This lack of representation was challenged as well by a veteran of New Orleans' civil rights movement: "We went to jail. A lot of people died for us to *have the right to vote for who we want to represent us.* This governance mess is like ... R-A-C-I-S-M. It's vicious, it's malicious, and it's got to stop." She concluded, "These two people [Pastorek and Vallas] don't have [the] right to control us as a people" (Fieldnotes, 2010). In sum, there was a palpable sense that education entrepreneurs in New Orleans, assisted by white policymakers, have been the real beneficiaries of charter schools in the RSD.

All of this takes on added significance when one considers the history of the high school where the public hearing occurred. As mentioned earlier, McDonogh No. 35 was established in 1917 as the city's first black public high school (DeVore & Logsdon, 1991). It is telling that almost 100 years later community members would gather there to debate the effect of current reforms on educational equity. What would lead community members to protest reforms that charter school advocates portray so positively? The next chapter provides part of the answer.

Notes

1 In the United States, Reconstruction was the period following the Civil War (1865–1877) during which southern whites sought to restore their racial power despite the emancipation of blacks and federal intervention. A similar period of massive resistance occurred during the civil rights movement of the mid-20th century, when whites attempted to defend inequitable racial conditions despite black protest and federal intervention. I use the term *Reconstruction* in this book to underscore the ways in which disaster in New Orleans provided the conditions for restoring white control over the city's

largely black public school system (and other dimensions of urban infrastructure). This power had been partly compromised by white flight to surrounding suburbs after the civil rights movement and the increasing presence of black leaders in local government from the late 1970s to 2005.

2   The withdrawal of federal support for blacks is what enabled the Old South to "redeem" itself (Du Bois, 1935). In New Orleans today, the withdrawal of government responsibility for public infrastructure—turning the city's public schools over to privatization by white entrepreneurs—has allowed the birth of a "new" New Orleans.

References

Anderson, J. D. (1988). *The education of Blacks in the South, 1860–1935*. Chapel Hill, NC: University of North Carolina Press.

Armao, J. (2012, April 27). The Big Easy's school revolution. *Washington Post*. Available: www.washingtonpost.com/opinions/the-big-easys-school-revolution/2012/04/27/gIQAS4bDmT_story.html

Bell, C. C. (1997). *Revolution, romanticism, and the Afro-Creole protest tradition in Louisiana, 1718–1868*. Baton Rouge, LA: Louisiana State University Press.

Blassingame, J. W. (1973). *Black New Orleans, 1860–1880*. Chicago, IL: University of Chicago Press.

Blassingame, J. W. (Ed.). (1977). *Slave testimony: Two centuries of letters, speeches, interviews, and autobiographies*. Baton Rouge, LA: Louisiana State University Press.

Briggs, X. (2005). *The geography of opportunity: Race and housing choices in metropolitan America*. Washington, DC: Brookings Institution Press.

Bring New Orleans Back Commission. (2006, January 17). Report of the cultural committee. New Orleans, LA: Author.

Buendía, E., Ares, N., Juarez, B. G., & Peercy, M. (2004). The geographies of difference: The production of East Side, West Side, and Central City School. *American Educational Research Journal, 41*(4), 833–863.

Buras, K. L. (2007). Benign neglect? Drowning yellow buses, racism. and disinvestment in the city that Bush forgot. In K. Saltman (Ed.), *Schooling and the politics of disaster* (pp. 103–122). New York, NY: Routledge.

Buras, K. L. (2008). *Rightist multiculturalism: Core lessons on neoconservative school reform*. New York, NY: Routledge.

Buras, K. L. (2012, March). Review of "The Louisiana Recovery School District: Lessons for the Buckeye State." Boulder, CO: National Education Policy Center.

Carr, S. (2009, November 24). Langston Hughes Academy's former financial manager booked on theft counts. *Times-Picayune*. Available: www.nola.com

Carr, S. (2010, January 13). Langston Hughes Academy books were "left in shambles," board chairman says. *Times-Picayune*. Available: www.nola.com

Chujo, K. (1999). The Negro Division: Public education policy for Black Louisiana, 1916–1941. In M. G. Wade (Ed.), *The Louisiana Purchase Bicentennial Series in Louisiana History: Education in Louisiana* [Vol. XVIII] (pp. 300–325). Lafayette, LA: Center for Louisiana Studies at University of Southwestern Louisiana.

Ciravolo, G. L. (2002). *The legacy of John McDonogh*. Lafayette, LA: Center for Louisiana Studies at the University of Louisiana at Lafayette.

Cowen Institute. (2009, November). Creating a governing framework for public education in New Orleans: Charter school authorizers and charter school governance. New Orleans, LA: Author.

Cowen Institute. (2010). The state of public education in New Orleans: 2010 report. New Orleans, LA: Author.

Delpit, L. (2012). *"Multiplication is for white people": Raising expectations for other people's children*. New York, NY: New Press.

Desdunes, R. L. (1911/1973). *Our people and our history: Fifty Creole portraits* (edited by D. O. McCants). Baton Rouge, LA: Louisiana State University Press.

DeVore, D. E., & Logsdon, J. (1991). *Crescent City schools: Public education in New Orleans, 1841–1991*. Lafayette, LA: Center for Louisiana Studies at the University of Southwestern Louisiana.

Dingerson, L. (2008). Unlovely: How the market is failing the children of New Orleans. In L. Dingerson, B. Miner, B. Peterson, & S. Walters (Eds.), *Keeping the promise?: The debate over charter schools* (pp. 17–34). Milwaukee, WI: Rethinking Schools.

Du Bois, W. E. B. (1935/1992). *Black Reconstruction in America, 1860–1880*. New York, NY: The Free Press.

Evans, F. W. (2011). *Congo Square: African roots in New Orleans*. Lafayette, LA: University of Louisiana at Lafayette Press.

Foner, E. (1990). *A short history of Reconstruction, 1863–1877*. New York, NY: Harper & Row.

Foner, E., & Mahoney, O. (1995). *America's Reconstruction: People and politics after the Civil War*. Baton Rouge, LA: Louisiana State University Press.

Gabor, A. (2013, September 20). The great charter tryout: Are New Orleans's schools a model for the nation—or a cautionary tale? *Newsweek*. Available: http://mag.newsweek.com/2013/09/20/post-katrina-the-great-new-orleans-charter-tryout.html

Gehman, M. (1994). *The free people of color: An introduction*. New Orleans, LA: Margaret Media.

Grace, A. G., & Citizens' Planning Committee for Public Education in New Orleans. (1940). Tomorrow's citizens: A study and program for the improvement of the New Orleans public schools. New Orleans, LA: Orleans Parish School Board.

Grande, S. (2004). *Red pedagogy: Native American social and political thought*. Lanham, MD: Rowman & Littlefield.

Hall, G. M. (1992). *Africans in colonial Louisiana: The development of Afro-Creole culture in the eighteenth century*. Baton Rouge, LA: Louisiana State University Press.

Harris, C. I. (1995). Whiteness as property. In K. Crenshaw, N. Gotanda, G. Peller, & K. Thomas (Eds.), *Critical race theory: The key writings that formed the movement* (pp. 276–291). New York, NY: New Press.

Harvey, D. (1973). *Social justice and the city*. Baltimore: Johns Hopkins University Press.

Harvey, D. (2006). *Spaces of global capitalism: Towards a theory of uneven geographical development*. New York, NY: Verso.

Hill, P., Campbell, C., Menefee-Libery, D., Dusseault, B., DeArmond, M., & Gross, B. (2009, October). *Portfolio school districts for big cities: An interim report*. Seattle, WA: Center on Reinventing Public Education.

Hill, P., & Hannaway, J. (2006, January). The future of public education in New Orleans. In M. A. Turner & S. R. Zedlewski (Eds.), *After Katrina: Rebuilding opportunity and equity into the new New Orleans* (pp. 27–35). Washington, DC: Urban Institute.

Horsford, S. D. (2011). *Learning in a burning house: Educational inequality, ideology, and (dis)integration.* New York, NY: Teachers College Press.

Isaacson, W. (2007, September 6). The greatest education lab. *Time Magazine.* Retrieved from www.time.com/time/magazine/0,9171,1659767,00.html

Kaminski, M. (2011, October 8). The Big Easy's school revolution. *Wall Street Journal.* Available: http://online.wsj.com/article/SB10001424052970203388804576616802947504250.html

Kelley, R. D. G. (1997). *Yo' mama's disfunktional! Fighting the culture wars in urban America.* Boston, MA: Beacon Press.

King, J. E. (Ed.). (2009). *Black education: A transformative research and action agenda for the new century.* New York, NY: Routledge.

Kopp, W. (2001). *One day, all children: The unlikely triumph of Teach for America and what I learned along the way.* New York, NY: PublicAffairs.

Lewis, P. F. (2003). *New Orleans: The making of an urban landscape.* Santa Fe, NM: Center for American Places.

Lipman, P. (2011). *The new political economy of urban education: Neoliberalism, race, and the right to the city.* New York, NY: Routledge.

Louisiana State Advisory Committee. (1961). The New Orleans school crisis [Report of the Louisiana State Advisory Committee to the United States Commission on Civil Rights]. Baton Rouge, LA: Author.

McKittrick, K., & Woods, C. (2007). "No one knows the mysteries at the bottom of the ocean." In K. McKittrick & C. Woods (Eds.), *Black geographies and the politics of place* (pp. 1– 13). Cambridge, MA: South End Press.

Medley, K. W. (2003). *We as freemen: Plessy v. Ferguson, the fight against legal segregation.* Gretna, LA: Pelican Publishing.

Meese, E., Butler, S. M., & Holmes, K. R. (2005, September 12). *From tragedy to triumph: Principled solutions for rebuilding lives and communities.* Washington, DC: Heritage Foundation.

Michna, C. (2009). Stories at the center: Story circles, educational organizing, and the fate of neighborhood public schools in New Orleans. *American Quarterly, 61*(3), 529–555.

Mind Trust. (2011). Creating opportunity schools: A bold plan to transform Indianapolis public schools [report prepared by Public Impact]. Indianapolis, IN: Mind Trust. Available: www.themindtrust.org/files/file/opp-schools-full-report.pdf

Mirón, L. (2008). The urban school crisis in New Orleans: Pre- and Post-Katrina perspectives. *Journal of Education for Students Placed at Risk, 13,* 238–258.

Morris, J. E. (1999). A pillar of strength: An African American school's communal bonds with families and community since *Brown. Urban Education, 33*(5), 584–605.

Morris, J. E., & Monroe, C. R. (2009). Why study the U.S. South? The nexus of race and place in investigating black student achievement. *Educational Researcher, 38*(1), 21–36.

New Orleans Parent Organizing Network. (2009). New Orleans parents' guide to public schools (3rd ed.). New Orleans, LA: Author.

Ng-A-Fook, N. (2007). *An indigenous curriculum of place: The United Houma Nation's contentious relationship with Louisiana's educational institutions.* New York, NY: Peter Lang.

Osborne, D. (2012). *Born on the bayou: A new model for American education.* Washington, DC: Third Way.

Plessy and Ferguson Foundation. (2013). Homepage. Available: http://plessyandferguson.org/

Ravitch, D. (2013). *Reign of error: The hoax of the privatization movement and the danger to America's public schools.* New York, NY: Knopf Doubleday.

Reckdahl, K. (2009, February 11). Plessy and Ferguson unveil plaque today marking their ancestors' actions. *Times-Picayune.* Available: www.nola.com

Recovery School District (RSD) & New Orleans Public Schools (NOPS). (2008, November 6). Superintendents' amendments: Recommendations to the Louisiana Board of Elementary and Secondary Education (BESE). New Orleans, LA: Authors.

Ritea, S. (2006a, August 12). Public schools compete for kids. *Times-Picayune.* Available: www.nola.com

Ritea, S. (2006b, August 5). Schools to help confused parents. *Times-Picyune.* Available: www.nola.com

Robertson, C. C., & King, J. E. (2007). Boŋ Feerey: A teaching and learning methodology for healing the wounds of distance, displacement, and loss caused by Hurricane Katrina. *Journal of Black Studies, 37*(4), 469–481.

Sanders, R. (2009). The Louisiana Recovery School District: The post-Katrina saga of Thurgood Marshall School. Available: www.researchonreforms.org

Scott, J. T. (2009). The politics of venture philanthropy in charter school policy and advocacy. *Educational Policy, 23*(1), 106–136.

Scott, J. T. (2013). A Rosa Parks moment? School choice and the marketization of civil rights. *Critical Studies in Education, 54*(1), 5–18.

Smith, N. (2012, January). The Louisiana Recovery School District: Lessons for the Buckeye State. Washington, DC: Thomas B. Fordham Institute. Available: www.edexcellence.net/publications/the-louisiana recovery-school-district.html

Souther, J. M. (2006). *New Orleans on parade: Tourism and the transformation of the Crescent City.* Baton Rouge, LA: Louisiana State University Press.

Stovall, D. (2013). Against the politics of desperation: Educational justice, critical race theory, and Chicago school reform. *Critical Studies in Education, 54*(1), 33–43.

Sublette, N. (2008). *The world that made New Orleans: From Spanish silver to Congo Square.* Chicago, IL: Lawrence Hill Books.

Tang, E. (2011). A Gulf unites us: The Vietnamese Americans of Black New Orleans East. *American Quarterly, 63*(1), 117–149.

Tate, W. F. (2008). "Geography of opportunity": Poverty, place, and educational outcomes. *Educational Researcher, 37*(7), 397–411.

Thevenot, B. (2009, May 17). Local school principals' pay reaches new heights. *Times-Picayune.* Available: www.nola.com

Truitt, A. (2012). Vietnamese visions of reform in the charterization of New Orleans. *Amerasia Journal, 38*(3), 52–74.

Times-Picayune. (2010, February 27). Editorial: Lesson of Langston Hughes. Available: www.nola.com

Tough, P. (2008, August 17). A teachable moment: Education in post-Katrina New Orleans. *New York Times Magazine.* Available: www.nytimes.com/2008/08/17/magazine/17NewOrleanst.htmo?pagewanted=all&_r=0

Tourgée, A. W. (1879/1991). *A fool's errand: A novel of the South during Reconstruction.* Prospect Heights, IL: Waveland Press.

Walker, V. S. (1996). *Their highest potential: An African American school community in the segregated South.* Chapel Hill, NC: University of North Carolina Press.

Washington, J. M. (Ed.). (1992). *I have a dream: Writings and speeches that changed the world.* New York, NY: HarperCollins.

Watkins, W. H. (2001). *The white architects of black education: Ideology and power in America, 1865–1954.* New York, NY: Teacher College Press.

White, M. A. (2002). Paradise lost? Teachers' perspectives on the use of cultural capital in the segregated schools of New Orleans, Louisiana. *Journal of African American History, 87*(2), 269–281.

Yosso, T. (2006). Whose culture has capital? A critical race theory discussion of community cultural wealth. In A. D. Dixson & C. K. Rousseau (Eds.), *Critical race theory in education: All god's children got a song* (pp.167–189). New York, NY: Routledge.

2

THE ASSAULT ON BLACK CHILDREN BY EDUCATION ENTREPRENEURS

Charter Schools, Whiteness, and Accumulation by Dispossession

We did a different model [in New Orleans]. We decided to take the failing schools away from the school district. ... And in doing that, the local policies go away, the collective bargaining agreement goes away. ... So out comes the building, the students, and the money and a fresh start. ...

There are still people in the minority community angry that we took over the schools and that we disenfranchised them.

—Leslie Jacobs, charter school advocate and architect of
Louisiana's Educational Assessment Program
(Charter Revision Commission, 2010)

They came back and said, "Oh, you no longer have jobs. The district no longer exists. We're going to split it up, make some charters. The state's going to take control of everything."...I asked one state legislator, "How could you do that with us being displaced and still abide by open meetings law?" Because when you do stuff like that, you have to post notice. You have to invite the public. You have to get their input. ... He said, "Well, what we did was we called up a few people that we knew was back in town and invited them over to my house, and we sat down and began to dismantle the district."... This is the kind of underhanded tactics that was going on while our family members were still floating in the waters of Katrina, while our schoolchildren were still floating in that water.

—Veteran public school teacher in New Orleans
(Interview, 2008)

Leslie Jacobs speaks with promise about the fresh start provided by a different educational model in New Orleans. As a former member of the Orleans Parish School Board (OPSB) and the Louisiana Board of Elementary and Secondary Education (BESE), and member of New Orleans' white business elite, she commands attention and is able to circulate a number of claims about what is best for the "minority community." Paul Hill, a nationally recognized conservative who leads the Center on Reinventing Public Education, echoes Jacobs. He writes with his colleagues:

> [A] "portfolio school district" is ... based on a simple set of ideas: a district that provides schools in many ways—including traditional direct opera-tion, semi-autonomous schools created by the district, and chartering or contracting to independent parties—but holds all schools ... accountable for performance. ... Many things traditional school districts were originally built to do ... are at odds with operation of schools by diverse providers and replacing schools and staff that do not perform. Adopting a portfolio model means rebuilding a school district from the ground up. ... Traditional edu-cators, and citizens who do not want their schools to change, inevitably feel insulted and dispossessed.
>
> (Hill et al., 2009, pp. 1–2)

Much like Jacobs, Hill presents a "simple set of ideas" about how to improve urban school performance. Yet, as one black veteran public school teacher indi-cated, these so-called reforms are rapacious. Notably, they are not only rapacious in their effects; the process of implementing these reforms, far from being demo-cratic, has been more like a deadly assault on black schools and neighborhoods.

Educational reformers such as Jacobs and Hill make some key assertions (Buras & Apple, 2005; Saltman, 2010). First, they argue that a market-driven, com-petitive model of education is best. This portfolio model (invoking the language of business is not accidental) allegedly ensures high-performing and accountable schools, since low-performing schools run by inept "service providers" will fail to generate the allegiance of clients and be removed. Second, they assert that doing away with local politics and bureaucracy (references to teacher unions are not accidental either) will lead to fresh and innovative practices. That is, freed from the shackles of regulatory government and labor protections, schools will be able to deliver a nonstandardized curriculum and to do so more efficiently and cost effectively. Third, they claim that knowledgeable consumers are able to equitably navigate the newly renovated system of schools based on access to performance data. Jacobs has made clear that in New Orleans "we are a system of schools ver-sus a school system" and that "every single school is a school of choice" (Charter Revision Commission, 2010, pp. 10–11).

Hill and his colleagues (2009) stress that "there is only one way to judge a portfolio district"—namely, by its capacity to "create a process of continuous change under which ... the quality of schools available [and] the district's overall responsiveness to needs in the community ... will steadily improve" (p. 47). Hill's words resonate with a newly emerging movement around social entrepreneurship and conscious capitalism. As one of the leading proponents indicates, conscious capitalists establish organizations to address specific problems and "reject Milton Friedman's argument that a corporation's primary responsibility is to its share-holders" (Miester, 2010, p. 17). Instead, all businesses "should have a purpose beyond profits." Accordingly, "the more we can get entrepreneurs to step up and be conscious capitalists, the less we're going to need regulations" (p. 17). Entre-preneurs assert that educational markets and school choice advance equity and opportunity for communities long harmed by a state monopoly on public educa-tion. Is this the case? Is this the intent?

The experiences of families such as Michelle Mosby and her six-year-old granddaughter La-Aarea cast doubt on reformers' assertions. Mosby hoped to get La-Aarea into first grade at Akili Academy, a charter school in the Recov-ery School District (RSD), but learned several weeks before the end of summer that it was already too late. To complicate matters, Mosby, "who works the cash register in a cafeteria, does not have a flexible work schedule or well-placed con-tacts to help her navigate the complicated new landscape" (Carr, 2009, para. 7). Meanwhile, La-Aarea was attending a direct-run school in the RSD, one that Mosby disliked because of its large classes, inadequate homework, and the seeming disengagement of her granddaughter, who never mentioned school. Like most parents and caregivers, Mosby sought "a good school close to where she lived and worked" (para. 25). She next tried Success Preparatory Academy, a brand new charter school in the RSD, but discovered a sign on its door that the first grade was full. She was invited to complete an application for the waiting list but was informed that applications were only accepted in the afternoon between one and four o'clock. During the first week of school, Mosby was still seeking a place-ment. Many schools were full or simply did not return her calls, and she could not afford to miss work to continue her search (Carr, 2009). There was no choice: La-Aarea would remain at the same school she attended the previous year, one of the direct-run RSD schools considered to be a "dumping ground" for the children not selected by charter schools (UTNO, LFT, & AFT, 2006).

Lawmakers and entrepreneurs say they are engaged in a socially conscious effort to advance equity and improve public schools. Rather than allowing the traditional profit motive to define their efforts, they frame their work as *conscious capitalism* in action. All the while, New Orleans' urban space economy is reshaped along racial lines, leading to the criminal dispossession of black working-class communities and the teachers and students who have contributed to the city's culture and history.

In this chapter, I critically analyze the policy ecology—the complex set of rela-tionships that have influenced education reform in New Orleans—and the city's corresponding urban space economy. This includes the role of federal and state governments in zoning southern space as an experimental site for charter school reform and alternative teacher recruitment; the role of local government, particu-larly the Bring New Orleans Back Commission (BNOB), in envisioning a racially inspired, market-based plan for reconstruction of the city and its schools; the role of non-state policy actors, such as Tulane University's Cowen Institute for Public Education Initiatives, New Schools for New Orleans (NSNO; charter school incubator), and teachNOLA (an alternative teacher recruitment initiative), in advancing the takeover and privatization of New Orleans Public Schools (NOPS) by education entrepreneurs; and the role of the state-run Recovery School District (RSD) and School Facilities Master Plan (SFMP) in establishing the blueprint for which schools would be rebuilt and where, as well as the uneven urban space economy produced as a result. I discuss the effects of these actors and organizations on working-class communities of color, including black veteran teachers and students, and challenge the notion that charter schools are a panacea for race and class inequities.

First, let me say something about events just prior to the takeover and chartering of New Orleans public schools, linking the history in chapter 1 to the present era of racial reconstruction.

New Orleans Public Schools: A Recent History

As mentioned, *Brown v. Board of Education* in 1954 led to mass white flight from the city's public schools. In the fifty years following *Brown,* New Orleans lost two-thirds of its white population (Lewis, 2003). Despite shifting racial demographics, NOPS did not have its first black superintendent until 1985, and from 1996 to 2005 the district had nine interim or permanent superintendents (DeVore & Logsdon, 1991; UTNO et al., 2006). Throughout the 1990s, the district suffered ongoing financial crises. Per-pupil spending in 1998 was $5,000 in New Orleans compared with nearly quadruple this amount in suburban public schools nationally (Saltman, 2007b).

The state takeover of Orleans Parish began in June 2005. At that time, the Louisiana Department of Education entered into a memorandum of understanding with the OPSB, which authorized the state to manage the district's $30 million deficit. Interestingly, the state's financial management would be accomplished by contracting with Alvarez and Marsal, a private accounting firm. In turn, Alvarez and Marsal suggested that some of the district's operations, such as food service, payroll, and transportation, be privately contracted (Mirón, 2008). Thus, the grounds for public school decentralization and privatization had been laid through historic and racially targeted neglect, generating the educational "crisis" that entrepreneurs have allegedly stepped in to resolve (Buras, 2007, 2009; Saltman, 2007a).

Despite these oppressive conditions, New Orleans developed one of the strongest black teacher unions in the nation, United Teachers of New Orleans (UTNO), with a long history of struggle for equal pay for black and white teachers and more adequate educational resources (Randels, 2010).[1] A large portion of the city's black middle class was composed of public school teachers. By 2005, veteran teachers in New Orleans had taught for decades in horrendously underfunded schools and had more than earned their pensions. For reformers, all of this needed to be fundamentally altered; state takeover of New Orleans public schools, combined with groundbreaking charter school reform, would provide the means for change. Hurricane Katrina provided the window of opportunity in August 2005. In the minds of reformers, damage or destruction to 80 percent of the city's public schools created an absolute space for calculated reconstruction and profit making.

Prior to August 2005, the locally elected OPSB controlled 128 public schools in the city of New Orleans. After August 2005, the state-run RSD assumed control of 107 of the city's public schools and chartered the majority of them, while only a handful of schools remained under local governance through OPSB. Thus, by 2009–2010, the majority of schools were charters (51 of 88 schools enrolling 61 percent of students), with more than 30 different providers in two different school districts (Cowen Institute, 2010)—the RSD in New Orleans governed by the state's BESE and NOPS governed by the OPSB (see Figure 2.1). While a smaller number of traditional, direct-run schools remained in each district, the operation of charter schools by education entrepreneurs took precedent. This would be the new model of education reform in New Orleans, one that conscious capitalists claimed was in the best interest of still-displaced communities.

Whiteness, Accumulation by Dispossession, and the Urban Space Economy

In this chapter, I question the notion of socially conscious capitalism and argue that what is happening in New Orleans is, instead, unconscionable and has little to do with improving school performance for children of color. Educational reforms in New Orleans are not designed to respond to oppressed communities or to enhance public school performance, even if they are often couched in such language. Rather, this is a feeding frenzy, a revivified Reconstruction-era blueprint for how to capitalize on public education and line the pockets of white entrepreneurs (and their black allies) who care less about working-class schoolchildren and their grandmothers and much more about obtaining public and private monies and an array of lucrative contracts.

Schools are performing just as reformers tacitly, if not explicitly, intend because the educational reform model is not about improving urban education. As mentioned in chapter 1, these reforms are a form of *accumulation by dispossession,* which David Harvey (2006) defines as a process in which assets previously belonging to one group are put in circulation as capital for another group. In New Orleans, this has included the appropriation and commodification of black children, black schools, and black communities for white exploitation and profit. As I show, this process is intimately connected to the production of an *urban space economy* (Harvey, 1973) premised on capital accumulation and the politics of white supremacy. Here again, Harvey understands the city as a built environment that embodies the conditions and spatial ordering necessary for profitmaking to proceed. Since every economic-spatial project is also a racial one, I also rely on Cheryl Harris's (1995) critical race theory of *whiteness as property.* According to Harris, white identity has historically enabled its possessors to use and enjoy a host of benefits and assets and to exclude communities of color from such entitlements. In New Orleans, white entrepreneurs have seized control of a key asset in black communities—public

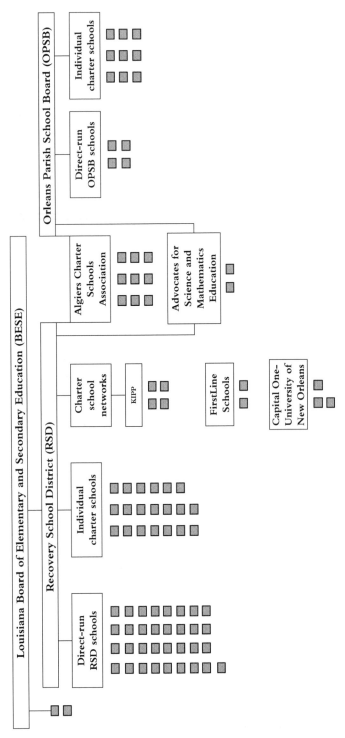

FIGURE 2.1 Diagram of the organization of New Orleans public schools, 2009–2010

schools—and through state assistance, charter school reform, and plans for recon-struction, have built a profitable and exclusionary educational system that threat-ens to reinforce rather than challenge the political economy of New Orleans.

Kalamu ya Salaam, a New Orleans poet and teacher, describes the interconnec-tions between political economy, race, and schooling, particularly with regard to the city's cultural tourism industry:

> Education is ground zero in the systemic exploitation of black people in New Orleans—ground zero because public schools are the direct feeder for the nec-essary, albeit unskilled, labor needed for the tourist-oriented economy....In New Orleans they are building more hotels every day. Where will the bell-hops and maids come from?...Our schools are the way they are because the economy...continues to require a labor force to clean, cook, and serve.
>
> (Buras et al., 2010, pp. 66–67)

Salaam's complex analysis resonates with the ecological framework I seek to elabo-rate on in this chapter (see also Lipman, 2011; Omi & Winant, 1994; Tate, 2008). According to Marcus Weaver-Hightower (2008), policy ecology "consists of the policy itself along with all of the texts, histories, people, places, groups, traditions, economic and political conditions, institutions, and relationships that affect it or that it affects" (p. 155). This is what Harvey (2006) refers to as the socioecological *web of life,* or the critical analysis of *space-time* at a variety of geographical scales. Figure 2.2 presents a visual representation of the web of federal, state, and local actors that shaped the racial-economic reconstruction of public schools in New Orleans during the years immediately following the storm. (Figure 6.1 provides additional detail about this network over the past decade.)

Before undertaking my analysis, allow me to say something about the spatial frames used to illuminate the perspectives of education actors. I ask for readers' patience. The spatial frames described below may seem at first to be painfully theoretical. However, they ultimately help to expose what is at stake in viewing place and urban space in one way as opposed to another. Do entrepreneurs situate their work in the history of schools and neighborhoods or do they view schools as ahistorical places ripe for transformation along the lines they envision? Providing a vocabulary to talk about the *meanings* of place is essential to the analysis and the project of building schools that are connected to the people and communities they serve. Let us consider for a moment some different ways of thinking about space and then keep these in mind during the analysis of charter school reform in New Orleans. It becomes apparent that entrepreneurs and community members have strikingly different views on schools and neighborhoods.

Absolute space is fixed, bounded, calculated, timeless, and presumed to have the precision of Cartesian geometry: a current grid of city streets, a map of school buildings. *Relative* space-time pertains to relationships between objects and depends on what is being observed, why it is being observed, and who is doing

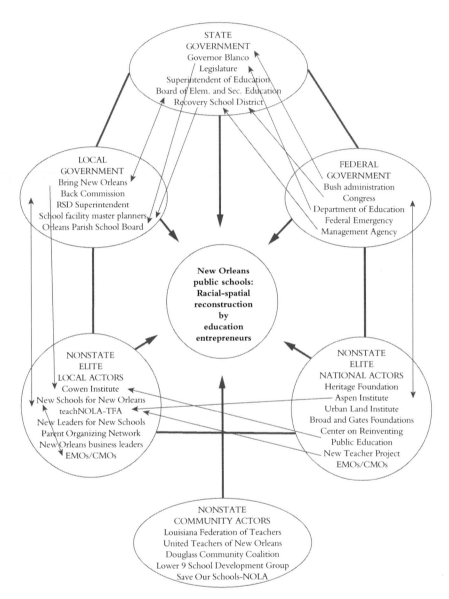

FIGURE 2.2 Policy ecology of New Orleans public schools: Racial–spatial reconstruction

the observing. There are multiple possible geometries depending on one's point of reference: the flow and movement of students from homes to schools. *Relational* space-time is representative of the past, present, and future swirling through and across space; rather than referring to what exists at a single point in time, it requires an aesthetic reading of where "mathematics, poetry, and music converge if not merge" (Harvey, 2006, p. 124): sitting in a newly renovated school and reminiscing about its past incarnations while seeing, through a window, a razed building where a future high school could have resided. Intersecting this matrix is another series of spatial frames: *perceived* space (as sensed through sight, sound, and touch), *conceived* space (as envisioned or represented), and *lived* space (infused with complex meanings generated from daily life, emotion, experience, and imagination) (Harvey, 2006; Lefebvre, 1974).

Taken together, these spatial frames illuminate the stakes of particular policy choices and put in sharp relief whose interests are most squarely served by current school reforms and the urban space economy they produce. The remaking of New Orleans' educational landscape after 2005 involved both systematic federal and state intervention and the actions of local education entrepreneurs and allies in city government. As such, I begin by mapping the web of influence from Washington, DC, to Louisiana's state capital in Baton Rouge and, ultimately, to New Orleans.

When Things Go South: Remaking the Racial, Economic, and Political Geography of New Orleans from Washington, DC, and Baton Rouge

In the mid-1990s, Cecil Picard—a member of the Louisiana state legislature who later became state superintendent of education—helped pass SB1305, which allowed charter schools in several of the state's school districts for a five-year trial period. This trial was only a shadow of what ultimately was to happen in New Orleans. To say that *things went South* in August 2005 alludes to the devastation of homes, schools, and neighborhoods as well as a relative geographic description of how monies and policies traveled from Washington to Baton Rouge and from Baton Rouge to New Orleans. Within days of the hurricane's strike on August 29, 2005, the conservative Heritage Foundation had begun issuing reports on "principled solutions for rebuilding lives and communities" on the Gulf Coast. In a report on September 12, it warned against Congress taking any steps that would "cause dollars to be used inefficiently" (Meese, Butler, & Holmes, 2005, p. 1). Infused with the language of choice, entrepreneurialism, and markets, the Heritage Foundation offered the following guidelines for education:

> New approaches to public policy issues such as enhanced choice in public school education should be the norm. The critical need now is to encourage investors and entrepreneurs to seek new opportunities within these cities. Bureaucrats cannot do that. The key is to encourage private-sector

creativity—for example, by declaring New Orleans and other severely damaged areas "Opportunity Zones."

(Meese et al., 2005, p. 1)

Conscious capitalists conceived of the Gulf Coast, particularly the city of New Orleans, as an experimental space for deregulation, so-called innovation, and private entrepreneurial investment.

Three days after the Heritage Foundation report was issued, President George W. Bush (2005) delivered a national address from Jackson Square and urged that rebuilding efforts address "deep, persistent poverty in the region," a condition that "has roots in a history of racial discrimination" (para. 17). His answer: Congress should create a Gulf Opportunity Zone in Louisiana, Mississippi, and Alabama where the government "will take the side of entrepreneurs as they lead the economic revival of the Gulf Region" (para. 20). The very next day, Heritage followed up with "how to turn the president's Gulf Coast pledge into reality," stressing that "Congress should use existing federal charter school funding to encourage the development of charter schools" (Butler et al., 2005, para. 24). Such political-economic reconstruction of southern space, or regional zoning, was a federal mandate for state leaders—one soon to be bolstered by political pressure and strategic funding. Within two weeks of the storm, on September 14, U.S. Secretary of Education Margaret Spellings (2005) issued a letter to state leaders:

> Because charter schools are exempt from many State and local education rules, they may be uniquely equipped to serve [storm affected] students. Accordingly, the [U.S.] Department [of Education] is prepared to consider requests for statutory and regulatory waivers of various requirements under the CSP [Charter School Program] and other federal statutes and regulations over which the Secretary of Education exercises administrative authority.
>
> (para. 2)

In addition, Spellings' letter stated that $20 million was available "to assist States and charter schools to meet the immediate needs of students" (para. 3). Written requests for federal charter school funds were to be submitted by September 23—just nine days later—or they would expire.

State leaders in Louisiana had plans of their own. A displaced representative of the Louisiana Federation of Teachers (LFT)[2] reported receiving a call from Superintendent Picard even before the Federal Emergency Management Agency (FEMA) had hit the ground to address the crisis unfolding in New Orleans, where residents were stranded and dying in the hurricane's wake. The LFT representative recalled Picard saying:

> The schools are going to be closed for at least a year. I mean, it's bad, but at the end of it all, we are going to have a brand new school system and it's

going to be the bright new city of great opportunity for all children. ... New Orleans is going to be a much smaller city because the folks that have been in New Orleans, the poor, have had no opportunities and now they are arriving in places [that promise much more].

On one hand, New Orleans was destined to be a new city with educational opportunity for *all* children; on the other, it was going to be *smaller* with *fewer poor people*. These two maps of the future were irreconcilable and betrayed deeper contradictions. Which map would be the blueprint?

A makeshift headquarters was set up in Baton Rouge for high-ranking state officials to reengineer the city. There was an immediate attempt to install Rod Paige, Bush's former secretary of education, as superintendent of education in Orleans Parish; however, according to an LFT representative, it failed because a supermajority vote of the Orleans Parish School Board was required but not secured. Nonetheless, the move for Paige signaled federal influence. Even more alarming, according to this representative, was that there was talk of "the social re-engineering of a [Republican] city." In other words, there were political aspirations (some of which have come to pass) that New Orleans could be racially reconstructed so that the largely black Democratic stronghold of New Orleans would be weakened and the state's white Republican forces could have greater electoral sway; this would also have implications for local politics, shifting the racial balance of constituencies. In fact, a study in 2008 revealed that "the number of voters in the New Orleans area has fallen sharply, with African-Americans and registered Democrats losing the most ground" (Krupa, 2008, para. 1).[3] The potential for radical shifts in the political landscape could have provided context for Picard's geographic imagination—did the poor (and black) residents not want to return, or were they not wanted back?

In November 2005, Louisiana governor Kathleen Blanco called a special legislative session in Baton Rouge. One LFT representative recalled, "We were hearing rumors that of all the things we could concentrate on [after] the greatest national disaster to hit a state or city—we're going to concentrate on school reform." After hearing about a potential state takeover of New Orleans schools, the LFT approached Blanco, who reportedly assured the organization that "everything was going to be fine." That legislative session became the occasion for passing Act 35, which redefined what constituted a "failing" school so that most of the New Orleans public schools could be deemed failing and placed in a state-run Recovery School District.[4] Act 35 enabled 107 of the 128 schools to be folded into the RSD, whereas only 13 schools could have been assumed before the legislation was passed (UTNO et al., 2006).

On the floor of the state legislature where the bill was circulating, an LFT representative asked why all of a sudden the denotation of failure had shifted upward, with the School Performance Score (SPS) cut point now just below the state average (i.e., shifting from 60 to 87.4), and what exactly a "failing school" was. A white suburban senator reportedly responded, "A failing school is whatever we say it is." The LFT representative reflected on the meaning of the senator's statement:

> The definitions are as we define them and the process is not driven by any
> kind of real data. It's driven by the powers, and the powers now had a very
> clear charge. And the charge was these schools are going to be taken over
> and they're going to be reformed, and they're going to be sold out, they're
> going to be chartered.

This exercise of raw power, revealing the indeterminate nature of the law and its
malleability in serving dominant interests (Crenshaw, Gotanda, Peller, & Thomas,
1995), has been a central dynamic of education reform in New Orleans. The
circuit of power was not limited to Baton Rouge alone. It seems that, figuratively,
Governor Blanco had a gun placed to her head by federal officials. An LFT representative said that the options presented to her were limited: "You're either going
to turn [New Orleans] this way, it's going to become the largest experiment for
charter schools—we're going to reengineer this, or you're not going to get the
money [for reconstruction]."

Around this same period in 2005, Blanco signed Executive Orders 58 and 79
suspending certain provisions of charter school law, such as the need to consult and
obtain the votes of affected faculty, staff, and parents before converting an existing
public school into a charter school (LFT & AFT, 2007). In a letter regarding the
executive orders, the LFT expressed a number of fundamental democratic concerns:

> Current charter school law provides for a community and faculty buy-in
> expressed by a favorable vote by both for a very good reason. The success
> of such an experimental school is largely dependent upon this active buy-
> in. ... Teachers who wish to return to their now "forced-charter" schools must
> first accept the vacating of their negotiated contract, forfeiture of many legal
> rights, and embrace conditions of employment imposed upon them. They
> must also accept a unilaterally developed education plan spelled out in the
> charter application. Otherwise, these dedicated professionals cannot return.

Even more crucially, teachers "may have served with ... commitment for decades
only to see their sense of place and their careers snatched from them." Ultimately,
the letter concludes, "a charter school decree ... disenfranchises the stakeholders"
(LFT, 2005). Such decrees were executed with a speed, precision, and scope that
are terrifying. And disenfranchisement was not a by-product—it was a goal.

Strategic conversations about the development of "human capital" in New
Orleans (read: teachers) were proceeding simultaneously in Washington, DC, at the
Aspen Institute, a self-described nonpartisan education and policy studies institute
headed by Walter Isaacson (Aspen Institute, n.d.). Born in New Orleans, Isaacson
worked for the local *Times-Picayune* newspaper and later as CEO of CNN. In 2003
he became president and CEO of the Aspen Institute. In addition, he was serving
as chairman of the board of Teach for America, which recruits college graduates
who are not yet certified as teachers to teach in urban schools.[5] As a witness to

exchanges at the Aspen Institute in Washington, an LFT representative pondered the dominant discourse there:

> We have a problem with teaching, the sustainability of the model. What do you do with the pension issue? The cost issues associated with it? Health care? We all know as teachers get older the cost of health care [rises]. What if we have a teacher quota: it is five years. Young people brought from quality universities, recruited by TFA [Teach for America], who would come. Until they decided what they really wanted to do with their lives, they would teach. There is no expectation of a pension. They would do this service.

On November 30, 2005, the announcement went out: 7,500 New Orleans teachers and school employees were informed that they would be fired and lose health insurance on January 31, 2006 (LFT & AFT, 2007; UTNO, LFT, & AFT, 2007a). In a piece titled "Go Southeast, Young Man," Isaacson (2006) lauded the unfolding educational innovations as a "civic revival," writing, "A system of competing charter schools has sprung up, nurtured by the state and fostered in Washington" (para. 11). It did not feel like a revival to veteran teachers. They had been fired en masse without due process and without any regard for either their contributions as educators or their hard-won rights and entitlements. When the New Orleans Public School system was dissolved and reorganized as a mere shadow of itself, and the state-run RSD was installed, veteran teachers who had worked for 20 to 30 years effectively lost all protections and entitlements guaranteed by UTNO's collective bargaining agreement. That is to say, the collective bargaining agreement was nullified because the district with which the agreement was negotiated no longer existed. This was unconscionable, but the state had no intention of rectifying it; rather, the state had engineered it.

One major issue was related to the cost of health insurance for those teachers and retirees who remained in the revamped system: premiums threatened to rise to over $1,000 per month. As an LFT representative recounted, during the infamous November legislative session, two elderly, retired teachers in their 80s planned a trip to Baton Rouge to request appropriations to offset escalating premiums:

> It was getting toward the end [of the session] and ... there was no quorum. So you had these old folks sitting in there with their nice little ties on, taught for 35 years each in the system, and they are going to tell them there is not going to be a meeting [without a quorum]. Now of course the administration brought them around to meet different people. ... There were about ten of them [legislators] that came out. "Oh, something will work out." The bottom line is, nothing did. There was no money and the increases occurred.

The representative contends, "There is still no willingness to accept responsibility that you broke something down. ... People work their entire lives. You have an obligation. They had the expectation. ... This is a moral imperative." Meanwhile, despite the inhumane and criminal nature of their actions, many state legislators at the session donned buttons on their shirts that read "Rebuild It Right." Plans in Washington and Baton Rouge to oust vested, unionized, experienced teachers who were "expensive," and to recruit exploitable, cheap, itinerant teachers with little expectation of benefits, were under way in New Orleans.

Another demonstration of unbridled power was exemplified when Lisa Keeling, a teacher for 21 years, returned after a period of displacement to teach at her former school. Yet, when Keeling arrived at school, she was greeted by a principal she did not recognize who asked what she was doing there (LFT, n.d.). According to an LFT representative, she was informed, "You don't work here anymore. But since you're here, why don't you get your stuff out." Her school had been taken over and chartered without teacher or community input. One can only imagine what it must have been like for Keeling to reenter this lived space, where she had countless memories of students and years of emotional attachment, only to discover that the one place that felt like home had been taken over and completely reconstituted. Such a moment crystallizes the meaning of accumulation by dispossession. To educational privatizers, the school was conceived as an empty shell ripe for transformation. But for Keeling, its hallways were pathways to a past she knew well, its present was painfully unrecognizable, and the future she imagined returning to was stolen. Keeling made her way north to the legislative session where she, too, was rebuffed.

The federal government created a Gulf Opportunity Zone, while President Bush spoke of addressing persistent inequities in the region. State officials in Louisiana alluded to building a bright new city and better schools for all children. Despite this socially conscious discourse, the flow of money and corresponding legislation evidenced a very different set of commitments. As their actions reveal, federal and state authorities in alliance with national policy actors sought to construct an urban space economy in New Orleans that served the interests of education entrepreneurs far more than the students, parents, and veteran teachers presumably at the center of reform. I argue that the racial and spatial dimensions of the project were evident—black veteran teachers were to be removed and replaced; their "sense of place" was to be snatched in the most literal sense.

The Bring New Orleans *Back* Commission?

In addition to understanding the federal and state roles, it is equally essential to understand the roles of local government and education entrepreneurs in advancing racial-economic reconstruction and the ways in which national policy actors supported reform initiatives on the ground in New Orleans. Beyond Baton Rouge, the dynamics of reform were likewise unfolding in New Orleans. In October 2005, Mayor Ray Nagin established the Bring New Orleans Back Commission (BNOB). Similar to Blanco's Louisiana Recovery Authority, BNOB's leaders included business elites (Buras, 2005). Among the appointees was James Reiss, a shipping and real estate mogul and chair of New Orleans Business Council, who declared, "Those who want to see this city rebuilt want to see it done in a completely different way: demographically, politically, and economically" (Cooper, 2005). Joseph Canizaro, another appointee and real estate multimillionaire, connected BNOB with the Urban Land Institute, which raised $1 million to assist in rebuilding the Gulf Coast. This fund was initiated with a stipend from its J. C. Nichols Prize for Visionaries in Urban Development program. Notably, Nichols "was an influential real estate 'pioneer' from Kansas City…who played a key role in promoting the use of racial covenants…to keep African Americans…out of neighborhoods" (Arena, 2005, para. 5). In this way, BNOB evidenced a deeply relational and disturbing conception of space and time. To Bring New Orleans *Back* was really to tap a legacy of racial exclusion that stretched far and wide and to invoke this past as the city's future—a bright new city where whiteness as property will pass as socially responsible land use.

A range of subcommittees were constituted under BNOB, among them city planning, economic development, culture, and education, and each was tasked with envisioning and formulating a component of the larger plan for reconstruction. Headed by Tulane University president Scott Cowen, BNOB's education committee issued its plan in January 2006, advocating a "world-class public education" in the form of an all-charter school district. Using an educational network model, providers would operate groups of charter schools coordinated by network managers, and principals would be given oversight on budgets, hiring, and firing. This would be a portfolio district, a system of schools rather than a school system traditionally controlled by a presumably inefficient central office (BNOB, 2006).

BNOB's education committee made two notable recommendations: first, the district create a fair, rules-based system for placing students in their school of choice (p. 16); second, the district design a comprehensive scorecard to assess school and network performance and make scorecard results publicly available (BNOB, 2006, p. 18). These recommendations are particularly significant because they have never been fully implemented. The lack of these two items—fairness in student access and accountability in charter school performance—is noteworthy since they are the aspects of school choice that ensure democratic processes and could act as policy levers leading to greater oversight.

Many on the education committee agreed that free-market schooling was indeed the way forward, including Scott Cowen, Leslie Jacobs, Cecil Picard, and Mary Garton, executive director of Teach for America of Greater New Orleans. The stakeholder advisory committee that supported BNOB's educational effort also included some conspicuous figures: Steven Bingler, owner of Concordia architects, a firm with stakes in consulting and school building contracts; Brian Riedlinger, who would manage the Algiers Charter School Association, a network of charter schools; and Kathy Riedlinger, who would act as principal at Lusher, a selective admissions charter school. The committee also touted its consultation of "top education experts" such as Wendy Kopp, Teach for America's founder; Mike Feinberg, founder of the Knowledge Is Power Program (KIPP); and Sarah Usdin, a founding partner of the New Teacher Project and soon-to-form New Schools for New Orleans (NSNO), a charter school incubator. Moreover, it consulted with the Gates Foundation, Broad Foundation, and Annenberg Institute—groups that would later support the materialization of BNOB's vision either politically or financially.

As BNOB's plans were being issued, the federal government had already begun providing millions of dollars for the establishment of charter schools in New Orleans ($45 million in the first ten months after the storm) (UTNO, LFT, & AFT, 2006). Meanwhile, Paul Hill and his colleague Jane Hannaway (2006) issued a report on schooling in New Orleans for the Urban Institute. Their view was unequivocal: "The leadership of the state of Louisiana and the city of New Orleans should treat the school system as a laboratory" (p. 11).

The Cowen Institute for Public Education Initiatives: New Schools, New Teachers, and New Leaders for *New* Orleans

The actions of federal, state, and local government created an opportunistic space into which education entrepreneurs quickly stepped. In fact, the role of elite nongovernmental policy actors in remapping the city's schools was fundamental, including an entrepreneurial university and an array of locally situated, but nationally funded, charter school and human capital recruitment organizations—all of which aimed to advance what was portrayed as an innovative experiment in reengineering public education.

In its report, BNOB's education committee suggested the need to transform itself into an "Implementation Oversight Committee" (BNOB, 2006, p. 36). Enter the Cowen Institute for Public Education Initiatives at Tulane University, which provides shelter for a host of pro-charter school and human capital recruitment organizations in New Orleans. A Cowen Institute representative explained that the links between BNOB's education committee and the Institute were never part of a preordained plan but, rather, evolved organically and for strategic purposes. When the committee's report was issued in January 2006 and hailed as a national "blueprint for what education reform looks like," a mayoral election was on the horizon and there were concerns that the blueprint could get "lost in the shuffle," particularly if Nagin, who instituted BNOB, lost at the polls.

A more serious concern pertained to negative public perceptions of BNOB and the need to strategically disassociate the educational blueprint from its origins, even as its content remained unchanged. At the grassroots level there was an increasing sense that the BNOB agenda was antithetical to the interests of poor and working-class African Americans who wished to return to the city. A representative of the Cowen Institute shared:

> We recognized that no matter what happened, it [the education blueprint] couldn't be housed within the mayor's office. ... One of the [BNOB] Commission meetings ... was a presentation about where people could live. ... It was a public meeting [with 600 residents] and there was this big map with dots, and it was like you're looking—"That red dot is actually where I live and red means that's going to be green space."... Everyone then thought of the land use plan. ... [And] anything attached to [BNOB] was almost like a four-letter word. ... They were so up in arms about shrinking New Orleans' footprint.

For this reason, even if the education blueprint was part of a more comprehensive plan to take over and commodify public assets in black neighborhoods, it had to be given new grounding.

In the end, as a Cowen representative explained, education reformers recognized that Tulane could "move something along," particularly since it is "the largest employer in the city—we have more political capital in the state and DC than any other entity." The need was all the more pressing as "new nonprofits were arising," such as New Schools for New Orleans and New Leaders for New Schools, "yet [without] a lot of coordination between anybody." It was envisaged that Tulane could be a "convener of all of these." The Cowen Institute opened its doors in March 2007, fashioning itself as an "action-oriented think tank that informs and advances solutions—through policies, programs, and partnerships—to eliminate the challenges impeding the success of K–12 education" (e.g., see Cowen Institute, 2010, p. i).

An oft-repeated exultation at the Cowen Institute is that no one there has an educational background. This is seen as positive because, according to an Institute representative, in schools of education:

> They spend all of their research capacity and money and resources on academic theory and curriculum. ... But the problem is over here. ... [The schools] can't even buy books because the money is being mismanaged, or the principals can't even fire bad teachers.
> ... That's about management. That's not about academics and curriculum.

By contrast, the staff at the Cowen Institute is "able to think about [education] from a business perspective because we have MBAs working who've studied corporate America and franchising."

According to the Cowen Institute, the central problem is a managerial one. It is not that there is no money to buy books, or that teachers are doing badly because there are no books; instead it is an issue of bureaucratic governance, and the theory is that if schools are open to market forces, they will improve. Therefore, one of the primary areas where the Cowen Institute has focused its resources is governance. For example, the institute generated a series of white papers on models of educational management (Cowen Institute, 2009a, 2009b, 2009c). While arguments for and against particular models are presented, the overarching impression is that local school boards are politicized and ineffective and that either state control, some level of mayoral control, or appointed leadership is preferable; a central office generates fraud and waste while decentralized decision making in budgeting, personnel, and school operations leads to improved outcomes and cost reduction; and, finally, charter schools are the wave of the future and state-level authorization, seemingly insulated from local matters, is likely to be a more impartial and productive process.

A more historicized and relational frame betrays the notion that the problem is a managerial one. Given that since the late 1970s the mayor, city council, and board of education in New Orleans have been more black, specifically Afro-Creole, than white (DeVore & Logsdon, 1991; Parent, 2004), this notion harkens back to Reconstruction-era discourse that African Americans have no capacity for self-government. While past instances of financial mismanagement in NOPS should not be dismissed, we must also recall the legacy of racialized neglect and disinvestment that plagued the schools, engendered shortfalls in the millions, and made it all but impossible to balance the budget (Buras, 2007).

When I questioned representatives at the Cowen Institute about its mission as an "action-oriented think tank," there was consistent denial that it was engaged in political work (e.g., see Cowen Institute, 2010, p. i). One representative underscored, "We don't advocate for an all-charter system because we don't feel there's adequate research to indicate that charters will outperform noncharters." Instead representatives present the Institute as an "honest broker" and an "objective observer." However, as soon as one steps through its doors and perceives the space, this presentation is challenged. Just beyond the main desk is an incubation room for charter schools. The fact is, the Cowen Institute provides free room and board to some of the most aggressive pro-charter school groups and human capital recruitment organizations in the city, including: New Schools for New Orleans (NSNO), a charter school incubator; an alternative teacher recruitment triad comprised of teachNOLA, the New Teacher Project, and Teach for America (TFA); New Leaders for New Schools (NLNS), a recruitment and professional development project for principals and charter school board members; and the New Orleans Parent Organizing Network, a group that organizes parents around school choice.

When asked to account for this contradiction, one Institute representative explained:

> I think the idea was just that Cowen had a lot of space and there were a number of organizations that needed space. ... The idea was to bring a lot of groups together that were working in the reform area so that there would be more back and forth around, "What are you doing?"

By sharing space, another representative said, the Institute is "able to find out what's happening in the trenches without being in the trenches."

Whether explicitly acknowledged or not, the Cowen Institute is indeed in the trenches. I assert that there are no circumstances under which an institution as elite as Tulane University would provide shelter for organizations without a congruence between the Cowen Institute's mission and their purposes. Nor was it a financial necessity for these groups to rely on the Institute for space, particularly since NSNO, TFA, and NLNS received $17.5 million from the Broad, Gates, and Doris and Donald Fisher foundations in December 2007 (Maxwell, 2007; Scott, 2009). Moreover, the spatial politics are apparent: the Cowen Institute and its partners are co-located because they share an agenda, and it does not seem by chance that they operate under the auspices of Tulane, a historically white institution uptown, while the actions of these organizations have serious consequences for black children and families who largely live downtown.

Initiatives Housed at the Cowen Institute

New Schools for New Orleans (NSNO), founded in early 2006, is committed to charter school and human capital development. More specifically, its strategy is fivefold as it seeks founders to *start* charter schools, principals to *lead* charter schools, teachers to *teach* in charter schools, members to *serve* on charter school boards, and investors and philanthropists to *contribute* to these efforts (see NSNO 2008a, 2008b, 2008c). For example, its Incubation Program provides "resources to new school founders in the year before opening" and announces, "If you are an experienced, dynamic, entrepreneurial educator...then this is your chance" (NSNO, n.d., p. 7). From 2007 to 2010, the organization launched ten charter schools, seeded three local charter management organizations, and provided 21 start-up grants that have supported over 90 percent of newly approved charter schools (NSNO, 2010b).

NSNO has partnered with the national organization New Leaders for New Schools (NLNS) to recruit, train, and place principals and other school leaders in the public schools of New Orleans. "In schools, just as with businesses, strong leadership breeds results," reads its literature (NSNO, 2008a, para 1). NSNO (2010b) boasts the training of 36 charter school boards for over 90 percent of charter schools in the city. To facilitate this effort, NLNS maintains a Board Bank that includes the names and résumés of parties wishing to serve on charter school boards and makes them available to schools. The qualifications that NLNS expects from Board Bank members reveal the raced and classed dimensions of charter school governance:

- Expertise in law, real estate, financial management, governance, marketing, fund raising, community organizing/outreach, education, or strategic planning
- Personal experience with entrepreneurship
- Willingness to leverage personal and professional networks on behalf of the school (NSNO, 2010a)

It is safe to say that very few working-class parents—most of whom are African American in New Orleans—command the social, economic, and political capital, much less the spare time, to participate on such a board. In this way, whiteness is perpetuated as a form of property, as those who possess forms of capital closely linked to class and race status benefit from and exercise disproportionate power over public schools attended by African American students.

An additional "human capital" initiative is teachNOLA, a teacher recruitment collaboration with the New Teacher Project, a national organization that "works with clients on a fee-for-service basis" to place "alternate route teachers" in "high-need schools" (TNTP, 2010). The New Teacher Project itself won the Social Capitalist Award in 2008 from *Fast Company* magazine (TNTP, 2007). Building on this ethos, teachNOLA claims to have "eliminated the city's teaching shortage so that there can now be an increased focus on long-term quality" (NSNO, 2010b). Skirting the fact that the shortage was engineered through state policy, teachNOLA placed new teachers in 96 percent of the city's charter schools from 2007–2010 (NSNO, 2010b).

New Schools for New Orleans also seeded the New Orleans Parent Organizing Network, tasked with providing information to parents on school choice. Among the Network's projects was the 90-page *New Orleans Parents' Guide* (NSNO, 2007). The earliest guide suggested that parents seeking to enroll a child determine which documents are required by a given school in order to apply or register, including report cards and test scores that "can help *properly place* [italics added] your child" (p. 9). Parents are also offered guidance on how to "choose" a school: review 70 pages of information to "identify schools," then arrange visits, tour the schools, observe classes, interview principals and teachers, and possibly apply—that is, if one's child qualifies and the application deadline has not passed (pp. 9–15). Clearly, such processes are navigated more easily by parents with surplus time, readily accessible transportation, intact documents, physically undamaged homes, monetary resources, and education, thereby advantaging more privileged families as well as families with "able" and "high-achieving" children (see also Apple, 2001; Ball, 2003). This provokes questions about student admission and familial access to what are supposed to be public spaces and institutions. NSNO consistently states its support for chartering "public" and "open enrollment schools," but such qualifiers serve to mask exclusionary practices that are occurring (NSNO, n.d.). While *open enrollment* may refer to schools that do not rely on traditional neighborhood attendance boundaries for student admission but instead admit students citywide, this does not mean that such schools are necessarily *open access* with respect to admissions policies.[6]

Whether in terms of how boards are constituted or in terms of how student and familial challenges are addressed, the charter school movement in New Orleans is closely bound to the protection of whiteness as property, as the clearest beneficiaries are upper-class white (and a few black) entrepreneurs who seek to capitalize on public assets for their own advancement while dispossessing the very communities the schools are supposed to serve. A veteran teacher reflected on the mass firing of educators and the charter-driven state takeover:

> I explain the dismissal as a hostile takeover, a power struggle [by] those who wanted the control of the millions of dollars that was involved in education in Orleans Parish. …
>
> This was primarily controlled by African Americans who were able to allot contracts and do all the necessary things that they needed to do to control their own destiny. The powers that be [were] not pleased with that. They were looking for years to find ways to wrest control back from the district because the district served a majority African American population.

Notably, while charter school advocates frequently refer to "fraud" that predated current reforms, there is much less talk about the fraudulent manner in which the schools were taken over or the ways in which their charterization enables the channeling of public monies into private hands through "legal" means.

The Recovery School District and School Facilities Master Plan: The Master's Plan Indeed

The state-run Recovery School District (RSD) has been a key partner in advancing the project of conscious capitalism, turning over public schools to education entrepreneurs for a "fresh start." Historic and willfully fostered racial inequities prepared the grounds for their assault on black schools and neighborhoods, while the School Facilities Master Plan (SFMP) provides the blueprint for racial-spatial reconstruction of New Orleans' urban space economy.

In 2006, many students in the RSD, who were nearly twice as likely to be low-income, were still without teachers, books, buildings, and school buses (Ritea, 2006; UTNO et al., 2006). By January 2007, the Southern Institute for Education and Research declared that New Orleans had "the most balkanized school system in North America" (McElroy, 2007). After Cecil Picard passed away, Paul Pastorek—a corporate attorney and former member of BESE—took his place as state superintendent of education (Font, 2009). While schoolchildren in New Orleans went without books, Pastorek became the highest paid state education superintendent in the South, making a salary of $411,000. Paul Vallas, who was partly responsible for the closure and privatization of schools in Chicago and Philadelphia, assumed the role of RSD superintendent for a salary of $252,689 (Thevenot, 2009). Those responsible for leading the project of accumulation by dispossession would be well paid for their labor, while the needs of veteran teachers and students would be neglected, if not consciously dismissed.

The start of the school year in 2007 was no more promising. By this time, the city had 82 public schools, and 42 were charters—most of them with selective admissions criteria, enrollment caps, and other barriers to entry (UTNO, LFT, & AFT, 2007b).

The development of the SFMP for Orleans Parish by school officials and private consultants was also under way from October 2007 to July 2008 (RSD & NOPS, 2008a). The SFMP determines which schools remain open, merit renovation or new construction, or get closed—decisions with clear implications for working-class and middle-class communities of color who resided where destruction from the hurricane was most substantial.[7] It landbanks more than 60 existing schools; that is, the schools are either to be "retained" (remain closed indefinitely), "redeveloped," or "converted" for public or private uses (RSD & NOPS, 2008a, p. 58). Each of these possibilities has direct and disparate financial consequences for entrepreneurs and targeted schools and communities.

According to the RSD and OPSB, "The creation of the master plan presented a unique opportunity to engage the community" (RSD & NOPS, 2008a, p. 38). However, rather than using the language of community, the plan is filled with terms such as *inputs, outputs, Facility Condition Index, population trends,* and *recovery profiles.* Working-class communities of color were denied a voice in shaping the SFMP in any meaningful way. After a series of public meetings between October 2007 and July 2008—meetings that many residents described as a farce, since decision making was already under way by master planners—the SFMP "draft" was released in August 2008 (RSD & NOPS, 2008a). There was to be a 30-day window of public comment before the final plan was set. Around this time, Hurricanes Gustav and Ike prompted another round of evacuations. Concerned about parents' and students' ability to weigh in before the deadline, Save Our Schools–New Orleans, Louisiana (SOSNOLA) petitioned the RSD for a 90-day extension of the comment period to January 1, 2009. The petition argued that citizens needed additional time "to hold meaningful conversations within … communities so as to make informed decisions regarding our thoughts on the plan" and concluded with the line, "OUR Schools. OUR Future. OUR plans." As one resident wrote with his signature on the petition, "To ram this Master Plan through with such a brief public comment period is unconscionable" (SOSNOLA, 2008). However, the planners were not moved by the petition; they extended the period of comment by only two weeks. In the end, a representative with SOSNOLA said, "The schools that are going to be rebuilt under the [SFMP] are basically at the whim of the superintendent and the folks who are in charge." Dismissing the request for additional time for public comment, the RSD released its amendments to the draft master plan in early November 2008 (RSD & NOPS, 2008b).

The SFMP is intimately related to the production of New Orleans' urban space economy. The plan patently reflects the racial, economic, and spatial vision of the master planners, education entrepreneurs, and their uptown neighborhood allies rather than the city imagined by black working-class neighborhood residents. First and foremost, the SFMP adopted an absolute and highly technical conception of space—one divorced from the lived experiences and historical relations that communities share with longstanding neighborhood schools. This ahistorical focus on facilities can be seen in the blueprint, which states that "the master plan describes the maintenance and development of an infrastructure and physical plants that will support the needs of educational delivery" (RSD & NOPS, 2008a, p. 13).

Second, the plan weds demography and topography to produce *accumulation by dispossession* (Harvey, 2006). One of the "selection parameters" for determining where schools will be opened, renovated, or built is enrollment projections, which do not account for the ways in which class, race, and state policy have enabled and disabled the reconstruction of specific neighborhoods—or the fact that it is even harder to return to and rebuild neighborhoods when there is no school nearby. The plan fails to account for the ways in which the SFMP itself plays a fundamental role in shaping the deconstruction and reconstruction of communities along race- and class-based lines.

Third, the geography of where schools will be landbanked, demolished, or built is wholly racialized and connected to elite conceptions of a less populous city. One community member expressed concern about the master planning process and possible closure of Frederick Douglass High School, the only open-access high school in the Bywater neighborhood (see Figure 2.3). "If we close down all of the high schools, and you know your children have nowhere to go to school," policymakers presume, "then you'll leave." "They've tried everything that they can to get people out [of this city]," she averred.

Finally, an uneven urban space economy was produced through the phased nature of the blueprint—an example of what Lipsitz (2007) calls the "spatialization of race" and the "racialization of space." Although the SFMP includes six different building phases, only Phase 1 was actually funded when the plan was developed. The estimated cost of the entire plan is approximately $2 billion, yet only $685 million had been secured through FEMA and Community Development Block Grants.[8] A representative of the grassroots parent organization SOSNOLA stated, "I call it Phase 1 and Phase Never." The reality is, for the foreseeable future only schools in Phase 1 will receive support for rebuilding, which means only certain neighborhoods will have schools. Even before the development of the SFMP, Cynthia Willard-Lewis, who represents downtown neighborhoods on the city council, warned, "The reality check is that the schools below Canal Street were X-ed off the map" (Tisserand, 2007, para. 35). In addition, phasing of the plan engendered a splintered spatial imaginary that divided communities from one another as each sought to secure a place in Phase 1 of the blueprint.

Sadly, a spatial analysis of the distribution of schools across the city does not require sophisticated use of geographic information systems, although I did use such technology; a pencil, however, would suffice. Canal Street, which divides uptown from downtown and borders the French Quarter, not only demarcates natural high ground from vulnerable low ground and white space from black space, but it likewise marks a long history of racism, territorial segregation, and economic exploitation of black labor. For example, one of the major thoroughfares intersecting Canal Street is called St. Charles Avenue on the uptown side and Royal Street on the downtown

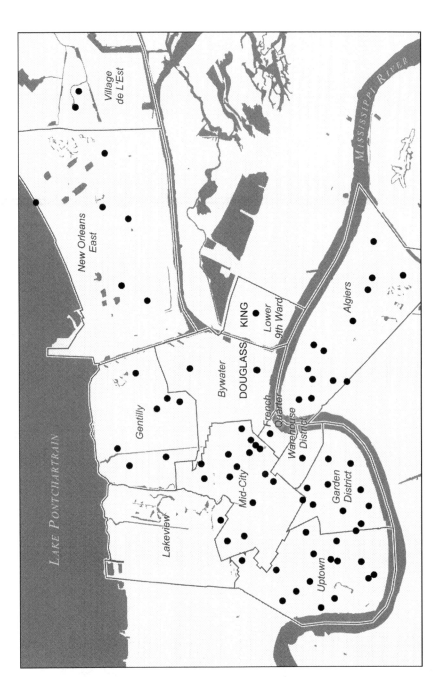

FIGURE 2.3 Map of public school locations in New Orleans

Note: Since charter schools push out traditional schools and/or take over space when they close, co-located schools are repre-sented by a single bullet.

side, a reminder of segregation. Today it is a stark dividing line that separates a high density of public schools relocated uptown under the SFMP (RSD & NOPS, 2008a) and the mere handful of public schools reopened or rebuilt downtown.

Figure 2.3 shows school locations in New Orleans in 2009–2010 after five years of reform. Simply laying a pencil where the French Quarter divides uptown from downtown reveals the mass concentration of schools uptown and the gross absence of schools downtown, even though the majority of the students who attend public schools live in the downtown neighborhoods. Downtown neighborhoods in Figure 2.3 include Bywater, the Lower 9th Ward, New Orleans East, and Village de L'Est. Figure 2.4 shows that these areas are heavily populated by African Americans, unlike most uptown areas—Warehouse District, Garden District, and Uptown—where schools have been rebuilt. It is also interesting to note that for black neighborhoods in uptown areas, schools were rebuilt peripherally rather than centrally; they are located on the outer edges of uptown neighborhoods that are heavily African American or where black neighborhoods border predominantly white uptown territory. Across the Mississippi River in Algiers, a more substantial number of schools were rebuilt, but these were also some of the first schools, due to limited damage, to be taken over and chartered through the Algiers Charter School Association, with hundreds of veteran teachers fired; they are also the least accessible schools for the majority of black students, who reside on the opposite side of the river in downtown New Orleans. In sum, schools are most sparse downtown where the majority of black students reside. This uneven geography impacts student access, transportation issues, and neighborhood restoration more generally. It is common to see elementary-aged children at bus stops before sunrise and after sunset in New Orleans. There is no such thing as walking to a neighborhood school; if children miss the bus, they miss school, or working-class families must orchestrate transportation to locations relatively distant from where they live if that is the only "choice" available.

The spatialization of race and the racialization of space (Lipsitz, 2007) are clearly evident, particularly as public schools are geographically reorganized, commodified, and wedded to the perpetuation of racial and economic power and subordination. An independent analysis by policy scholar Bruce Baker (2011) affirms the uneven geography discussed above and information from the Greater New Orleans Community Data Center (2011) affirms that a density of school-aged children remain in neighborhoods where schools have not been rebuilt, a fact that renders master planners' demographic planning problematic.

To provide a very real glimpse into what is happening under the SFMP, I offer as an example the story of the Lower 9 School Development Group (L9SDG) at the end of the next chapter. This moves us from an overarching discussion of the SFMP's racial-spatial politics to a living example of how the decisions of elite policy actors are affecting and dispossessing grassroots communities.

Martin Luther King Elementary School in the Lower 9th Ward (see Figure 2.3) was only rebuilt due to the civil disobedience of its principal, veteran teachers, and

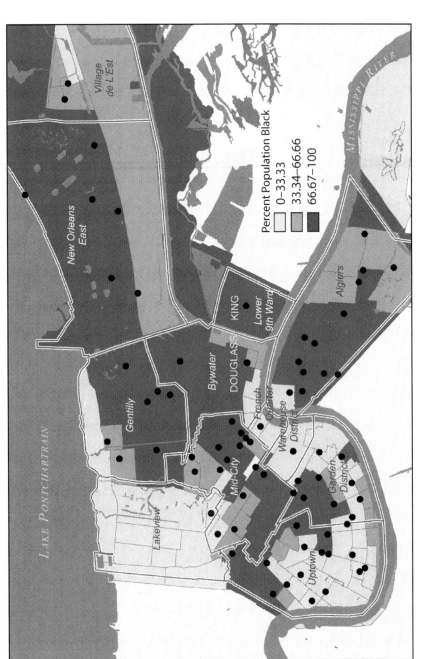

FIGURE 2.4 Map of public school locations in New Orleans, with racial geography

Percent Population Black
0–33.33
33.34–66.66
66.67–100

LAKE PONTCHARTRAIN

Mississippi River

Lakeview

Village de L'Est

New Orleans East

Gentilly

Mid-City

Bywater

DOUGLASS

KING

Lower 9th Ward

French Quarter

Warehouse District

Garden District

Uptown

Algiers

community members (Buras, 2011a). Predating current reforms by a decade, it was forced to charter—the only means for possibly reopening. Since its reopening, the school has reached capacity at 800 students, has a waiting list of over 500, and is running a small high school on its current campus.

As the Lower 9 School Development Group (L9SDG) attests, the neighborhood is in desperate need of a high school. Under the SFMP, three of the five schools that existed in the Lower 9th Ward have either been demolished or are slated for demolition, and a fourth has been indefinitely closed (RSD & NOPS, 2008a). Yet the RSD received millions from FEMA for damage to these schools. This money was not allocated to the Lower 9th Ward, but instead it was placed in a general fund and is being used for other Phase 1 projects (L9SDG, 2010). Although Phase 2 includes a Lower 9th Ward high school, it was planned as a meager $5 million addition to King Elementary (RSD & NOPS, 2008b). L9SDG formed to collect petitions from families for a proposed high school in the neighborhood. It also sponsored a billboard demanding RSD funding for neighborhood schools, which read, "Lower 9th Ward Stakeholders Ask ... Where's the Money?" A representative of the group asks, "Who made a decision that we didn't want a school back in this area? ... To take my money and place it in some arbitrary fund and say we're going to do whatever we want to do—I think that's criminal" (see also Buras, 2011b; L9SDG, 2010). More will be said about this and the SFMP at the end of the next chapter. All in all, the SFMP has been a fundamental part of building the "new city" envisioned by Picard and like-minded policymakers.

New Orleans—Socially Conscious Capitalism?

The race and class dynamics producing the urban space economy of New Orleans involve not only local policy actors but powerful actors at the state and federal levels as well. From nationally influential conservative foundations and the corresponding exercise of power by federal authorities, to Louisiana lawmakers and state education officials, to local politicians, business leaders, and education entrepreneurs, an experimental plan for reconstructing the public schools of New Orleans was consciously envisioned and enacted. It is essential to understand this complex policy ecology and its effects on working-class communities of color. The dispossession of such communities has been fostered through exclusionary decision making by elite policy makers and the capitalization of the public institutions on which these communities depend. At the same time, accumulation by dispossession has not advanced without resistance from affected grassroots communities (e.g., see Buras et al., 2010). Rather, they have critically assessed and challenged these circumstances by articulating their concerns and mobilizing against this assault—demanding, in essence, that whiteness as a form of property is exposed as racially exploitive and racially redistributive.

As the next chapters show, what is currently happening in New Orleans is not socially conscious capitalism. It is simply unconscionable.

Notes

1 UTNO is the local affiliate of the American Federation of Teachers. I interviewed union representatives from these organizations as well as veteran teachers affiliated with UTNO. UTNO has represented the majority of black veteran educators in the city for decades. In this chapter and subsequent ones, I do not identify any of those I interviewed through UTNO by name or by role, nor do I differentiate them from one another by pseudonym.

   More generally, I use *representative* to refer to more than one person within an organization and *affiliate* to refer to those associated with an organization outside of an official capacity.

2 LFT is the state affiliate of the American Federation of Teachers, a national teacher union.

3 In fact, voter turnout in historically black areas of the city dropped almost 60 percent from 2003 to 2007, while turnout in largely white areas dropped only 27 to 36 percent during this same period. Statewide and citywide implications are equally apparent: "The days when local candidates could appeal to Orleans' overwhelmingly black electorate and receive a handful of white votes to win office may be a thing of the past" (Krupa, 2008, para. 23).

4 Act 35 targeted Orleans Parish by (1) analyzing SPS scores in Orleans Parish to provide a listing of the scores to be used in drafting the legislation so the highest number of OPSB schools could be taken over; (2) raising the SPS cut point immediately after the storm to 87.4; (3) specifying that the state's authority to take over schools applied only to districts with more than 30 "failing" schools (Orleans Parish is one of the few districts in the state with more than 30 schools—50 of 64 districts have fewer than 30 schools); and (4) neglecting to take over "failing" schools in three other districts, while taking over the vast majority of "failing" schools in Orleans Parish (see UTNO et al., 2006; Civil District Court, 2012).

5 It should also be mentioned that Isaacson sits on Tulane University's board and was also appointed vice chair of Governor Blanco's Louisiana Recovery Authority, which included executives from banks, shipyards, investment firms, real estate, construction, architectural, and lumber companies, oil industries, and restaurants (Buras, 2005).

6 The Recovery School District launched "OneApp" in February 2012, providing families with a single application for RSD schools. Although a lottery is used to determine school assignments, various admission and retention priorities continue to operate formally and informally.

7 Two private firms were hired by the RSD to develop the SFMP—Parsons, a management and planning firm with a deficient construction history in Iraq, and Concordia, an architecture and planning firm founded by Steven Bingler, a member of the stakeholder advisory committee for the BNOB education committee and brother-in-law of Sarah Usdin, founder of NSNO (Myers, 2007; RSD, 2007). In the case of Parsons, U.S. taxpayers paid the firm $62 million for its construction of the Baghdad Police Academy, which is notable for its shoddily built brick walls, cracking concrete, faulty electrical box wiring, and plumbing that leaked human waste through light fixtures and ceilings (Myers, 2007).

8 Senator Mary Landrieu made an announcement in August 2010 that FEMA would provide a $1.8 billion grant to the RSD (Chang, 2010). This has intensified grassroots concerns over transparency and the politics of decision making and shaped the ongoing struggle over the SFMP.

References

Apple, M. W. (2001). *Educating the "right" way: Markets, standards, God, and inequality.* New York, NY: RoutledgeFalmer.

Arena, J. (2005, November 23). *The Urban Land Institute, J. C. Nichols, and the ethnic cleansing tradition. New Orleans Independent Media Center.* Available: http://neworleans.indymedia.org/news/2005/11/6415.php

Aspen Institute. (n.d.). *Walter Isaacson: President and CEO of the Aspen Institute.* Available: www.aspeninstitute.org/walterisaacson

Baker, B. (2011, September 9). Friday afternoon maps: New Orleans, race, and school locations. School Finance 101 Blog. Available: http://schoolfinance101.wordpress.com/2011/09/09/friday-afternoon-maps-new-orleans-race-school-locations/

Ball, S. J. (2003). *Class strategies and the education market.* London: RoutledgeFalmer.

Bring New Orleans Back Commission [BNOB]. (2006, January 17). *Rebuilding and transforming: A plan for world-class public education in New Orleans.* New Orleans, LA: Author.

Buras, K. L. (2005). Katrina's early landfall: Exclusionary politics behind the restoration of New Orleans. *Z Magazine, 18*(12), 26–31.

Buras, K. L. (2007). Benign neglect? Drowning yellow buses, racism, and disinvestment in the city that Bush forgot. In K. Saltman (Ed.), *Schooling and the politics of disaster* (pp. 103–122). New York, NY: Routledge.

Buras, K. L. (2009). "We have to tell our story": Neo-Griots, racial resistance, and schooling in the other South. *Race Ethnicity and Education, 12*(4), 427–453.

Buras, K. L. (2011a). "We're not going nowhere": Race, urban space, and the struggle for King Elementary School in New Orleans. *Critical Studies in Education, 54*(1), 19–32.

Buras, K. L. (2011b). Challenging the master's plan for the Lower Ninth Ward of New Orleans. *Z Magazine, 24*(5), 19–22.

Buras, K. L., & Apple, M. W. (2005). School choice, neoliberal promises, and unpromising evidence. *Educational Policy, 19*(3), 550–564.

Buras, K. L., Randels, J., Salaam, K. Y., & Students at the Center. (2010). *Pedagogy, policy, and the privatized city: Stories of dispossession and defiance from New Orleans.* New York, NY: Teachers College Press.

Bush, G. W. (2005, September 15). Text of Bush speech. Available: www.cbsnews.com

Butler, S. M., Carafano, J. J., Fraser, A. A., Lips, D., Moffit, R. M., & Utt, R. D. (2005, September 16). *How to turn the president's Gulf Coast pledge into reality* (Webmemo 848). Heritage Foundation. Available: www.heritage.org/research/reports/2005/09/how-to-turn-the-presidents-gulf-coast-pledge-into-reality

Carr, S. (2009, November 10). Grandmother struggles to navigate system. *Times-Picayune.* Available: www.nola.com

Chang, C. (2010, August 26). $1.8 billion from FEMA for Hurricane Katrina school rebuilding is "worth the wait," Sen. Mary Landrieu says. *Times-Picayune.* Available: www.nola.com

Charter Revision Commission. (2010, January 28). *Proceedings* [Transcript]. Jacksonville, FL: Author.

Civil District Court for the Parish of Orleans. (2012, June 20). *Eddy Oliver et al. v. Orleans Parish School Board et al.* [Reasons for judgment]. New Orleans, LA: Author.

Cooper, C. (2005, September 8). In Katrina's wake—Old-line families escape worst of floods and plot the future. *Wall Street Journal*, p. A1.

Cowen Institute. (2009a, November). *Creating a governing framework for public education in New Orleans: School district political leadership.* New Orleans, LA: Author.

Cowen Institute. (2009b, November). *Creating a governing framework for public education in New Orleans: The central office and the school.* New Orleans, LA: Author.

Cowen Institute. (2009c, November). *Creating a governing framework for public education in New Orleans: Charter school authorizers and charter school governance.* New Orleans, LA: Author.

Cowen Institute. (2010). *The state of public education in New Orleans.* New Orleans, LA: Author.

Crenshaw, K., Gotanda, N., Peller, G., & Thomas, K. (Eds.). (1995). *Critical race theory: The key writings that formed the movement.* New York, NY: New Press.

DeVore, D. E., & Logsdon, J. (1991). *Crescent City schools: Public education in New Orleans, 1841–1991.* Lafayette, LA: Center for Louisiana Studies, University of Southwestern Louisiana.

Font, P. (2009, March 9). The gospel according to Paul. *Baton Rouge Business Report.* Available: www.businessreport.com

Greater New Orleans Community Data Center. (2011). *The loss of children from New Orleans neighborhoods.* New Orleans, LA: Author.

Harris, C. I. (1995). Whiteness as property. In K. Crenshaw, N. Gotanda, G. Peller, & K. Thomas (Eds.), *Critical race theory: The key writings that formed the movement* (pp. 276–291). New York, NY: New Press.

Harvey, D. (1973). *Social justice and the city.* Baltimore, MD: Johns Hopkins University Press.

Harvey, D. (2006). *Spaces of global capitalism: Towards a theory of uneven geographical development.* New York, NY: Verso.

Hill, P., Campbell, C., Menefee-Libery, D., Dusseault, B., DeArmond, M., & Gross, B. (2009, October). *Portfolio school districts for big cities: An interim report.* Seattle, WA: Center on Reinventing Public Education.

Hill, P., & Hannaway, J. (2006, January). *The future of public education in New Orleans.* Washington, DC: Urban Institute.

Isaacson, W. (2006, June 8). *Go southeast, young man.* Aspen Institute. Available: www.aspeninstitute.org/node/2953

Krupa, M. (2008, April 23). City's political landscape has shifted. *Times-Picayune.* Available: www.nola.com

Kvale, S. (1996). *InterViews: An introduction to qualitative research interviewing.* Thousand Oaks, CA: SAGE.

Lefebvre, H. (1974). *The production of space* (Donald Nicholson-Smith, Trans.). Malden, MA: Blackwell.

Lewis, P. F. (2003). *New Orleans: The making of an urban landscape.* Santa Fe, NM: Center for American Places.

Lipman, P. (2011). *The new political economy of urban education: Neoliberalism, race, and the right to the city.* New York, NY: Routledge.

Lipsitz, G. (2007). The racialization of space and the spatialization of race: Theorizing the hidden architecture of landscape. *Landscape Journal, 26*(1), 10–23.

Louisiana Federation of Teachers [LFT]. (n.d.). *Imagine just for a moment* [Broadside]. Baton Rouge, LA: Author.

Louisiana Federation of Teachers [LFT]. (2005, November 2). *Letter to Blanco regarding Executive Orders 58 and 79.* Baton Rouge, LA: Author.

Louisiana Federation of Teachers [LFT] & American Federation of Teachers [AFT]. (2007, January). *The chronology: Scenario of a nightmare.* Baton Rouge, LA: Author.

Lower 9 School Development Group [L9SDG]. (2010, January 16). *What is L9SDG?* Available: http://l9sdg.blogspot.com/

Maxwell, L. A. (2007, December 13). Foundations donate millions to help New Orleans schools' recovery. *Education Week.* Available: www.edweek.org

McElroy, E. J. (2007, January 30). *Statement to friends of public education.* Washington, DC: American Federation of Teachers.

Meese, E., Butler, S. M., & Holmes, K. R. (2005, September 12). *From tragedy to triumph: Principled solutions for rebuilding lives and communities.* Washington, DC: Heritage Foundation.

Miester, M. (Ed.). (2010). The rise of conscious capitalism. *Freeman, 26*(2), 17.

Mirón, L. (2008). The urban school crisis in New Orleans: Pre- and post-Katrina perspectives. *Journal of Education for Students Placed at Risk, 13,* 238–258.

Myers, L. (2007, January 31). Did Iraq contractor fleece American taxpayers? Government report says flagship project was turned into hall of horrors. *MSNBC.com.* Available: www.msnbc.msn.com/id/16909438/

New Schools for New Orleans [NSNO]. (n.d.). *Transformations* [Informational folder]. New Orleans, LA: Author.

New Schools for New Orleans [NSNO]. (2007, August). *New Orleans parents' guide to public schools.* New Orleans, LA: Author.

New Schools for New Orleans [NSNO]. (2008a). *Lead.* Available: http://newschoolsforneworleans.org/

New Schools for New Orleans [NSNO]. (2008b). *Serve.* Available: http://newschoolsforneworleans.org/

New Schools for New Orleans [NSNO]. (2008c). *Start.* Available: http://newschoolsforneworleans.org/

New Schools for New Orleans [NSNO]. (2010a). *Charter board member qualifications.* Available: http://newschoolsforneworleans.org/

New Schools for New Orleans [NSNO]. (2010b). *Our impact.* Available: http://newschoolsforneworleans.org/

New Teacher Project [TNTP]. (2007, December 3). *The New Teacher Project wins Fast Company magazine and Monitor Group's social capitalist award.* Available: www.tntp.org/newsandpress/120307_TNTP.html

New Teacher Project [TNTP]. (2010). *About us: Our business model.* Available: www.tntp.org

Omi, M., & Winant, H. (1994). *Racial formation in the United States: From the 1960s to the 1990s.* New York, NY: Routledge.

Parent, W. (2004). *Inside the carnival: Unmasking Louisiana politics.* Baton Rouge, LA: Louisiana State University Press.

Randels, J. (2010). Passing on a torch. In K. L. Buras, J. Randels, K. Y Salaam, & Students at the Center, *Pedagogy, policy, and the privatized city: Stories of dispossession and defiance from New Orleans* (pp. 101–103). New York, NY: Teachers College Press.

Recovery School District [RSD]. (2007, June 13). *Two companies awarded the contract to develop master facility plan for Orleans Parish public schools* [Press release]. Baton Rouge, LA: Author.

Recovery School District [RSD] & New Orleans Public Schools [NOPS]. (2008a, August). *School facilities master plan for Orleans Parish.* New Orleans, LA: Authors.

Recovery School District [RSD] & New Orleans Public Schools [NOPS]. (2008b, November 6). *Superintendents' amendments: Recommendations to the Louisiana Board of Elementary and Secondary Education*. New Orleans, LA: Authors.

Ritea, S. (2006, August 12). Public schools compete for kids. *Times-Picayune*. Available: www.nola.com

Saltman, K. J. (Ed.). (2007a). *Schooling and the politics of disaster*. New York, NY: Routledge.

Saltman, K. J. (2007b). Schooling in disaster capitalism: How the political right is using disaster to privatize public schooling. *Teacher Education Quarterly, 34*(2), 131–156.

Saltman, K. J. (2010, June). *Urban school decentralization and the growth of "portfolio districts"* [Policy brief]. East Lansing, MI: Great Lakes Center for Education Research and Practice. Available: http://greatlakescenter.org/docs/Policy_Briefs/Saltman_PortfolioDistricts.pdf

Save Our Schools–New Orleans, Louisiana [SOSNOLA]. (2008). Extend school facilities master plan public review period [Petition]. Available: www.thepetitionsite.com/1/SOSNOLA-ExtendReviewPeriod

Scott, J. (2009). The politics of venture philanthropy in charter school policy and advocacy. *Educational Policy, 23*(1), 106–136.

Spellings, M. (2005, September 14). Letter from the secretary of education to states affected by Hurricane Katrina. Washington, DC: U.S. Department of Education.

Tate, W. F. (2008). "Geography of opportunity": Poverty, place, and educational outcomes. *Educational Researcher, 37*(7), 397–411.

Thevenot, B. (2009, May 17). Local school principals' pay reaches new heights. *Times-Picayune*. Available: www.nola.com

Tisserand, M. (2007, August 23). The charter school flood. *The Nation*. Available: www.thenation.com/article/charter-school-flood

United Teachers of New Orleans [UTNO], Louisiana Federation of Teachers [LFT], & American Federation of Teachers [AFT]. (2006, November). *"National model" or flawed approach? The post-Katrina New Orleans Public Schools*. New Orleans, LA: Author.

United Teachers of New Orleans [UTNO], Louisiana Federation of Teachers [LFT], & American Federation of Teachers [AFT]. (2007a, June). *No experience necessary: How the New Orleans school takeover experiment devalues experienced teachers*. New Orleans, LA: Author.

United Teachers of New Orleans [UTNO], Louisiana Federation of Teachers [LFT], & American Federation of Teachers [AFT]. (2007b, October). *Reading, writing, and reality check: An early assessment of student achievement in post-Katrina New Orleans*. New Orleans, LA: Author.

Weaver-Hightower, M. (2008). An ecology metaphor for educational policy analysis: A call to complexity. *Educational Researcher, 37*(3), 153–167.

3

KEEPING KING ELEMENTARY SCHOOL ON THE MAP

Racial Resistance and the Politics of Place in the Lower 9th Ward

> Those who want to see this city rebuilt want to see it done in a completely different way: demographically, politically, and economically.
>
> —James Reiss, real estate investor, chair of New Orleans Business Council, and Bring New Orleans Back Commission member (Cooper, 2005)

> Don't come back, there's nowhere for you. This is a new place, a new city, a new time.
>
> —Ms. Strong, veteran teacher at King Elementary School in the Lower 9th Ward, describing policymakers' viewpoint on rebuilding black communities (Interview, 2008)

> I guess a lot of people thought if you keep them [black residents] down so long they'll surrender. It don't work like that here. This is all we have. This is home. We're not going nowhere.
>
> —Mr. Fritz, veteran teacher at King Elementary (Interview, 2008)

When one enters the public library in the Lower 9th Ward of New Orleans, there is an easel. The easel displays a large photograph. On one side is a picture of the waterlogged library that was destroyed when more than 20 feet of water surged through the neighborhood from a levee breach after the storm in 2005. The other side has a picture of the renovated library, a mirror image of the current space (Fieldnotes, 2008). The photograph provides a visual marker of time and space—a kind of "then" and "now"—and suggests a complex history. Educational struggles go back more than half a century in the 9th Ward and include the establishment of Martin Luther King Elementary School (hereafter King Elementary), which shares space with the public library and came into being over a decade before the events of 2005.

Sitting at a table with Ms. Perks, the school librarian, I noticed a children's book on Ruby Bridges, the courageous African American first grader who desegregated the William Frantz School amid white mobs in 1960.[1] Ms. Perks pondered, "I was reading [this] book yesterday and I said, 'That school, it's historical. What Ruby Bridges went through, it's unreal.' And things really haven't changed that much. The school is closed" (Interview, 2008). Unfortunately, the racially motivated closing of schools in New Orleans is not a thing of the past. It is a thing of the present as well. A case in point is King Elementary.

The destruction of the Lower 9th Ward provided education entrepreneurs and their state allies with an "unprecedented opportunity" to rewrite the geography of New Orleans along more exclusionary lines. But there was one problem: a long history of black activism in the Lower 9th Ward as well as veteran teachers and a principal at King Elementary with no intention of allowing such dispossession to occur. King's principal, Ms. Gaines, explains, "We're not strangers to struggle" (Interview, 2008). With most of the city's public schools rapidly swept into a state-run Recovery School District (RSD) intent on creating the nation's first charter school system, the Lower 9th Ward community had little "choice" after 2005. They could attempt to reopen by chartering the school or cease to exist.

Based on oral history interviews with veteran teachers, administrators, and community members affiliated with King Elementary as well as school and community observations, this case study traverses time and space, documenting the

FIGURE 3.1 Destruction in Lower 9th Ward after 2005 levee break

community's history of racial resistance and recent struggles for educational equity, including the fight to keep King Elementary on the map. These struggles are examined in the context of attempts to undermine the reconstruction of black neighborhoods and create a space for entrepreneurial control of public education through charter school reform and alternative teacher recruitment. As I will show, efforts to rebuild King Elementary in this newly reformed landscape reveal a distinct commitment to equity, culture, and a shared sense of place—the antithesis of the vacuous market-based policies that have guided New Orleans school reform. I argue that such commitments have enabled and energized grassroots educational resistance despite well-financed entrepreneurial efforts.

As with previous chapters, two crucial points of departure will be to more fully understand *whiteness as a form of property* (Harris, 1995) in education entrepreneurship and how processes of *accumulation by dispossession* (Harvey, 2006) represent a redistributive geography of race and class power—one simultaneously confronted by grassroots resistance. This requires situating King Elementary historically as well as detailing current tensions over schools and neighborhoods in a policy environment of targeted state disinvestment and market-based reforms that capitalize on public education.

In what follows, I first connect the reflections of teachers and community members to the critical theories that inform my analysis, providing an overview of concerns about communal assets and private venture in the Lower 9th Ward. I next offer a cultural and spatial description of King Elementary at present, which lays the groundwork for historical analyses of past and more recent struggles for educational access and equity. This includes grassroots efforts to rebuild the school after its destruction and amid elite plans to support privately managed charter schools elsewhere in the city. I also provide a glimpse into the place-based consciousness that informs pedagogy at King Elementary, unlike the ahistorical and decontextualized pedagogy present in many of the city's privately managed charter schools, where veteran teachers indigenous to the community have not been hired. In conclusion, I highlight the battle for a much-needed Lower 9th Ward high school, initially unsupported by master planners, and delineate what can be learned from the case study about the resources available to racially and economically oppressed communities threatened by charter school reform, venture philanthropy, and uneven geographic development.

Taking Property for Private Venture: Race, Urban Space, and Dispossession

A grandparent—once a leader with the Parent–Teacher Association at King Elementary—stressed, "If they [entrepreneurs] had their wish, they'd run us away from here." He quickly followed without wavering, "I've already told them, there's no way this side of heaven they can buy mine. ... You can't take my property for a private venture" (Banks interview, 2008).

Taking property for private venture, however, is the *modus operandi* of education entrepreneurs, venture capitalists, and their state allies. Consider that the Lower 9th Ward was once a cypress swamp and for years it has been rumored there is oil under the ground. In late 2005 after the storm, residents reportedly received letters from an oil company offering to buy their property. Mr. Piron, a teacher at King Elementary, explained:

Piron: We don't care about the oil underneath or the sky above.
Buras: The resource is right here [meaning the school and community].
Piron: That's because this is where we live. This is the community that we know. There's no place like the Lower 9th Ward in the City of New Orleans. Fats Domino right down the street. ... Many of New Orleans' musicians ... originally started down here.

Before there [were] homeowners in the suburbs, this is where people bought homes and bought property. No, the storm didn't take it away from us. Government going to try and investors going to try and take that away from us. ...

When these tracts of land apparently became available, oh man, they started falling out of the sky to get the land. And we're like, if you could put warehouses right off the [Industrial] Canal that would be convenient for the ship merchants, but what about our homes and our families? You can put condos up overlooking wetland sanctuaries [as] you're proposing to do. But what about us who live here? (Interview, 2008)

These words resonate powerfully with those of David Harvey (1973, 2006), who has sought to better understand *accumulation by dispossession*. This process has become familiar in metropolitan areas throughout the United States and unevenly developing urban centers worldwide. It includes:

- Commodification and privatization of land and the forceful expulsion of populations;
- Conversion of various forms of property rights into exclusive property rights;
- Suppression of rights to the commons;
- Commodification of labor power and the suppression of indigenous forms of production and consumption; and
- Colonial, neo-colonial, and imperial processes of appropriation of assets (including natural resources). (Harvey, 2006, p. 43)

In New Orleans, this process is intimately connected to the production of an *urban space economy* (Harvey, 1973) premised on capital accumulation and the politics of white supremacy. With support from state policymakers and venture philanthropists, white entrepreneurs in New Orleans have seized control of public schools in black communities and attempted to create a racial geography that furthers their economic interests, while ignoring the claims of communities of color to educational resources and urban space. Similar dynamics are unfolding in Chicago, New York City, and elsewhere, as I highlight in the concluding chapter.

As before, I draw on various "spatial frames" to illuminate the perspectives of education actors in relation to time and place (Harvey, 2006; Lefebvre, 1974). Think about the words of Ms. Strong that opened this chapter and her commentary on elite plans for the city's reconstruction: "Don't come back, there's nowhere for you. This is a new place, a new city, a new time" (Interview, 2008). Considering how different actors view space reveals the stakes of particular policy choices and puts in sharp relief whose interests are served most squarely by current reforms and the urban space economy they produce.

The previous chapter showed that policy actors at the federal, state, and local levels have contributed to a process of privatization and an inequitable racial-spatial redistribution of resources in New Orleans while acting under the banner of innovation and social entrepreneurship (see Buras, 2007, 2011b). It would be wrong, however, to assume that reforms proceed without resistance from the communities at the center of reconstructive efforts. Ms. LaBorde, a counselor at King Elementary, speaks with resolve on this point:

> We're not going to let this force of impoverishment, of racism—we're not going to let it ... determine whether or not we can return; whether we can function; whether we can educate our children, our community, be a support to our parents.
>
> (Interview, 2008)

This same spirit of resistance is reflected in the architecture of the school and the story behind how the school first came to be. Thus I offer a cultural and spatial description of King Elementary at present and then discuss the neighborhood's longer struggle for education. This ultimately provides context for understanding grassroots mobilizations around the school since 2005.

King Elementary School Now

If one proceeds from the public library into the main corridor of King Elementary, the first thing encountered is a glass case displaying artifacts and books on African American history and culture: W. E. B. Du Bois' *The Souls of Black Folk, Narrative of Sojourner Truth,* and seven candles representing the principles of Kwanzaa—unity, self-determination, collective work and responsibility, cooperative economics, purpose, creativity, and faith—which are evidenced throughout the school. Propped against the freshly coated, sky blue wall is a hand-painted canvas of freedom fighters Frederick Douglass and Thurgood Marshall, including Douglass' well-known proclamation: "If there is no struggle, there is no progress." Each hallway is a symbolically named byway such as "Civil Rights Boulevard" (Fieldnotes, 2008).

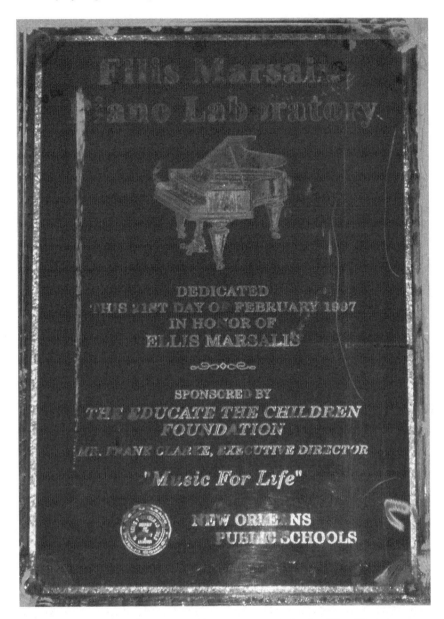

FIGURE 3.2 Rusted plaque by music classroom in Martin Luther King Elementary

Serving as a physical reminder that connects past and present, a rusted plaque salvaged from floodwaters hangs outside one of the music classrooms, the "Ellis Marsalis piano laboratory," which was originally "dedicated this 21st day of February 1997." In the cafetorium (or cafeteria-auditorium), which combines seating for lunchtime with a stage for school and community events, is a mural-like painting that stretches from the stage's floor to the ceiling. It is headlined "Realizing the Dream" and includes a larger-than-life painting of Dr. Martin Luther King, Jr. pensively gazing with his hands folded beneath his chin. Just below his hands is a silhouetted stream of marching civil rights activists postured with determination. In King Elementary, there is a relational sense of time and space, where history is a meaningful and ever-present guide for students and teachers.

FIGURE 3.3 Mural of Martin Luther King in cafeteria-auditorium of King Elementary

Connecting one hallway to the next is an audio system on which Principal Gaines broadcasts announcements. It is difficult to convey the enthusiasm of her voice, which communicates even the most pedestrian announcements with joyous energy. Continuing full circle on the first floor, there is a computer room designated as the "Learning Zone," where a sign announces "No interruptions— Literacy in progress." Hanging on a nearby wall are various photos of Dr. King and his family. In one he is accepting the Nobel Peace Prize. In another Coretta Scott King reads to their children. Posted below the photos is a quote by King that reads: "One of the most agonizing problems within our human experience is that few, if any, of us live to see our fondest hopes fulfilled. The hopes of our childhood and the promises of our mature years are unfinished symphonies" (Fieldnotes, 2008).

A desire to complete the symphony for the children is palpable in King Elementary. Rarely, if ever, do teachers use the word *student*. With remarkable consistency, the principal, teachers, and staff all speak of doing what is best for *our children*. When asked how he would characterize the philosophy of the school, Mr. Fritz stated with conviction, "There's only one philosophy. Everything is for the children." This sense of purpose, unity, and collective interest across generations is best conveyed by a story one of the teachers shared:

> I express to [the children], "It's important that you make it. It's important that you go to college or become a productive member of society. It's important because your little brothers and sisters are around watching you. It's important that you become doctors and lawyers and teachers and all those other dreams you have because Mr. [Piron's] going to get old one day, and he's going to need somebody to take care of him. And hopefully that doctor will be you. If I need a lawyer, the lawyer will be you. If I need to go to somebody's store, it'll be your store. And you'll remember me. ... Look out for me like I looked out for you."
>
> (Interview, 2008)

Mr. Dauphin, another teacher, explained it this way:

> Ms. Gaines refers to us quite often as a family and the reason why she does this is the teachers, especially here, take a very personal approach to the kids. These are our children, and they know they're our children.
>
> (Interview, 2008)

Not surprisingly, it was this temporal sense of community and the "fondest hopes" of Lower 9th Ward residents that led to the founding of King Elementary in the mid-1990s.

I turn to this history because it reveals why the struggle to rebuild King Elementary was so robust. It also reveals the rich legacy of racial resistance upon which the principal, teachers, and community members were able to draw when the school's fate was threatened by charter school reform and plans to remap New Orleans' urban space economy.

Recollecting the Lower 9th Ward's Educational Past: The Founding of King Elementary in Historical Context

The tract of land where King Elementary now stands did not always have a well-built school. Prior to King's development, Macarty Elementary School—a school built in 1861 and one at the center of a historic battle for educational equity in the late 1940s (as I discuss shortly)—stood there. By the 1940s, the school was plagued with "warped floors, mildewed ceilings, and overcrowding" (Baker, 1996, p. 152). This reality is part of the collective memory of King Elementary teachers, one of whom described Macarty Elementary as "a big, raggedy, wooden school, rat infested," emphasizing, "So there was a need for another school" (Piron interview, 2008). Most schools in the area were old and overcrowded explained Principal Gaines, who recollected: "I can remember many years ago, prior to the opening of [King Elementary], they had a groundbreaking. [But it] took place about 15 years before they actually started [to build the school]." What ultimately led to the school's construction was the activism of local women from the community, particularly Mama Griffin. Gaines tells it like this:

> It took Mama Griffin ... and others to go to the school board. ... Ms. Griffin would be there by herself most of the time. And whenever the school board would spend money, she would get to that mic[rophone]. "You better not be spending the money that's earmarked for King!" So it was that kind of thing, and it went on and on and on for years.
>
> She was a local community activist, a little short lady. But [many knew], "Don't mess with Mama Griffin." ... She had a lot of fire.
>
> So it took a lot. It took years and years until they finally said, "We're going to do the school."

Gaines, who grew up in the Lower 9th Ward, was principal of Joseph Hardin Elementary School at the time, and was recruited to open King Elementary. She, along with select teachers from each grade level, moved to King where a "community approach" was used to recruit the remaining teachers. She recalls, "We had someone from the district. We had two community persons. ... I think Mama Griffin was on that committee. ... And that's how we got our first staff" (Interview, 2008).

Thus the school opened in 1995 after a decade of community activism. Serving pre-kindergarten through eighth grade, it boasted a faculty on which 90 percent of the teachers had more than 20 years of experience. It dramatically improved test scores, attendance, and drop-out rates, although it "never sorted students or shied away from those who offered the greatest challenges" (Ritea, 2006, p. 3).

The founding of King Elementary in the mid-1990s cannot be appreciated apart from black educational activism that has historically characterized the Lower 9th Ward. The efforts of Mama Griffin and Principal Gaines are informed by the legacy of African American predecessors as well as the history of white supremacy in New Orleans. Significantly, two of the major legal challenges advanced by the NAACP (National Association for the Advancement of Colored People) around school desegregation were lodged by Lower 9th Ward residents protesting the poor and unequal educational facilities designated solely for black children.

The first case, *Rosana Aubert v. Orleans Parish School Board*, was filed in 1948 on behalf of Wilfred Aubert, a dock worker and community activist who had school-aged children and sought to equalize public school facilities (DeVore & Logsdon, 1991, p. 226). It is highly relevant that the school which inspired Aubert to seek legal counsel was Macarty Elementary—the school attended by his own children and the one that stood where King Elementary now stands. The second case, *Earl Bush v. Orleans Parish School Board*, was filed in 1952 on behalf of Earl Benjamin Bush to force the desegregation of the city's public schools (DeVore & Logsdon, 1991, p. 232).

With massive resistance to integration after *Brown v. Board of Education* in 1954—protestations of White Citizens' Councils, foot dragging and evasion by the Orleans Parish School Board, and the passage of countless segregationist bills by the Louisiana State Legislature—Federal Court Judge Skelly Wright crafted a school desegregation plan in 1960 that encompassed elementary schools, beginning with the first grade. In turn, the school board negotiated a compromise that entailed district authorities screening applicants whose families wished for them to transfer and integrate the schools. For a host of unsubstantiated reasons, the superintendent rejected most of the transfer requests, siphoning off all but 5 of 135 applications by black students (Baker, 1996; DeVore & Logsdon, 1991).

Both of the schools chosen by the school board for desegregation were in the 9th Ward—William Frantz Elementary School in the Upper 9th Ward and McDonogh No. 19 Elementary School in the Lower 9th Ward (Baker, 1996; Carl, 2008). At all-white Frantz Elementary, six-year-old Ruby Bridges was escorted by federal marshals as she confronted the violence of the "cheerleaders," a group of white mothers who daily hurled racial insults, physical threats, and rotten eggs at Ruby. The three first graders who entered McDonogh No. 19 had similarly harrowing experiences, along with their parents and families, yet they persisted for the collective good of the black community. The traces of this history are indisputably present in the actions of Mama Griffin and the King Elementary community.

In the Lower 9th Ward, community members know well that whiteness as a form of property has shaped educational access or the benefit of attending well-resourced schools while excluding African Americans from these spaces. In the case of Frantz and McDonogh No. 19, Judge Leander Perez—founder of the White Citizens' Council movement in southern Louisiana and boss of nearby St.

Bernard Parish—welcomed fleeing white students who boycotted the two schools (Carl, 2008). White parents sought to purchase land for a segregated private school and ran a fundraising campaign guided by the motto, "Buy a square foot of freedom for the 9th Ward Private School" (Carl, p. 19). Opening in 1961, the 9th Ward Elementary School was attended by white students who, by and large, originally attended Frantz and McDonogh No. 19 (Carl, 2008).

This was the structure of racial domination that Lower 9th Ward residents had a history of challenging. In fact, the King Elementary community developed strategies of grassroots resistance on the very same ground contested almost a half century earlier by Rosana Aubert, Ruby Bridges, and others. Such resistance was crucial in the face of the white entrepreneurial assault on black schools and neighborhoods in 2005.

We Shall Not Be Removed: Homecoming and the Struggle to Rebuild King Elementary

In 2005, struggles for access and educational equity intensified in the wake of destruction. Amid efforts to obstruct their right to return, the principal, teachers, and staff at King Elementary literally stood their ground and conveyed on no uncertain terms: We shall not be removed. The challenges have been immense, as plans to dispossess black veteran teachers and working-class communities of color rapidly unfolded after the storm. Seeing the Lower 9th Ward inundated with water was devastating enough. However, Mr. Piron noted:

> The most crushing blow came when we heard the announcement over television that all school teachers in Orleans Parish School District were fired, and we were sitting there perplexed because we had a union. We had a contract that should have been honored.
> .... To lose our jobs in such a manner was just chilling and heartbreaking.
> (Interview, 2008)

When asked how he explained teachers' dismissal, Piron responded without hesitation:

> I explain the dismissal as a hostile takeover, a power struggle between those who wanted the control of the millions of dollars involved in education in Orleans Parish. ...
> This was primarily controlled by African Americans who were able to allot contracts and do all the necessary things that they needed to do to control their own destiny. The powers that be [were] not pleased with that. They were looking for years to find ways to wrest control back from the district because the district served a majority African American population.
> (Interview, 2008)

Racialized teacher union-busting was only the beginning of the attempted process of accumulation by dispossession by the white power structure of Louisiana (see also Buras, 2011b; Buras et al., 2010). In the midst of this, the school district was taken over the by state. The message was "You no longer have jobs. The district no longer exists. We're going to split it up, make some charter [schools]. The state's going to take control of everything." Indeed, "all of this happened within a matter of weeks" (Piron interview, 2008).

The principal and a board member at King Elementary were able to return quickly and understood that chartering the school "was the only way we could [reopen]" (Charbonnet interview, 2008). They initiated discussion with the teachers and most agreed to return. Before beginning work on the charter proposal for King Elementary (notably for a decade-old school with an established record of success), Principal Gaines decided it was important to venture to the state capital in Baton Rouge. A message had to be sent:

> Hey, we know what's going on. We know what you all are trying to do. But, if there is any indication coming out that you are going to print that King [Elementary] was taken over because it's a failing school, you better watch and see our attorneys because we're going to sue.
>
> (Interview, 2008)

The state had little intention of supporting the return of King Elementary. Mr. Charbonnet, a King board member, explained, "After the state put out its timeline for when they were going to open certain schools in certain areas, we knew that we were going to have a fight on our hands" (Interview, 2008). Quite plainly, there was not a single school in the Lower 9th Ward on the list.

Principal Gaines and a number of teachers from King Elementary proceeded with writing a charter proposal—the only means they saw for possibly reopening the school in a newly reformed, charter school-driven policy environment. Teachers met periodically at hotel restaurants, public libraries, university campuses, and spared homes to write and refine the proposal while the city was still reemerging. Nonetheless, Gaines emphasized:

> [We] were really, really anxious about it and wondering whether or not they would accept it. Because you've got to understand, we didn't have a management company, and we didn't want a management company because we felt we could manage it. We'd been doing this so long together.
>
> (Interview, 2008)

Ultimately, King Elementary was the only state-approved charter submitted solely by a grassroots group; other charters were granted to schools collaborating with management organizations.

Despite all of the work required to get the school's charter, approval was only the beginning. King Elementary still needed a building for 2006–2007, while the original site in the Lower 9th Ward was being renovated. This, too, proved to be a battle. The RSD offered the Charles Colton Middle School, which had problems with asbestos, termites, and other hazards. Principal Gaines and the teachers demanded access to a school building on Willow Street—a site in much better condition—but the RSD said it had other plans for that building. After renovation deadlines were repeatedly missed, King Elementary decided to hold school on the front steps of Colton Middle School to let the world know that teachers were ready to teach. The school was not alone in making its proclamation. It maintained a longstanding relationship with the Southern Christian Leadership Conference (SCLC), the national civil rights organization that Dr. King founded; key stakeholders were present. Moreover, parents and the Lower 9th Ward Community Council provided breakfast and lunch to the children. The teachers prepared lesson plans along with handheld signs that demanded "Open our school." It did not take long for the "riot police" to show up and they were not there to protect the children (Charbonnet interview, 2008).

The King Elementary community decided it would march to RSD headquarters two miles away. RSD superintendent Robin Jarvis was not there, so students took a seat and teachers continued to teach. SCLC also talked with the children about "Dr. King and his struggle to bring equality during the 1960s." The superintendent finally arrived and "agreed to a closed-door meeting with five or six key people and no cameras" (Charbonnet interview, 2008).

As a result, the well-maintained building on Willow Street became available and this is where King Elementary students were taught for the remainder of the 2006–2007 academic year. Needless to say, the refusal of the Lower 9th Ward community to be dispossessed was the most important lesson of the year.

On August 13, 2007, King Elementary returned to its original location in the Lower 9th Ward, where renovations had occurred throughout the previous year. On that momentous day, Principal Gaines expounded on the meaning of "home" before an exhilarated community:

> Dr. King said, "They dared to dream." And after the disaster that devastated this area and our school, we dared to dream. ... We are glad to be home and indeed this is a homecoming.
>
> (Mos Chukma Institute, 2008)

To designate the school as "home" is to invoke a notion of place that rarely applies to privately managed charter schools. Surely this sense of affiliation and solidarity was felt as the Zulu Warriors, Pin Stripe Brass Band, and Rebirth Brass Band led the teachers, children, and families into the newly renovated school, reminding everyone that this was the cultural heritage they had fought to preserve.

Mr. Piron testified before the second-line—or traditional march behind the brass band—entered the school: "They said we wasn't coming back! But we said this is our home and we're coming back and we're back! ... This *our* home and we *love* it!" (Mos Chukma Institute, 2008)

Pedagogy and the Politics of Place at King Elementary

Finally back home at King Elementary, Mr. Piron explained:

> Here at King, [we were] a safe haven *before* the storm, a safe haven *during* the storm, and a safe haven *after* the storm. How [the school] served as a safe haven after the storm: it was ... if not the tallest building in the Lower 9th Ward, one of the tallest. And so people came here in order to be above the water level.
>
> (Interview, 2008)

Piron notes that King's second floor is the highest point in the neighborhood. This is more than a reference to the number of storeys in the school; it is a relational and geographic recognition of *social location*. The fact that schools in the Lower 9th Ward were destroyed had much to do with historic patterns of segregation, lack of access to high ground, and an uneven geography of opportunity (Landphair, 2007). The place-based consciousness exhibited by Piron permeates the culture and pedagogy of King Elementary.

The Mos Chukma Institute (meaning "Good Child" in the Houma language) was founded at King Elementary in 2006 by Ms. Mount, a native of New Orleans and a Black Indian (Pawnee, Seminole, and Creole). The institute welds therapy, art, and place-based education to promote student resiliency and community agency, especially amid the loss of schools, homes, and neighborhoods. One artistic installation created by students was a two-sided box, with one alcove entitled "Memory Box: Grief and Loss" and the other "Hope Box: Dreams and Wishes." Children inserted words, pictures, and handcrafted artifacts on each side to represent their feelings and experiences. The memory box included crumbled blue paper representing waters of destruction and displacement, and a house with the words "respect my people" on its roof. The hope box, by comparison, contained homes surrounded by green trees and papers inscribed with words such as "fell down but back up again" (Fieldnotes, 2008). Such sentiments are personal and political, reflecting the struggles engendered by racially motivated state policies.

In the first grade class of Ms. Green, a veteran teacher of more than 30 years, Ms. Mount guided the children in an activity:

> Take a deep breath in our nose and our mouth. ... This time when you breathe, breathe in everything you need. Breathe in all the love, joy, the support, the happiness. Breath out what you don't need. Breathe out any worry or concern or unhappiness.
>
> (Mos Chukma Institute, 2008)

FIGURE 3.4 Memory box made by Martin Luther King Elementary students

In Mr. Casey's class, Ms. Mount leads the meditation of 20 engrossed third graders:

> We're holding the sun down behind our eyes. I want you to look out through your eyes and see what you see with the sun behind your eyes. All the good things you see for yourself: all the happiness; the activities you like to do; your family together and happy; your home good and whole.
>
> (Mos Chukma Institute, 2008)

Drawing upon indigenous traditions, Ms. Mount reminds students as she works throughout the school: "[The Indians] go out and dance for the earth, for the earth's renewal, just like we're working on renewing New Orleans." With students seated in chairs, she leads them in collectively generating a rhythm by tapping their hands in their laps: "I want you to see yourself held between the sun and the earth. We feel strong in King. We feel strong on the earth. And we're happy students, aren't we? [Students shake their heads in affirmation]." In this emotive geography of community, Ms. Mount situates the school in relation to sun and earth and as part of a larger whole. She invokes a collective sense of well-being and belonging. She invokes the words of Chief Seattle of the Suquamish Indians, which rest at the heart of Mos Chukma Institute and King Elementary:

> Teach your children what we have taught our children: that the earth is our mother. Whatever befalls the earth befalls the children of the earth. This

we know—the earth does not belong to man, man belongs to the earth. This we know—all things are connected like the blood that unites one family. ... Man did not weave the web of life; he is merely a strand in it. Whatever he does to the web, he does to himself.

(Mos Chukma Institute, 2008)

The sense of shared geography and shared destiny at King are utterly missing from privately managed charter schools across the city—a point taken up in chapter 5.

One girl discusses her desire to return home to the Lower 9th Ward. Although she is back in New Orleans, her family is not yet back in the neighborhood. Mr. Penzato, artist and videographer for Mos Chukma Institute, questions, "Have you thought about your future, and how that's going to look when you're back home?" In response, the girl thoughtfully reflects: "My mama was thinking of a family day together so we could rebuild my grandma's and my auntie's and my house. That was going to be a family day and after that we can have a picnic." She continues her exchange with Ms. Mount:

Girl: I always wanted to sit by the oak tree. But the oak tree is not there to see. It blew up [in the storm].
Mount: But there's still some trees, aren't there?
Girl: My family was thinking about the tree I used to sit by. I was going to plant another one.
Mount: Oh, that's perfect. That's a great idea. It will grow up with you, won't it?
Girl: (bright affirmative smile)

This narrative portrays that uprooting, whether of trees, families, or schools, cannot destroy one's sense of home and the deep desire to renew the community from which one has been separated.

In the spirit of this place-based pedagogy, one community member emphasized, "We must not forget that King sits on sacred ground" (Mos Chukma Institute, 2008). The reference to sacred ground is germane in the Lower 9th Ward, where working-class African Americans settled, fought for schools, and built homes that have been passed down through generations. In 2005, the 9th Ward as a whole had one of the highest rates of black working-class home ownership in the nation (Common Ground, 2006). Mr. Dauphin, a veteran teacher at King Elementary, told the story of his own family's roots in the Lower 9th Ward:

People came from the rural areas, most like my grandfather's generation. ... They grew sugarcane. They worked in the rice fields. ... That whole generation came here to the big city. As a result, they were limited because this was in the 1940s ... and they would have to go to the segregated section. The Lower 9th Ward was one of those areas. ... It was lower ground, so it was cheaper.

He went on to note, "Many people took out their loans and they started working and paying for their houses, and they ended up eventually paying for it. ... Houses were generally handed down." After 2005, he reports, officials were "talking about shrinking the city's footprint." The King community asserted otherwise, Dauphin explains: "The idea is to understand that if the school is here, the community can come back. The community can't come back without the school" (Interview, 2008).

With deep emotion, Mr. Piron likewise shared the sacrifices made by his parents to purchase a house in the Lower 9th Ward:

> My parents—the first house they ever bought was...a couple of blocks from the levee. And I watched them work hard, hard, hard to buy a house. [I] watched them live their days out in that house. My father died in that house. ... And I'd never give it up because I know what they put into it. So this is my home, and when I say home, I'm not talking about a building. I'm talking about a home of love, a community of caring, and I can't turn my back on that because if my children so see fit, then that'll be their home, and they can talk about the legacy that comes with it.

For Lower 9th Ward students, teachers and community members, schools and homes are invaluable intergenerational assets situated on sacred ground. This sense of place is dramatically different from the calculus of market exchange and profit

FIGURE 3.5 Home in Lower 9th Ward with "Roots run deep" yard sign

that guides private charter school operators and venture capitalists, who aim to tailor an urban space economy that serves their possessive interests. It is the former sensibility, not the latter, that shapes the place-based pedagogy at King Elementary.

BOX 3.1   THE WETLAND WARRIORS PROGRAM AT KING ELEMENTARY

At King Elementary, seventh and eighth grade students have the opportunity to participate in a homegrown program called Wetland Warriors. The program is a collaboration between science teachers at King and Bayou Rebirth, an organization that raises awareness about the need for wetland restoration. The lead teacher is Mr. Dauphin, who values the program because "it took science where I've always thought science should be: out of the classroom" (Interview, 2009). As Wetland Warriors, students visit the wetlands surrounding the Lower 9th Ward and southern Louisiana. Before heading out to the bayou, students research "the wildlife, plants, flora, and fauna" that they will see and they learn about "saltwater intrusion," which is partly responsible for destruction of wetlands (Interview, 2009). Once prepared, they take canoe trips, identify regional plants and animals, record findings on clipboards, and test for water quality (e.g., salinity level). They also gather specimens and later dissect them. "I never thought I was going to be dissecting a crawfish or [fresh water] fish," shared one student in the *Warrior Weekly,* the program newsletter (2009, p. 2). Another aspect of their work includes "propagating swamp grass," explained Mr. Dauphin. "We actually grew some out in the yard [here at King], and the kids got all into it. We later planted it in Bayou Savage" (Interview, 2009).

Students write reports about what they learn and contribute to the *Warrior Weekly* during their course of study. Mr. Dauphin brings his own sense of place to his work with the program:

> I grew up in New Orleans. We called [the wetlands] the weeds. The things that came out of there, unless you were hunting or fishing, were considered nuisances. But [ultimately] you come to more of a symbiotic-type relationship to understand that we're part of the environment and the environment is us, and we have to get along together in order for one to sustain the other. We can't abuse it because if we abuse it, then it won't protect us. The kids are getting it.
>
> (Interview, 2009)

In this way, students connect their knowledge of science to the water-scape that surrounds them and develop a healthy and more sophisticated relationship with the environment. On their reports, Mr. Dauphin has students write their name on a line labeled *scientist,* encouraging students to see themselves as able custodians of the environment; this includes special education students who participate in the program. In reflecting on the Wetland Warriors program, Mr. Dauphin concluded with pride:

> It's all about the children. Many times when we went out there into the swamp, I came back [to King] and teachers laughed at me because I'm covered in mud and I'm soaking wet from perspiration. And they're saying, "Oh, you guys were in the swamps again." But it was for [the children]. Once you get to the point where you understand that the commitment has to be for the children, [nothing else matters].
>   I've got some scientists coming along....
>
> (Interview, 2009)

This place-based curriculum enables King's students to understand their role in rebuilding and sustaining the community. As one student penned in a poem entitled "The Wetlands":

> We need to save them now
> 'Fore it's too late....
>
> (*Warrior Weekly*, 2009, p. 4)

King Elementary and the Difference from Privately Managed Charter School Start-Ups

King Elementary is not like most charter schools in New Orleans. Ms. LaBorde explained, "I have to pause and say King... is not chartered in the usual sense." While many of the city's charter schools have sought to distinguish themselves from traditional public schools, King Elementary, founded as a traditional public school, only applied for a charter out of "absolute necessity." LaBorde attests, "If we were going to be able to move [quickly] and educate our children of color here in New Orleans [after 2005], we had to do it like that. It was about survival" (Interview, 2008). The majority of teachers at King Elementary are black veteran teachers with years of experience and deep roots in the community. Most of those teaching in New Orleans' charter schools are transient white recruits from outside the city with no teaching experience whatsoever (see chapter 5). Principal Gaines opposed this approach by reformers:

> You could read between the lines that said, "Hey, we're going to go in a different direction. We're going to go with Teach for America.... And we're going to recruit. We're going to do a nationwide recruit."

> So what you're saying is you don't want me [as a veteran teacher]. . . . I'm part of the problem that you perceive.
>
> (Interview, 2008)

By contrast, at King Elementary, veteran teachers are respected. King's staff developer, Ms. Hunter, emphasized that professional development was not about outside experts "talking at you, saying how it's supposed to be when you've done it for 30 years" (Interview, 2008). Rather, she stressed dialogue among experienced teachers.

Further, King Elementary predated current reforms and is "tried and true" in its success as opposed to start-up charter schools with no record of student achievement and no connection to surrounding communities. Principal Gaines articulated her anxiety about such charter schools:

> Those of us who are here for the long haul, [who] live in New Orleans, we're very concerned that charters, the ones that are going up, that they're as sincere as we are. And that they do extra to pull kids in and keep them in.
>
> It concerns me that so many are coming up . . . without track records. You know, you've got so many charters schools. . . . You got a charter school for this. You got a charter school for that.
>
> (Interview, 2008).

Her words call into question whether or not so-called diverse providers of education services can ever fulfill the promise of neighborhood public schools, as King Elementary does.

Finally, unlike most charter schools in New Orleans, King Elementary is not operated by a private management company. The school's work is overseen by a board of local persons who are longtime residents of the community. While King Elementary has appreciated the freedom to determine its own schedule, tailor professional development to teachers' needs, and purchase educational materials of its own choosing, chartering has also presented substantial challenges, particularly financial ones. For example, the state provided charter start-up funds but they came as a reimbursable grant. Ms. Charbonnet, board liaison, pondered: "You had to spend it before you had it. Now, how could we spend what we didn't have?" (Interview, 2008) The school had to seek a line of credit with a bank and later negotiate and manage its own contracts with vendors. "If we had signed up with the RSD, the cost of busing would have sent us to bankruptcy court," said Charbonnet (Interview, 2008). Meanwhile, many privately managed charter schools have millions of dollars at their disposal, especially when philanthropic monies are considered (Chang, 2010; Harden, 2013; Maxwell, 2007).

These differences and the sense of place that animate King Elementary are important to the community's educational future. Although King had come home, Alfred Lawless High School, the only secondary school in the Lower 9th Ward, still needed to be rebuilt. Needless to say, this was not a priority for master planners.

FIGURE 3.6 Alfred Lawless High School in Lower 9th Ward

The Struggle for a Lower 9th Ward High School

The politics of place at King Elementary reveal that struggles over urban space are historically inflected, culturally grounded, and deeply political. Education entrepreneurs and policymakers view New Orleans as an absolute space where history can be effaced in the interest of calculated development. The School Facilities Master Plan (SFMP) issued by the RSD and New Orleans Public Schools (NOPS) in August 2008 determined which schools would remain open, be renovated, or be closed (RSD & NOPS, 2008).

Under the SFMP (RSD & NOPS, 2008), three of the five schools in the Lower 9th Ward prior to 2005 have been demolished or are slated for demolition and a fourth has been indefinitely closed. Meanwhile, the RSD has received millions from the Federal Emergency Management Agency (FEMA) for damage to these schools. This money was not allocated to rebuild schools in the Lower 9th Ward, but instead was put in a general fund to support school construction in largely white neighborhoods uptown—all of this despite the fact that the vast majority of students in the city's public schools are African American and live downtown. Most of the renovated and newly built spaces would be given to privately managed charter schools.

The Lower 9 School Development Group (L9SDG) was organized to fight for rebuilding a neighborhood high school (Buras, 2011a). Despite RSD claims that the master plan used demographic information to create neighborhood "recovery profiles," which were then presumably used to determine where schools would be rebuilt, a demographic profile prepared at the behest of L9SDG in 2008 revealed a dramatically different picture: within a two-minute drive of King Elementary, there were 493 school-aged children (ranging from age 0 to 19). Within a five-minute drive of King, there were 4,752 school-aged children.

Among its many actions, L9SDG collected petitions from families in support of rebuilding the high school. It also wrote to Congress requesting a federal investigation of the use of public monies by the RSD, urging: "We have endeavored to work in tandem with local and state school officials, but it has proven to be to our community's detriment. After five years of trying to rebuild schools and other essential infrastructure in our neighborhood, we feel that we have exhausted our options" (L9SDG, 2010).

Mr. Preston, a member of L9SDG, questioned, "Who made a decision that we didn't want a school back in this area? To take my money and place it in some arbitrary fund and say we're going to do whatever we want to do—I think that's criminal" (Interview, 2009).

Through its own efforts, L9SDG commissioned architectural plans for a high school where the former high school once stood. In 2010, the group sponsored a billboard demanding RSD funding. It read, "Lower 9th Ward Stakeholders Ask … Where's the Money?" (Fieldnotes, 2011). Prompted by their ongoing activism, RSD officials in 2011 committed to building a high school (Fieldnotes, 2011;

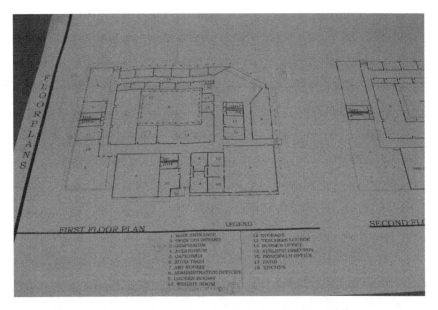

FIGURE 3.7 Architectural plans for rebuilding Alfred Lawless High School

L9SDG, 2011). Despite these promises, ground had not been broken for the high school at the time of this writing. Much like Mama Griffin, L9SDG has not backed down and seeks to ensure the high school is built.

"We've come this far by faith and we're going to continue"

The SFMP reflects an absolute and technical conception of space—one divorced from the lived experiences and historical relations that communities share with longstanding neighborhood schools. In the same way, a recent report by New Schools for New Orleans, entitled *New Orleans-Style Education Reform: A Guide for Cities (Lessons Learned, 2004–2010)*, presents the city as site of urban innovation (Brinson, Boast, Hassel, & Kingsland, 2012). New Orleans is described as a "charter school market" where entrepreneurship will "drive continual progress" (p. 12). A human capital initiative focused on recruiting "new talent" is emphasized. The report's section on the history of New Orleans public schools before 2005 is only two short paragraphs and singularly emphasizes "failure" and "bankruptcy" as reasons for philanthropic and private-sector intervention (a critical response to the *Guide for Cities* appears in chapter 6). For entrepreneurs, space ultimately is devoid of any explanatory or meaningful past.

In contrast, King Elementary has a shared commitment to equity, culture, and place. This accounts for why the community was able to mount such resistance, even in the face of well-funded entrepreneurial forces. As a lived space, King Elementary stands as a reminder of past struggles for racial equity and a testimony to aspirations for a more just future. From the painting of Frederick Douglass to the mural of Martin Luther King, from the sacrifices of Ruby Bridges to the unrelenting efforts of Mama Griffin, the history of racial oppression and a legacy of grassroots resistance provide motivation to fight for equity in the present. Inspiration also comes from a rich cultural heritage that includes "Fats Domino right down the street" and the brass bands that energized the second-line procession into the newly renovated school. Entrepreneurs may be committed to making money, but they, especially as outsiders to the community, will never possess the ineffable determination that comes from a genuine sense of place: "This [is] *our* home," proclaimed Mr. Piron, "and we *love* it!" Indeed, King Elementary and the historic family homes that once surrounded it reveal an intergenerational, culturally grounded conception of "property" that is unknown to investors. Theirs is a de-contextualized and de-territorialized approach to reform. Place-based consciousness, possessed by teachers and students indigenous to the community, is an invaluable resource in the struggle against accumulation by dispossession.

As Principal Gaines (Mos Chukma Institute, 2008) shared among students and teachers:

> The biggest thing that I thought I would never have to do is say to people in New Orleans that children of color deserve an education, and a first

class education. And it has been a struggle for all of us—it's been a struggle getting to this point. But we've come this far by faith and we're going to continue.

The struggle to defend public schools in black working-class neighborhoods would not be limited to the Lower 9th Ward. Not far from King Elementary, long-time residents in the Upper 9th Ward confronted the possible closure of Frederick Douglass, the only remaining open-access high school in the neighborhood, by master planners. As the next chapter reveals, the efforts of teachers, students, and community members to support Douglass, in spite of scarce economic resources for all-black high schools, would be threatened by attempts to "reinvent" the school and neighborhood. For elite policymakers, a charter school operator with no connection to the community appeared to hold greater promise.

Note

1 Frantz was in the Upper 9th Ward on the other side of the Industrial Canal, a waterway built in the early 1920s that separates the Lower 9th Ward from the Upper 9th Ward.

References

Baker, L. (1996). *The second battle of New Orleans: The hundred-year struggle to integrate the schools.* New York, NY: HarperCollins.

Bring New Orleans Back Commission. (2006, January 17). Rebuilding and transforming: A plan for world-class public education in New Orleans. New Orleans, LA: Author.

Brinson, D., Boast, L., Hassel, B. C., & Kingsland, N. (2012). New Orleans-style education reform: A guide for cities—Lessons learned, 2004–2010. New Orleans, LA: New Schools for New Orleans. Available: www.newschoolsforneworleans.org/guide

Buras, K. L. (2007). Benign neglect? Drowning yellow buses, racism, and disinvestment in the city that Bush forgot. In K. Saltman (Ed.), *Schooling and the politics of disaster* (pp. 103–122). New York, NY: Routledge.

Buras, K. L. (2011a). Challenging the master's plan for the Lower Ninth Ward of New Orleans. *Z Magazine, 24*(5), 19–22.

Buras, K. L. (2011b). Race, charter schools, and conscious capitalism: On the spatial politics of whiteness as property (and the unconscionable assault on black New Orleans). *Harvard Educational Review, 81*(2), 296–330.

Buras, K. L., Randels, J., Salaam, K. Y., & Students at the Center. (2010). *Pedagogy, policy, and the privatized city: Stories of dispossession and defiance from New Orleans.* New York, NY: Teachers College Press.

Carl, J. (2008). School vouchers come to New Orleans: Tuition grants and the Ninth Ward Elementary School, 1954–1968 [draft]. Paper presented at the History of Education Society Annual Meeting, St. Petersburg, Florida, November 6–9, 2008.

Chang, C. (2010, August 7). Charter incubator to get grant: It will help turn around more schools. *Times-Picayune.* Available: www.nola.com

Common Ground. (2006). New Orleans in numbers: Pre- and Post-Hurricane Katrina snapshot. New Orleans, LA: Author.

Cooper, C. (2005, September 8). In Katrina's wake—Old-line families escape worst of floods and plot the future. *Wall Street Journal,* A1.

DeVore, D. E., & Logsdon, J. (1991). *Crescent city schools: Public education in New Orleans, 1841–1991.* Lafayette, LA: The Center for Louisiana Studies at the University of Southwestern Louisiana.

Harden, K. (2013, October 28). Implementation of i3 education grants being questioned. *Louisiana Weekly.* Available: www.louisianaweekly.com/inplementation-of-i3-education-grants-being-questioned/

Harris, C. I. (1995). Whiteness as property. In K Crenshaw, N. Gotanda, G. Peller, & K. Thomas (Eds.), *Critical race theory: The key writings that formed the movement* (pp. 276–291). New York, NY: The New Press.

Harvey, D. (1973). *Social justice and the city.* Baltimore, MD: Johns Hopkins University Press.

Harvey, D. (2006). *Spaces of global capitalism: Towards a theory of uneven geographical development.* New York, NY: Verso.

Landphair, J. (2007). "The forgotten people of New Orleans": Community, vulnerability, and the Lower 9th Ward. *Journal of American History, 94*(3), 837–845.

Lefebvre, H. (1974). *The production of space* (D. Nicholson-Smith, Trans.). Malden, MA: Blackwell.

Lower 9 School Development Group. (2010, October). Letter to Congress [Document]. New Orleans, LA: Author.

Lower 9 School Development Group. (2011, August 8). Lower Ninth Ward School Development Group victorious in pressuring RSD to build high school in the Lower Ninth Ward [Press release]. New Orleans, LA: Author.

Maxwell, L. A. (2007, December 13). Foundations donate millions to help New Orleans schools' recovery. *Education Week.* Available: www.edweek.org

Mos Chukma Institute. (2008). Transcendent dreams [digital video]. New Orleans, LA: Author.

Recovery School District, & New Orleans Public Schools. (2008, August). School facilities master plan for Orleans Parish. New Orleans, LA: Authors.

Ritea, S. (2006, August 1). Dream team. *Times-Picayune.* Available: www.nola.com

Warrior Weekly. (2009, June 26). Newsletter. New Orleans, LA: Martin Luther King Elementary School.

4

THE CLOSING OF DOUGLASS HIGH SCHOOL

Counterstories on the Master's Plan for Reconstruction

What it has gotten to is the fact that if [policymakers] close down all of the high schools and your children have nowhere to go to school, then you'll leave. They've tried everything that they can to get people out [of the city].

— Bywater resident reflecting on the possible closure of Frederick
Douglass High School by the Recovery School District and
school facility master planners (Interview, 2008)

If we're waiting for a master plan, then why are we already talking about closing the school [Douglass], which is so important to this community? Who is making this master plan? Who are the resources? Are they New Orleanians? Are they people from outside of New Orleans?

— Douglass teacher addressing RSD superintendent Paul
Vallas at a public meeting on the school's
possible closure (Fieldnotes, 2008)

I'm agnostic when it comes to what buildings stay or go.

— Paul Vallas at public meeting on Douglass'
possible closure (Fieldnotes, 2008)

A granite "Memorial Arch" stands behind Frederick Douglass High School in the historic Bywater neighborhood of New Orleans' Upper 9th Ward. The arch, 29 feet high, 21 feet wide, and 7 feet thick, was constructed following World War I and dedicated in 1919 to recognize the military service of Upper 9th Ward residents. Adorned with embossed bronze plaques, it includes several lists of names: White men killed in action or who died in service; white men in active service; and colored men who died in service or continued in active service (*Times-Picayune*, 1919). Separate plaques for white and black soldiers are a reminder of the racial inequities and segregation that have shaped Douglass High School since its beginnings.

FIGURE 4.1 Memorial Arch by Frederick Douglass High School in Bywater

This all-black high school was not originally called Frederick Douglass, a name adopted in the mid-1990s to honor the legacy of the once-enslaved black abolitionist. It opened in 1913 (and was rebuilt in the late 1930s) as all-white Francis T. Nicholls High School and was named after a Confederate general who acted as Reconstruction governor of Louisiana after the Civil War (*Rebel Yell*, 1966, June 2, p. 10). As an all-white public high school, Nicholls was well-resourced, known for its 1930s Art Deco architecture, and envied for its large auditorium. With desegregation in the late 1960s, white flight and state neglect shaped what was quickly becoming an all-black high school. Although Douglass High School was spared substantial flood damage in 2005, it had not been painted since 1988 and lacked air-conditioning in a climate that regularly exceeds 100 degree temperatures (Baum, 2007; Carr, 2008). Despite this history of race-based neglect and the seeming record of "failure" that followed, Douglass established a number of successful programs and was considered the heart of the Bywater community. Recall the efforts of Students at the Center (SAC) and the Frederick Douglass Community Coalition, mentioned in chapter 1, to develop Plessy Park as a nearby civil rights education site that would include the writings of Douglass students and teachers. Not only was this effort thwarted by the reforms of 2005—the existence of Douglass itself was in question by the state-run Recovery School District (RSD) and school facility master planners. Reflecting in 2008 on the possibility of Douglass' closure and the building's takeover by the Knowledge Is Power Program (KIPP), a well-funded national charter school operator, then principal Allen Woods predicted: "I guarantee you there will be air-conditioning in the auditorium in 2012—when we're not here" (Carr, 2008, para. 49).

In this chapter, I draw on archival documents from Nicholls and Douglass; classroom observations of Students at the Center; writings and digital media from SAC students at Douglass; Douglass teacher, alumni, and community interviews; and fieldnotes from public meetings to chronicle the struggle over Douglass' future. Amid mass charter school development and the school facilities master plan aimed at reconstructing New Orleans' education landscape, Douglass remained one of the only open-access public high schools downtown. The community's spirited effort to honor the school's African American legacy and acquire greater resources from the RSD, in opposition to master planners' support for privately managed charter schools and a "new" New Orleans, provides another striking case study of resistance to current reforms and their costs.

To contextualize the struggle over Douglass, I open with an introduction to the Bywater neighborhood, Students at the Center (a nationally recognized writing and digital media program at Douglass), and the grassroots cultural and educational coalitions that supported Douglass in 2005. Traversing time and space, I next provide a history of all-white Nicholls High School and white resistance to Nicholls' desegregation in the late 1960s. In what follows, I chart the school's transformation as a result of white flight and the efforts of Douglass' black students and teachers to create a legacy of their own. Special attention is given to SAC as a historically grounded curriculum model and an illustration of what Douglass accomplished in spite of state neglect; student and teacher counterstories from the classroom and the community shed light on the struggle against dispossession by policymakers. Finally, I document that despite such efforts, RSD officials and master planners threatened to close Douglass, ignored community appeals for further investment, and ultimately handed over the building to KIPP Renaissance, a newly established high school in the KIPP New Orleans charter school network. Douglass students would not be welcome by KIPP nor would they and their families be the focal point of the riverfront development project, "Reinventing the Crescent [City]," just a few blocks away. Instead, the dispossession of black teachers and students at Douglass, and an urban space economy organized around the interests of an entrepreneurial white middle class, were the primary dynamics underway. This would have serious implications for the future of the surrounding community, especially longtime residents who had worked to realize the potential of Douglass as a community institution dedicated to racial equity rather than exclusion.

The Bywater Neighborhood, Frederick Douglass High School, and the Place of Culture

The Bywater neighborhood is located in New Orleans' Upper 9th Ward, down river from the French Quarter and adjacent to the Industrial Canal that separates the Upper and Lower 9th Wards. Plantations covered the area during New Orleans' early history. In the mid-1830s, large estates were broken apart and street grids were developed to accommodate houses in the area, especially as the city grew. Creole cottages and shotgun singles and doubles were built and continue to characterize Bywater's unique architecture today. Creoles of French, Spanish, African, and Native American ancestry resided in the area and were later joined by German, Irish, and Italian immigrants (Bywater Neighborhood Association, 2013; Ehlinger & Associates, 1998).

Francis T. Nicholls High School opened in 1913 and was located on the site of a former plantation. Nicholls (later Douglass) was redesigned and rebuilt in 1938–1939 as a Public Works Administration project during the Great Depression and included an elaborate auditorium. It occupies an entire square block and is approximately six blocks from the Mississippi River (Bywater Neighborhood Association, 2013; Ehlinger & Associates, 1998). First attended by white students and then by black students—histories charted later in the chapter— Douglass was occupied by the National Guard in the weeks following the storm (Anderson, 2005).

Some of the same classrooms at Douglass had been occupied by SAC since 1998. SAC is a writing and digital media program that builds on the voices and histories of New Orleans' black youth through courses offered in several public high schools, including Douglass. It was founded in 1996 by veteran public school teacher and teacher unionist Jim Randels and two of his students, and subsequently co-taught with poet and producer Kalamu ya Salaam, a respected figure in the Black Arts Movement. SAC builds on the history of racial resistance in New Orleans and is partly rooted in the tradition of the *griot*, or West African storyteller. It is guided by the tenet that oppressed communities must tell their stories to survive and challenge racism. Producing student anthologies, a newspaper called *OurVoice*, plays, radio broadcasts, and digital videos—what is described as "writing with text, sound, and light"—SAC has built on students' experiential knowledge and formulated a pedagogy rooted in the voices, cultures, and histories of marginalized youth, their families, and neighborhoods (Buras et al., 2010).

Recollections by Salaam in November 2005 convey the spirit of SAC's pedagogy as well as the culture of Douglass and the Bywater neighborhood. Salaam returned to New Orleans to discover immense destruction, but looked forward to the homecoming planned for the Douglass school community. He followed a second-line formed around the Young Tuxedo Brass Band, which headed to St. Paul's Church in Bywater. "People seep out of houses," Salaam recalled, "and a few are actually crying with joy" to be home. Upon passing Colton Middle School, "the band went into a dirge and that slow two-step they do to express grief." When the growing crowd reached St. Paul's, Salaam reminisced:

> Two young black women took turns dancing with the grand marshal of the second-line. Now being a grand marshal is no job for apprentices. You got to be carrying on in fine style. My man looked to be in his sixties dancing like he was still 32, plus you know he had a store house of moves from his years of dancing in the streets.
>
> By now, I am becoming emotional. Homesick. Critically ill. Somebody come see about me. I'm walking around laughing and joking with the students, with fellow SAC staff, with the band members whom I know, with friends who have joined us. ...
>
> Immediately after lunch we were to journey a couple of miles over to Douglass, which was walking distance. At the homecoming meeting we talked about where to go from here, what moves to make, what kind of response to mount to the ongoing abandonment. No public schools, No public hospitals. No this. No that. No. No. No.
>
> (Buras et al., 2010, p. 155)

For Salaam and others, Douglass and the surrounding community evoke a range of emotions, all tied to the deep cultural connection they share with this place. Fortunately, Douglass was in decent shape; only the band room had flooded. But what would Douglass' future hold in light of disinvestment by policymakers and the aggressive push for charter schools?

By this time, approximately 20 public schools in New Orleans had been chartered and the state was rumored to have plans to take over and charter the remaining ones.[1] Salaam shares, "We had a lot of discussion about charters and decided that we didn't want to go the charter route, even though we recognized that we might be forced to do so" (Buras et al., p. 156). In the tradition of SAC, everyone participated in the discussion: "Sitting in a big circle, we listened to each other— high school students, teachers, staff, community activists, civil rights veterans— everyone taking a turn speaking their hearts and minds, responding to the issues before us" (p. 156). Despite the difficulties at Douglass, SAC helped build a culture of caring, a shared sense of school ownership, and a respect for collective wisdom.

There is no denying that Douglass had its share of problems, but they were not the community's fault. New Orleans journalist Sarah Carr (2008) explains it this way:

> By any objective standard, Douglass had failed for years, with abysmal test scores and graduation rates, frequent fights, and scattershot attendance. But a close look at the school's history tells a much more complex story of a struggling urban school. ... It underscores the crippling effect of instability and the near-impossibility of reviving failing schools without consistent leadership, support and money—assets Douglass has long lacked.
>
> (para. 7)

In short, Douglass suffered from state abandonment, not community indifference. The community, as I will show, had a record of investing its cultural resources in the school to support students in whatever way possible. This included SAC, Crescent City Peace Alliance, Douglass Community Coalition, and other local groups.

One longtime Bywater community member—whose sons, granddaughter, and nieces attended Douglass—warned, "Don't fault the children." She continued: "When you close the school down, you're not punishing anybody else except for [the] children, and they don't deserve to be punished just because they did not get what they were supposed to get" (Interview, 2008). Her words are an essential reminder that despite the history of racial neglect, "Everyone was struggling to accomplish something, [and Douglass] was changing" (Interview, 2008). She recalls that prior to 2005, the school band would march through the streets and play music, emphasizing, "That's a big part of my heritage in this neighborhood." After 2005, neighbors who previously "fussed" about hearing the band now missed its presence and the students. Nonetheless, policymakers were hell bent on doing whatever they could to undermine grassroots efforts to improve Douglass and the community. They simply wanted to "get people out." This resident pondered the "building blocks" or strategies of accumulation by dispossession that were used (Harvey, 2006). First, the levees broke and everyone was forced to leave; next, people were told to wait before returning; upon returning, they were intimidated and arrested for minor, even contrived, infractions, such as driving too slowly down a pothole-filled street; building permits were delayed; "Road Home" monies were stalled; rent and insurance were raised; and finally, public education would be denied to youth in the neighborhood (Interview, 2008).

These strategies threatened to have tragic consequences. The 9th Ward as a whole had one of the highest rates of black working-class home ownership in the nation before 2005 (Common Ground, 2006). Waukesha Jackson (2005), a school-aged resident, reflects proudly on the 9th Ward's past:

> [In the 1940s] the area was home to both white and black families. It was one part of the city where black people could buy houses. ... For many years the Ninth Ward was a picture of stability, with strong black families in homes that many of them owned. ...
>
> Today the 9th Ward is predominantly black. ... The men join the military or do carpentry work. They work offshore and some of them are foremen on the riverfront. The women may sit with the elderly, do housecleaning, or work at hotels. ...
>
> Women play a big part in the neighborhood. ... They run barrooms that act as home bases, and go to church together. ... They organize Nights Out Against Crime, have participated in political organizations like the Black Panthers, and joined social clubs like the Nine Times Social and Pleasure Club. They take care of the community and each other while juggling their losses and responsibilities.

(p. 36)

No doubt, many also supported Douglass.

The history of all-white Nicholls High School and white resistance to desegregation provide context for understanding Douglass' subsequent challenges. This history is important to consider, especially since charter school advocates in New Orleans criticize traditional public schools, especially black ones, for their alleged "failure" without connecting racism and inequitable state education policies to the problems experienced by those schools.

A Confederacy of Students and Teachers: Whiteness, Property, and the Southern Way of Life at Francis T. Nicholls High School

For white students and teachers at Nicholls, the Civil War of the 1860s never ended. Rebellion against any form of Reconstruction that promised greater racial equity was a prominent part of the school's culture from the outset. When the new facility for Nicholls was dedicated on May 2, 1940, the state superintendent of education ceremoniously proclaimed:

> Within these walls may there always be respect for the individual, consideration and concern for others. ... Let us progress by helping boys and girls develop a wholesome knowledge of values, and teach them to use their intelligence.
>
> (Ehlinger & Associates, 1998, p. 1)

Although white education officials envisioned Nicholls as a place where "wholesome" values were developed, white supremacy was nurtured on a daily basis. Teachers and students saw no contradiction between the two.

The school was named after Francis T. Nicholls, a Confederate general. The school mascot was the Confederate Rebel and the student newspaper, founded in 1941, was called *The Rebel Yell*. A news article this same year focused on Francois Bourgeois, a 97-year-old Civil War veteran and explained the significance of the yell:

> "Hy-eeee," the Rebel yell, spurred many Southern soldiers on to daring feats, according to Bourgeois.
>
> The name, "Rebel Yell," was given by Union soldiers and the general public to the high pitched shout used by Confederates in spirited charges and violent clashes.
>
> (Willoughby, 1941, paras. 1–2)

According to the newspaper, Bourgeois later "worked as an overseer" on the St. George Plantation as well as on the St. Peter Plantation "for Leon Godchaux, the sugar king" (paras. 5–6). All of this being praiseworthy, the article ended by assuring readers that Bourgeois "still retains his faith in the American way. Hy-eeeeeeee!" (para. 9)

In 1954, the year of *Brown v. Board of Education*, Nicholls' principal Daniel Allain wrote a message to the graduating class of "Rebelville," a familiar reference to Nicholls. "To all of you the day of June 7, 1954 means the termination of four years of learning and citizenship preparation for a long future life" (Allain, 1954, para. 1). Allain was right—Nicholls prepared white students for productive futures and to assume their place as first-class citizens in the racial order of New Orleans. A survey, completed as a master's thesis at Tulane University, assessed the achievements of those who graduated from Nicholls between 1940 and 1951 (Fagan, 1952). Forty-six percent of the graduates responded to questions about residence, marital status, work experience, and additional education. Most remained in New Orleans; 60 percent continued their education, 70 percent had served proudly in the armed forces, and 47 percent were gainfully employed. In sum, Fagan (1952) concluded, "Nicholls' graduates made normal adjustments to marriage, jobs, and community living," and "gave strong evidence that the school had been effective in realizing its major purposes." In 1961–62, one decade later, Nicholls ranked first among New Orleans public schools in Louisiana's annual State Rally Competition, which assessed students in subjects ranging from English and trigonometry to chemistry and biology. *The Rebel Yell* was designated the best high school newspaper in Louisiana (*Rebel Yell*, 1963).

By all standard measures, Nicholls was a "successful" white public high school. Hundreds of students, sometimes referred to as "Confederates," were commended for presence on honor roll and perfect attendance records (*Rebel Yell*, 1955, pp. 1, 3; 1956, p. 5). They attended high school in a new building. They won contests for academic accomplishments. They took a range of courses that prepared them for productive pursuits after graduation and further education. In sum, as a white public school in New Orleans, Nicholls was given the resources it needed to ensure students' upward mobility.

Nicholls' students considered themselves not only a thriving educational community, but an inclusionary one as well. On April 23, 1960, they gathered in the school's auditorium for the annual spring fair, centered on the "melting pot." Activities related to "the four major nationalities most common at Nicholls," noted as Spanish, German, Italian, and French (*Rebel Yell*, 1960, p. 3). Festivities that day included mock tours of European countries, a U.S. military tap dance, and choral performance of the "Star Spangled Banner." If the identification with European ancestry and white supremacist ideals and icons was a part of Nicholls' taken-for-granted culture, it would be laid bare and challenged during the desegregation of New Orleans public schools.

Gwendolyn Adams, a black student who transferred to Nicholls in 1967, "recalled six white teens from the neighborhood throwing her through the plate glass window of a grocery store across the street from the school" (Carr, 2008, para. 14). Black students desegregating the school encountered white students who were the living incarnation of Nicholls' Rebel mascot. In 1970, white students from Nicholls held Confederate flags and protested school desegregation outside the offices of Orleans Parish School Board (Figure 4.2).

During this same period, white students at Nicholls celebrated Robert E. Lee's birthday. Lee was Commander-in-Chief of the Confederate Army and, according to *The Rebel Yell*, was "so esteemed and flawless a gentleman that the only fault the critics could find with him was that he had no faults" (*Rebel Yell*, 1966, Jan 21, para. 1). Heroes honored by students on Confederate Memorial Day in 1966 included Jefferson Davis, president of the Confederate States of America, Francis T. Nicholls, and others "who gave their all in the War for Southern Independence" (*Rebel Yell*, 1966, June 2, para. 1). To be clear, Confederate Memorial Day was a statewide tradition in Louisiana, a reminder that Nicholls' white supremacist culture was endemic. It is certain that black students involved in desegregating New Orleans public schools, as targets of racial abuse and violence, found many faults with General Lee, President Davis, and their student allies. For whites, however, Nicholls was theirs—they had an unmistakable property interest in whiteness and let black students know they were trespassing (Harris, 1995).

By the late 1970s, Nicholls was an all-black high school. White students fled to private urban academies as well as public schools in surrounding suburbs. When they departed, so did public resources for Nicholls. What was once a grand auditorium would decay after decades of state neglect. Aged classrooms, never repainted, would show the wear-and-tear of daily use. In 2008, RSD superintendent Paul Vallas and master planners would refer to this as *deferred maintenance*

FIGURE 4.2 White students protest desegregation of Francis T. Nicholls High School

and use Douglass' "failure" to justify its closure and the provision of this historic space to a charter school operator (Fieldnotes, 2008). The struggles that ensued at Nicholls from the 1970s onward, however, were the direct result of abandonment by white education policymakers in New Orleans and Baton Rouge. These were the inequitable conditions under which black students and teachers labored in the attempt to make Nicholls a place where racially oppressed youth could develop their potential and the community's.

From Francis T. Nicholls to Frederick Douglass High School: Black Educational Resistance in Bywater

Ms. Rosalind Vicknair, who took over as Nicholls' librarian in 1976, described "strong academic, sports, and music programs" developed at the then black high school (Carr, 2008, para. 16). Although white families ultimately fled the school and neighborhood, and students and teachers were now black, Russell Constanza, a white administrator, acted as school principal from 1970–1987 (*Bobcat Journal*, 1987, p. 1). Despite ongoing white leadership for almost two decades, Vicknair reports "a great deal of school pride" (Carr, para. 17). One of the first things students did in the 1970s was to change Nicholls' mascot from the Rebel to the Bobcat. By the early 1980s, nearly 1,400 students were attending Nicholls, with a Chapter I application in 1982–1983 indicating that approximately 20 percent were low-income, likely a substantial underestimate. An index published by City Hall described the area as an "endangered" neighborhood, ranked 28 of 70 neighborhoods in terms of "blighted conditions" (Chapter 1 Application, 1982–1983).

Official statistics and reports, however, failed to capture the meaningful cultural and educational work occurring at Nicholls. In the 1980s, a Black Culture Club infused a sense of racial pride and self-determination into the school climate. The *Bobcat Yearbook* from 1983 showcases the annual Black Culture Assembly sponsored by the club, where students were invited to "a celebration of works by Black Artists" and shown "the wealth of talent in the Black race" (*Bobcat Yearbook*, 1983, p. 126). Scenes from Lorraine Hansberry's *A Raisin in the Sun,* a play about the poverty and racism experienced by a black family living in Chicago, were performed by students on stage in Douglass' auditorium (see Figure 4.3). Ms. Celestand, a teacher involved with the club, delivered Nikki Giovanni's poem "Ego Tripping" about the strengths of African culture and history, alongside students who did their own poetic readings (*Bobcat*, p. 127). Others wearing dresses, coats, and ties participated in a candle lighting ceremony that revolved around various elements of Dr. Martin Luther King's dream (*Bobcat*, 1983).

Mobilizations occurred in New Orleans during the 1990s to change school names from those of Confederate leaders and slaveholders. Minutes from a meeting of Orleans Parish School Board on March 27, 1995, indicate that members of the Nicholls community "requested that the school's name be changed to Frederick A. Douglass Senior High School" (p. 19). Mrs. Assata Olugbala, a concerned

Top: Troy Taylor and Lisa Domengeaux perform a dance routine to Michael Jackson's "Beat It."

Top Right: Farrow Taylor and April Reimoneng perform a scene from "Rasin In The Sun."

More To "Blackness" Than The Boogie

On Friday February 25, 1983 the Black Culture Club presented its annual Black Culture Assembly. The students body was treated to a celebration of works by Black Artists. The program was dedicated to the memory of Eubie Blake (1883-1983).

The purpose of the program was to show students the wealth of tal-

ent in the Black race. Material by various artists was performed by members of the Club. Pieces by the following artists was presented: Nikki Giovanni, J. W. Johnson, Mari Evans and Scott Joplin. Guest speakers for the program were A. Reiss Mullen and English department member Ms. T. Mendez.

126/Black Culture Assembly

FIGURE 4.3 Black Culture Club assembly at Frederick Douglass High School

citizen, spoke on the need to rename Nicholls after Douglass. The request was "unanimously" approved by members of the school board (p. 20).

The naming of Douglass was a testament to the tenacity of students and teachers, but this period was characterized as well by mounting challenges that flowed from strategic disinvestment in New Orleans' black public schools. By this time, Douglass was in disrepair and "custodians no longer stocked the building with essentials such as toilet paper and trash cans," evidence of the school's resource-starved environment (Carr, 2008, para. 21). Under such conditions, there was constant turnover in school leadership. Chris Burton, a member of SAC and a 2005 Douglass graduate, emphasized, "I don't know any organization that can withstand seven different leaders in the span of four years" (Carr, 2008, para. 9). Greta Gladney, a 9th Ward activist who helped create small learning communities at Douglass, echoed Burton's concerns: "Every time we established a relationship and foundation with the school's leadership, they were replaced, and we had to start all over again" (para. 25).

This was the context in which SAC and the Douglass Community Coalition began work at Douglass.

Students at the Center, Douglass High School, and Charter School Reform

Douglass was one of the lowest-ranked public high schools in New Orleans when SAC joined the school in 1998. SAC student Maria Hernandez attested that before 2005: "The state, using its accountability plan, was trying to shut down Douglass or take it over." Contributing to a much wider national effort focused on educational inequity, Hernandez notes that she and fellow students at Douglass "were running a campaign called Quality Education as a Civil Right" (SAC, 2007a, p. 17). As a result:

> A lot of people were *finally* looking at our school as more than just a place where criminals are reared, which is the impression you'd get if all you knew were news reports. The media always ran to the school to report a fight, but no one said anything when my classmates placed first in a competition against professional journalists for a series they wrote on public education at the 50th Anniversary of *Brown v. Board of Education.*
>
> (p. 18)

The work of SAC challenged typical conceptions of Douglass and provided a space for meaningful activism and education.

Ashley Jones, a SAC student who went on to complete a university degree and returned to teach in the program, shared her thoughts on evacuating New Orleans before the storm. SAC was at the forefront of her mind:

> Before I thought about the place I used to get my chicken sandwiches from on Freret Street or Ms. Sadie the iceberg lady right off of LaSalle Street...I saw Maria and Rodneka, Earlnika, Keva, and Daniel. I thought about Douglass High School and the gloomy hallways that always made me feel that I was in a scary movie or something. I wondered what would be next for them, no longer having Students at the Center. I thought about the schools

they may be forced to go to, those cold, stiff rooms where the real world never becomes a part of the lesson plan.

(in SAC, 2007a, pp. 19–20)

Likewise considering the future of Douglass, Randels called attention to the history of unequal power that has characterized the city, invoking well-known musical lyrics:

> Randy Newman, in his song about the 1927 floods in New Orleans when the business leaders of the city decided to break the levees and flood the poorer parts of Louisiana in order to save their city, sang "They're trying to wash us away." Maria and Ashley and all of us are living that in terms of our public schools.
>
> (in SAC, 2007a, p. 42)

Randels refers to charter school reform aimed at reconstructing the city's public education system along privatized lines. Maria Hernandez shared her worries: "We had been fighting to improve from within neighborhood schools, that don't have selective admissions. Now, with all schools being charters, no one will have the choice of truly public, neighborhood-based education" (SAC, 2007a, p. 18). It seemed the concept of *public* education was at stake, with open access neighborhood public schools, such as Douglass, threatened by the proliferation of selective and privately managed charter schools.

There was cause for worry. In 2007–2008, the RSD admitted no new ninth graders to Douglass—the entire ninth grade cohort consisted of those who had failed the previous year. Pondering the situation in early 2007, before the district's announcement that Douglass might be closed, Salaam surmised:

> My theory is that they're phasing out Douglass and want to turn it into a charter. They want the building. It's just like my friend says about Nigerian oil—"They want the oil, but they don't want the people." They want the "earl" [the word *oil* repeated with local inflection], but they don't want the people.
>
> (Interview, 2007)

Randels connects this to longstanding contention around the school, indicating, "There was always a segment of this city that would have liked this school to go away—that was going on before the storm" (Interview, 2007). Regrettably, Randels testifies, "There were deeper inroads of parents and students and graduates who were invested in the school and who were here working for it. And so the push back was deeper. That's been stripped away. There's not as much traction here as there was before the hurricane" (Interview, 2007).

Much of the 9th Ward was still without potable water and electricity in 2006 (Common Ground, 2006). Stop lights were not operating in 2007 (Fieldnotes, 2007). Black residents in Bywater struggled to recover schools and homes, while uptown whites had resumed their lives. This was not by chance.

Students at the Center: Place-Based Curriculum at Douglass

SAC's work is situated in New Orleans' past as well as its present. Randels empha-sizes, "SAC understands that its work is part of a long stream of movements for lib-eration and social justice" (SAC, 2007a, p. 171). The influences are many and include the historic civil rights movement in New Orleans, black writers and musicians, Free Southern Theater, the NOMMO Literary Society (founded by Kalamu ya Salaam), and local efforts to form a teacher union and improve educational conditions. SAC adopted the tradition of the story circle from Free Southern Theater, a cultural out-growth of the civil rights movement that ultimately housed itself in New Orleans (Free Southern Theatre, 1963; see also Breunlin, n.d.). The story circle is:

> a small group forum in which participants sit in a circle and move around the circle ... reflecting on a theme or concept. ... The story one tells must be grounded in one's personal experience. ... All participants are encouraged to listen ... without interrupting. After the circle has been completed, par-ticipants ask questions, summarize lessons learned from the stories, develop visual images and other creative responses ... and engage in other forms of "cross talk."
>
> (Randels in SAC, 2007a, p. 158)

Salaam, now a teacher with SAC, is a former member of Free Southern Theater. Keva Carr, a Douglass student, speaks rather profoundly about such experiences with SAC:

> The teachers were different: It wasn't simply always their input but ours as well. ... We sat in a circle. We told stories and discussed real issues. ... I love Students at the Center for what it brought to me. And I love myself for what I brought to it.
>
> (SAC, 2007a, p. 144)

For SAC, the story circle is a way of creating community (see also Crossroads Project, 2006; SAC, 2007b).

Randels says SAC is based on the recognition that "students need a place that's smaller, so it's providing that setting." No more than 15 students are in each class and no more than four classes are taught per day by the teachers, who co-teach classes such as creative writing and English literature. Importantly, Randels makes clear that SAC is based on "a decision to stay within an existing system of public schools and to recognize that those were not set up in ways that fully meet the needs of the students or the teachers." Rather than setting up alternative or charter schools, Randels instead chose to ask, "What happens if within [the public system], you create some alternate structures?" (Interview, 2007). Salaam describes SAC as "a catalytic agent" and asserts, "What we have with the students right now is something that I don't see in most other classes" (Interview, 2007).

At Douglass, SAC classes consist of teachers and students sitting in a circle, sharing their stories and writings, listening carefully, and engaging in critical dialogue—practices informed by an appreciation of the connection between reflection and action (Freire, 1993). That is, "the best education is a collective and social rather than an individual endeavor" and "students learn when they teach and when they apply to community improvement and liberation what they learn in the classroom" (Randels in SAC, 2007a, p. 166). In the process, Randels and Salaam are mentoring as well as learning from a generation of student writers and storytellers in New Orleans, whose work is closely connected to the surrounding community. A lineage, in fact, has developed: more experienced SAC students mentor non-SAC peers in their own high schools, and some work with elementary-aged students at nearby public elementary schools (e.g., see SAC, 2007b). Graduates of SAC have returned as teachers in the program after completing college degrees. Douglass student LaQuita Joseph explains what sets SAC apart:

> SAC is not only a class in a school where we all learn facts and figures, but it's more of a way of life. Because what we learn, we apply to our everyday life. In many classes you are taught about people who make changes, but in SAC we take this to another level. We are taught how to make change through our writings, videos, and jobs that are provided for us where we tutor the young students. This is true praxis, taking what we have learned and putting it into action.
>
> (in SAC, 2007b)

Below I offer a glimpse into SAC classrooms at Douglass, where each student's sense of place and history is the starting point of the curriculum.

SAC in the Classroom: Circle the Chairs

When class begins at Douglass, SAC students and teachers quickly grab the chairs, arranged in rows from the previous period, and form a circle where everyone sits. After a minute or two of informal exchanges, the first question is usually "Who wants to start?" Next begins the hard work of sharing one's writing aloud, listening fully to the writer, choosing two peers to provide comment, and engaging in an overall dialogue around the text (Fieldnotes, 2007).

The question of why such loss and tragedy are unfolding for families and schools in New Orleans was taken up during one of SAC's creative writing classes at Douglass in 2007. Welling up with emotion, one student read aloud the story of how death has been visited upon her family since Katrina. Her grandfather died on her sibling's birthday, while another close relative got cancer and passed away. Most students closely related to what they called her "tears on paper" and believed that few people outside of the city understood the pain that has plagued New Orleans, especially since 2005. It was far from insignificant, pointed out

Randels, that Douglass had 22 security guards and only two guidance counselors. He pondered whether or not students might "secure" themselves by getting to class on time and then mobilize for more counselors. Meanwhile, Salaam opened up his laptop and proceeded to share two poems he had written over a very brief period when he lost two friends (Fieldnotes, 2007).

Salaam has emphasized with respect to SAC's work, "These are not woe-is-me, feel-sorry-for-us-poor-downtrodden-negroes investigations; rather these are honest explorations of complex social situations" (in SAC, 2007a, p. 138). This was apparent during a subsequent creative writing class at Douglass, when a student delivered "What I Hope to Do with My Life." Dedicated to a deceased grandparent, the piece detailed her goal of finishing high school—the first to do so in her family—and becoming a preschool teacher. "School's not for me," she wrote, "but I will finish for my family." As the dialogue around kinship proceeded, Salaam added, "I like the way ya'll lookin' out for each other. Folks with very little do that. Those with everything are like 'me, me, me.' It's good that's happening [in our community]." Of course, each and every exchange did not enhance community. One ninth grader was rather resistant. He questioned Randels, who, in the spirit of SAC, repeated the pattern. "C'mon man," he uttered with frustration, "I ask you a question and you ask a question back!" This same student later refused to read his writing aloud (Fieldnotes, 2007). Such fits and non-starters reflected the wider context of the school. During my time with SAC, for example, a day at Douglass was disrupted and then terminated due to an electrical outage. When I queried a security guard about the problem, I was told the fire chief did not know what was wrong, but it "could take a week to fix it" (Fieldnotes, 2007).

Students' narratives of familial loss, the loss of a school day, and the potential loss of Douglass contrast starkly with the experiences of white students who once occupied this space. The differences are explained by a history of unequal racial power, a history addressed by SAC through its work with the Douglass Community Coalition.

SAC in the Community: Mapping Racial Resistance with the Douglass Community Coalition

In the early 2000s, the Frederick Douglass Community Coalition (DCC) was organized. The DCC involved various grassroots educational, cultural, political, and environmental groups in an effort to make Douglass High School the center of community organizing and development in the Upper 9th Ward. Involvement of community members in decision making over curriculum and educational policy was part of the vision (Weaving the Web, 2003).

In the wake of post-2005 charter school reform, DCC emphasized its commitment to:

> [public] schools that have no selective admissions requirements, honor the collective bargaining agreement of AFT Local 527 [United Teachers of New

> Orleans, the city's teacher union], and are part of a public school system that
> plans and fights for equitable and high quality education for all students.
>
> (SAC, 2007a, p. 194).

The educational principles of DCC, influenced by SAC pedagogy, stressed that "education is for community development as much as it is for individual achievement" (SAC, 2007a, p. 194). Moreover, DCC asserted: "Students should be meeting educational standards through studying the history of New Orleans and participating in its planning and rebuilding" (p. 194). Educational models included SAC's involvement of Douglass students as lead writers and researchers for Plessy Park; the Creole Cottage Program in which Douglass students learned math and social studies while rebuilding homes in the city; and science projects in biology and chemistry focused on air and soil quality in New Orleans and surrounding wetlands. Communal principles and practices were to inform all aspects of school life, with housing, health, social, and community organizations taking up residence at Douglass and providing support for curriculum through reciprocal relationships with students and teachers (SAC, 2007a).

Within this context, SAC's book entitled *The Long Ride* (SAC, 2005) was published. It was framed as a collection of student writings based on events that are part of the long struggle for civil rights and social justice in New Orleans. In the absence of Plessy Park, these writings served as an educational resource for public schools across the city and connected students' life experiences to a history of racial resistance they could call their own. In reality, *The Long Ride* covered more than New Orleans' civil rights history. Writings spanned African history from *Plessy* to present-day New Orleans. Salaam reflected on the purposes of the project:

> *The Long Ride* ... calls for student writers to "imagine" themselves within history and to write from their own perspective about factual events that took place before the student was born. We are fortunate in New Orleans; much of our history is documented. We are unfortunate in that 99% of the documentation is from the perspective of our historic exploiters. ...
>
> The SAC approach is both deconstructive and reconstructive. ... We suggest that our students question every historical fact and also ... insert themselves into the process of interpreting history. So we break down the written history ... and then we rebuild [it] using our own perspectives and emotions.
>
> (SAC, 2005, p. 40)

Unlike the ahistorical approach of entrepreneurs who seek to transform New Orleans public schools without knowing the first thing about the history of the people attending them, SAC students understand that history is theirs to claim and to build. It is something that literally shapes the ground they walk on.

In *The Long Ride,* for instance, Adrinda Kelly, a student in one of SAC's first classes, writes about the necessity of "recovering the unknown" of Africa:

> As a young girl, my classmates and I didn't think about Africa often. ... The truth is there wasn't much a bunch of public school students growing up in one of America's blackest cities ... could know about a place that we spent so much time trying to disassociate ourselves from. Africa, to us, was Kunta Kinte, slavery, dark skin and big lips. It was the Zulu parade at Mardi Gras with people in black-face handing out coconuts and beads. It was grass skirts and spears, rhythm and jungle. It was a lie, an embellishment, an embarrassment, a fantasy. And we didn't want it.

For Kelly, overcoming these distorted understandings became "a kind of birthright" (SAC, 2005, p. 8).

In another piece entitled "A Twelve Year Old Talks to Plessy," Gabrielle Turner imagined herself coming face-to-face with Homer Plessy, a historic member of her community:

> I saw the shiniest pair of shoes walk past me. I knew exactly who it was. It was Mr. Homer. He always had the best looking shoes in the neighborhood, because he was a shoemaker.
>
> Before I looked up I saw another pair of shoes that weren't so nice walking behind Mr. Homer. I looked up and saw Mr. Homer with his hands behind his back and handcuffs tightly on his wrist. ....
>
> A couple of days later walking home from school, I passed Mrs. Louise's house. Mrs. Louise lived in one of the shotgun houses on my street. ... She and three other women were sitting on her front porch talking. She leaned back in her old wooden chair with *The Crusader* newspaper in her hand and said, "That man, he was only trying to get us black folks equal treatment."
>
> (SAC, 2005, p. 69)

For Gabrielle, *Plessy* was not a Supreme Court case; Plessy was a shoemaker, a neighbor, and someone who fought for the rights of black people in New Orleans. She "saw" him right down the street from Douglass and learned about the meaning of his resistance on the front porch of "one of the shotgun houses on my street." The time, more than 100 years, that separated them was no longer there.

Similarly, Anastasia McGee attempted to "connect with maroon colonies" in New Orleans. She compared the choices she faced regarding which high school to attend in New Orleans to these rebels' commitment to still-enslaved peoples, writing:

> The maroons communicated and stayed with the slaves to help free them ... It made me think about the decisions I could have made to escape oppression at my current neighborhood school ... but I resisted some teachers'

and students' efforts to try and get me to go to … selective admissions high schools. … I made the decision to stay at Douglass High School long before I read anything about the maroons and the history, but reading it made me conscious about my decision. … Like the maroons, I believe in helping other people in my community and not just myself.

(SAC, 2005, p. 28)

A relational sense of place and historical memory are maintained by SAC through writings about and for community. Although Plessy Park had been postponed, Randels nonetheless emphasized: "It's interesting to wonder what actions … Plessy [and others] would be taking [today]. … These are the questions students are beginning to ask" (p. 55).

SAC Counterstories on the Master's Plan for New Orleans

These questions were at the center of another SAC collection of student writings focused on post-2005 education reform in New Orleans and the destructive effects of the city's master plans for black students, schools, and neighborhoods. Originally entitled *Katrina and Me* (2007a), parts of the anthology were later published as *Pedagogy, Policy, and the Privatized City: Stories of Dispossession and Defiance from New Orleans* through Teachers College Press (Buras et al., 2010).

This SAC anthology opened with a declaration that linked past times with the present: "To understand post-Katrina, you have to understand pre-Katrina." In contrast to policymakers and planners who wish to destroy remnants of the old and "start from scratch," SAC announced: "Students, teachers, and community supporters certainly want much better public education in New Orleans. We just don't believe scorching the earth is the way to do it" (SAC, 2007a, p. 11). New Orleans and its public schools have entered a new era, "but it is not a moment out of time" (p. 12). Understanding the past is indispensable if a more equitable New Orleans is to be imagined and constructed. This "is not a story that only those in power will tell," insisted SAC students and teachers from Douglass and other public high schools across New Orleans (p. 12).

Counterstories must be told in opposition to dominant narratives of reform. For critical race theorists and SAC, counterstories are accounts that challenge white majoritarian narratives and are based on the experiential knowledge of people of color (Apple & Buras, 2006; Delgado, 2000; Yosso, 2006; for more on counterstories, see chapter 6). They are essential in the context of New Orleans, where racially and economically destructive reforms have been packaged as a successful model to be replicated nationally. Douglass students speak from ground zero.

For SAC, the undermining of Douglass is part of a story that goes way back and includes how students and their families were abandoned in the wake of Hurricane Katrina. Trapped with her family in New Orleans East after the storm, student Deborah Carey recollects:

We listened to the radio about what was going on in the city: nothing, but bad news everywhere. All you could hear was people scrambling for help. National Guards my ass: They didn't even save us.

The so-called criminals of New Orleans saved us, stealing boats, trucks, 18 wheelers, and buses. Society calls these people animals, saying, "They don't deserve to be citizens."...

Seeing a big moving truck with at least 30 people in the back, one of the drivers asked us did we need a ride. We didn't even answer. We just hopped on, which reminded me of how slaves were treated: a whole lot of black folks packed up on a wagon escaping from master....

Whatever help we needed the state was supposed to provide. It was like our citizenship went down the stream right along with our houses, all forgotten about by our government.

(SAC, 2007a, pp. 29–30)

Building on Deborah's critique of being "forgotten" by the government, Maria Hernandez shared her concerns about the selective practices of charter schools and RSD endorsement of such reform:

With all the schools being charters, no one will have the choice of a truly public, neighborhood-based education....

I've lost my home, my friends, my school. I'm always on the verge of tears, but the worst part of it all is that the public officials—both elected and hired—who are supposed to be looking out for my education have failed me worse that the ones who abandoned me in the Superdome [during Katrina].

(SAC, 2007a, pp. 18–19)

Another SAC student from Douglass, Vinnessia Shelbia, elucidated, "Leaving out of New Orleans was hard, because there's no other place like it. But living in post-Katrina New Orleans is just as bad, because there's nowhere to live" (in SAC, 2007a, p. 81). Her family was forced to move into homeless shelters throughout the city due to escalating rents. These circumstances caused her to question: "It makes me wonder what kind of world we live in when children no older than 14 are experiencing these things" (p. 82). Recalling the violence that typified New Orleans before 2005—violence too often blamed on poor African Americans without addressing white racism—she posed the penetrating question: "New Orleans really is the murder capital, but now who's holding the gun?" In the final analysis, Vinnessia's narrative illuminates policymakers' disinvestment in public housing and public schools in New Orleans' black neighborhoods and stimulates questions about so-called urban renewal in other cities (e.g., *Times-Picayune*, 2007a, 2007b).

Randels illustrated the promises and perils that characterized schools before 2005 and the challenges that confront the public schools of New Orleans today.

He refers to Z, "a young man [at Douglass] who didn't always go to class" before the storm and whose "size and facial expression and body language might seem menacing to someone who sees him around school but doesn't really know him." Z approached Randels to teach him how to read—a powerful reminder that even before 2005, resources at Douglass were insufficient. One lesson to be learned, says Randels, is that "young people such as Z are eager to learn, given the right conditions" (SAC, 2007a, p. 190). Tragically, he disclosed, "Z won't be with us in the return to New Orleans. Word is he drowned in the storm." Randels' plea challenges the notion that charter schools provide an easy way out: "For the sake of young people like Z, I hope policymakers and national experts will listen to the lessons veteran New Orleans educators have learned from Z." That is to say, students at schools like Douglass can learn if the physical, economic, cultural, and human infrastructure is there.

SAC provides a roadmap to a more successful and more equitable public education system, rather than going the route of charter schools. Unfortunately, this is not what master planners had in mind, as many in the Douglass community were acutely aware. Salaam reflected: "I don't believe we're gonna win this one. I really do not believe we're going to win this one. But I do believe the story is important. We have to tell our story" (Interview, 2007).

The Fight for Frederick Douglass High School: Students Don't Know Their History?

In early April 2008, officials announced that Douglass might be closed, with students possibly transferred to trailers at a nearby site where a Law and Public Safety Academy (a high school focused on military, police, fire, and emergency medical services) would be opened (Fieldnotes, 2008). Fears only deepened when then RSD superintendent Paul Vallas (2008) presented a report on the status of elementary and high schools in mid-April—one that failed to even mention Douglass—and "claimed that the community had not cared about Douglass for the last 40 years" (SAC, 2008; see also daLuz, 2008). Clearly, Vallas did not apprise himself of student and teacher efforts to uplift the school through the Black Culture Club, SAC, DCC, and other initiatives.

In response to these announcements, teachers, students, members of SAC, Douglass alumni, community members, and local activists—many affiliated with DCC—organized a public meeting with RSD officials. Meeting in Douglass' auditorium on May 6, 2008, officials emphasized that the School Facilities Master Plan for Orleans Parish, which was under development and due to be released mid-summer, would include "recommendations" regarding which schools would remain open, be renovated, or be closed (RSD & NOPS, 2008). Vallas claimed there was a lack of funds for renovations throughout the RSD (thus the need to close schools and "consolidate") and provided an estimate by a construction company (one responsible for building a substandard police academy in Iraq) that indicated it would require millions to repair Douglass (Fieldnotes, 2008; Myers, 2007). Financial constraints, however, failed to account for *why* other schools—some in worse condition and some in more affluent areas—were already slated for support by master planners. These contradictions prompted one alumnus to ask: "Why would [officials] close the school ... when there is no other high school in this community and the building itself is a viable building?" Vallas stressed:

> The master plan will present some recommendations, will present recommendations, *recommendations* [this summer]. Those recommendations will be presented to the community and then there will be a window of opportunity for the community to provide additional input before the final recommendations are made. So that's the process.
>
> (Fieldnotes, 2008)

Although Vallas emphasized the tentative nature of the planning process, concerns persisted. "We know in the world of government," another community member professed, "there are recommendations, and then there are *recommendations*. There are recommendations that really are advisory and there are recommendations that are actually conclusions." "No, they're advisory," Vallas assured the community, "and the [state] superintendent [Paul Pastorek] has said this over and over again" (Fieldnotes, 2008).

An alumnus of the school pushed back, "We fought for this school in the 60s, 70s, 80s, and 90s. We have too much history here [to close the school]," referring, in part, to black student protests in the late 1960s to have the school mascot changed from a Rebel to a Bobcat (Fieldnotes, 2008; Interview, 2008). Vallas responded: "Kids don't know they're going to school at a historical landmark. They just know they're going to a building where the electricity doesn't work, where the technology has been antiquated." Vallas did not address the role of the state in producing those conditions.

Another oft-repeated message by Vallas, who attempted to distance himself from the School Facilities Master Plan, was: "I'm not going to get involved in the politics of where schools should go. I'm going to get involved in the politics of what schools should be." In his view, no relationship existed between Douglass' history, the surrounding community, and role of place in shaping what the school should be. A theater artist, one associated with SAC, assumed the floor and explained:

> Many buildings in this city were destroyed three years ago and this building wasn't, and I think that this is why you're experiencing such a strong resistance about the idea of this building being destroyed or taken away from us. ...
>
> I want to share with you that many sacred academic moments have occurred in this building. ... One of those things ... is learning about

Frederick Douglass, learning about Homer Plessy and the boldness and the work that came from his step so many years ago [to challenge segregation]. [Another is] a textbook that has been written about the civil rights movement... called *The Long Ride* and it was put together by [SAC].

I think the biggest strength of the [SAC] program is that students who are some of the poorest, some of the most oppressed students in our city, have learned how to identify their own oppression.... They have learned how to voice that and write about it and teach everyone else about it....

If you want to make a difference... you will read that book.... And you will do everything in your power to save this school and give it back to the hands of the people who built it.

(Fieldnotes, 2008)

During the meeting, a petition circulated that contested the closing of Douglass and called for a curriculum focused on college preparation, fine arts, and community service—all elements embodied in SAC. Meanwhile, officials stressed that a "steering committee" had been organized by the principal, and an RSD liaison appointed, to generate a proposal for the school's future (Fieldnotes, 2008).

At a DCC meeting the next day, one activist, invited to be a member of the "steering committee," expressed concern that the committee was "not for input but for rubber stamping" plans that school authorities had made already. Even more disheartening, she stated that "neither the principal nor consultant [who headed the committee] has any idea of [our] history of work and have not made efforts to be informed about the strengths of the neighborhood, school, or graduates" (Frederick Douglass Community Coalition, 2008).

In mid-May, just *two weeks after* the meeting with RSD officials and *three months before* the School Facilities Master Plan "recommendations" had been formally issued in August for community input, then state superintendent of education Paul Pastorek (2008) responded in writing to one of several letters from community activists regarding Douglass' possible closure, declaring:

The Douglass school will be repurposed—reused for another purpose, not demolished. Community involvement will be part of the process of school property disposition....

My question to you and your coalition—are you tied to the school building or to creating a world class academic school for the students?

Douglass was closed at the end of the 2009–2010 school year and the building was given to KIPP, a national CMO developing a network of charter schools in New Orleans. The historic space that was Douglass became KIPP Renaissance High School in 2010–2011 (Simon, 2009). Douglass students would not be welcome to attend. Whose renaissance was this? Master planners and those consulted by the Bring New Orleans Back Commission, which called for the city to develop the nation's first charter school district, included the founder of KIPP; founder of Teach for America; founder of New Schools for New Orleans; and the Broad Foundation, Gates Foundation, and NewSchools Venture Fund (BNOB, 2006). Community-led education initiatives could have provided the basis for state investment of resources at Douglass, but instead the interests and visions of edu-businesses such as KIPP came first.

From Frederick Douglass High School to KIPP Renaissance High School

KIPP is a national CMO founded by Teach for America alumni, which had 99 schools in 20 states and Washington, DC, at the beginning of the 2010–2011 school year (Miron, Urschel, & Saxton, 2011). KIPP Renaissance High School took over the space once belonging to Douglass and opened the doors in 2010–2011 to its first group of ninth graders. Adding a new middle school that year as well, KIPP-New Orleans charter school network operated seven schools and had plans to ultimately run 12 schools serving 5,300 students, approximately 15 percent of New Orleans' public school population (Thevenot, 2009). In anticipation of opening, KIPP Renaissance principal Brian Dassler stated, "I hope that as the Douglass community gets more familiar with us and as we get more familiar with the Douglass community, it will be a partnership" (Simon, 2009, para. 26). From the outset, however, it was unclear exactly what was meant by "partnership." KIPP officials, after all, expected KIPP Renaissance "to draw most of its students from other KIPP schools in the city" (Simon, para. 27). Douglass high school students, the ones who remained as the school was phased out, would not be served by KIPP Renaissance. In fact, only 40 percent of KIPP Renaissance's incoming class came from non-KIPP schools (Ruth, 2011).

Prior to opening, KIPP Renaissance mobilized over 1,000 volunteers that gave more than 7,000 hours of their time to prepare the building for its grand opening. Scores of mostly young white recruits cleaned, painted, and made repairs (KIPP Renaissance, 2010). Considering the public and private philanthropic monies that flow through the KIPP charter school network—the Fisher, Walton, Gates, and Broad Foundations have given countless millions (Ruth, 2011)—this was foreseeable. Vallas noted in 2008, "If a charter high school like KIPP goes in the Douglass building, the organization might bring outside money to help renovate the building" (Carr, 2008, para. 44). Again, no consideration was given to the question of why state and local officials failed to maintain the building or why master planners decided Douglass did not merit renovations. It appeared that state culpability would be masked with a fresh coat of paint. In the school cafeteria, however, Douglass' Bobcat mascot remained visible on the walls, a visual marker of the rift between the school's past and the future conceived by outside entrepreneurs (KIPP Renaissance, 2010). As predicted, when KIPP Renaissance opened, the auditorium had air-conditioning.

KIPP Renaissance boasted: "KIPP schools are nationally recognized for preparing underserved students for success in college and in life. Over 85% of KIPP graduates have gone on to college" (KIPP Renaissance, 2012). One local publication in New Orleans echoed KIPP's claims about success: "[KIPP schools in New Orleans] rank at high levels of student performance even though they're open-enrollment schools. Most of New Orleans' high performing schools...have admission standards that limit admittance to only the city's most talented students" (Ruth, 2011, p. 4). The reality of KIPP charter schools in New Orleans, however, was not nearly as shiny as the new paint on the walls of Renaissance High School. Statistics provided by the Juvenile Justice Project of Louisiana (JJPL), based on data from the Louisiana Department of Education, indicate that in 2011–2012, KIPP Renaissance had an out-of-school suspension rate of 27 percent (JJPL, 2013a). In 2012–2013, Renaissance's out-of-school suspension rate was 37 percent, among the highest in the city (JJPL, 2013b). KIPP, which embraces a "No Excuses" charter school model, has an extensive and punitive code of conduct that ranks "disciplinary infractions" by level and suggests corresponding "corrective strategies," including suspension and expulsion (KIPP New Orleans Schools, 2012–2013). This punitive code is presented as a positive component of KIPP culture and is linked to the alleged success of KIPP students (Mathews, 2009). A description of KIPP McDonogh 15 Elementary in New Orleans reads:

> Talking in the halls or to each other in class is strictly prohibited, and violations bring punishments of exile and silence during lunch breaks, detention instead of recreation periods and demerits that can add up to other punishments.
>
> (Ruth, 2011, p. 5)

Although KIPP has built its reputation based on a no-nonsense approach, JJPL (2013a) warns: "Ineffective discipline policies, like the over-use of suspension, frequently push students out of school and increase the likelihood that they will drop out and become involved in the juvenile justice system" (p. 3). It is difficult to understand how KIPP can, on one hand, boast a college-going rate of 85 percent while, on the other hand, exhibiting high suspension and attrition rates.

Rather than looking at KIPP *outcomes*, such as college-going rates, a national study of KIPP charter schools done by Miron and colleagues (2011) examined two *inputs*: students and funding. During 2008–2009, KIPP schools across the nation—94 percent of the ones in operation that year—were compared with local school districts. Findings affirm that KIPP schools have a high rate of attrition. Specifically:

- KIPP attrition exceeds local school districts, with approximately 15 percent of the students, on average, dropping from KIPP grade cohorts each year;
- Between grades 6–8, KIPP grade cohorts drop by 30 percent;
- A full 40 percent of black male students leave KIPP between grades 6 and 8; and
- Empty seats are not refilled, especially in the higher grades.

Further, although KIPP schools tend to enroll a higher percentage of black students and low-income students than local school districts, they enroll a lower percentage of students with disabilities and English Language Learners. Miron and colleagues (2011) conclude that "the departure of low-performing students helps KIPP improve its aggregate results" (p. iii). KIPP also focuses on start-ups rather than taking over traditional public schools that are failing. The researchers note that "KIPP's only effort to take over a traditional pubic school [Cole Middle School in Denver]—with a representative range of students and with the responsibility to serve all students that come and go during and between school years—ended in failure after only 2 years" (p. 30). Start-up charter schools, they point out, benefit from selective entry and selective exit, and do not need to fill seats for students who leave during and between school years.

For 2007–2008, KIPP finance data was evaluated for 42 percent of KIPP schools in operation that year; it was compared with finance data for local school districts and with national means for charter and traditional public schools (Miron et al., 2011). In order to provide a fuller picture of KIPP revenues, including public funds and private philanthropic monies, researchers had to review federal data as well as IRS Form 990 tax filings (since none of the KIPP schools reported private contributions). Regarding revenues, they found:

- KIPP received more per pupil in combined revenue than local school districts or the national means for charter and traditional public schools; and
- With public and private sources of revenue combined, KIPP received, on average, $18,491 per pupil, $6,500 more per pupil than local school districts.

Thus, not only does KIPP have selective entry and exit of students. KIPP has more economic resources to educate the students that enter and remain. It also benefits, as Miron and colleagues (2011) point out, from a cost advantage not accrued by traditional public schools serving a more diverse array of students. The study did indicate the KIPP New Orleans network had one of the largest discrepancies between its level of *government* funding and the host district (RSD) (p. 19). That said, in 2007–2008, KIPP New Orleans network registered $1,582,192 in private revenue and served 712 students, resulting in an additional $2,222 in per pupil *private* revenue (p. 21). Also, the researchers did not consider an additional benefit garnered by KIPP New Orleans network. Most charter schools in the RSD receive rent-free facilities (e.g., those having a Type 5 charter agreement with BESE). This would include the Douglass building given to KIPP Renaissance.

In sum, KIPP is able to make claims about higher student achievement because of selective entry; selective attrition of low-performing students; and higher levels of funding, among other advantages. Ultimately:

> If KIPP wishes to maintain its status as an exemplar of private management of *public* schools, rather than a new effort to *privatize* public schools, it will

need to convince policymakers and the public that it intends to recruit and serve a wider range of students and that it will be able to do so with sustainable levels of funding comparable to what other traditional public schools receive.

(Miron et al., 2011, p. 31)

Presently, KIPP "[depends] on local traditional public schools to receive and serve the droves of students who leave" (p. 30). This is especially true in the RSD, where direct-run schools have become the "dumping ground" for students not admitted or retained by charter schools, such as KIPP (UTNO, LFT, & AFT, 2006). The above findings are not an anomaly. Another study that focused solely on KIPP high schools in three urban districts in Texas (including Houston, KIPP's birthplace)—the previous study assessed elementary and middle schools—reached similar conclusions:

[In Texas], the data show that despite the claim that 88–90% of the children attending KIPP charters go on to college, their Black secondary school attrition rate surpasses that of peer urban districts. And this is in spite of spending 30–60% more per pupil.

(Vasquez Heilig, Williams, McNeil, & Lee, 2011, p. 172)

Based on such evidence, it is difficult to believe that KIPP Renaissance will accomplish what its name implies: rebirth or revival. Instead, KIPP Renaissance is most likely to exacerbate historic racial inequities in New Orleans.

Douglass held promise for the Bywater community. SAC and DCC were committed to serving all students and they had a rich legacy on which to build. SAC and DCC embraced pedagogic practices that centered the students, their culture, and their history, and connected each individual's education to community development and liberation. By contrast, KIPP culture is punitive. As the leader of one KIPP middle school in Houston stated, either adhere to KIPP culture or "find the door" (Smith, 2005). Further, the KIPP curriculum is not culturally relevant, place-based, or participatory in any critical sense. It revolves around rituals of compliance and memorization. Praising the "paternalistic" culture of KIPP schools, Whitman (2008) describes the chants, claps, rhymes, and finger-snapping that drive instruction throughout the day (or what school leaders call "KIPP-notizing"). He describes KIPP's SLANT rubric that requires all students in class to Sit up straight, Listen, Answer and ask questions, Nod your head if you understand, and Track the speaker (p. 156). He offers the following description by researchers of the first day of summer school in Bay Area KIPP schools:

The staff welcomes the new students . . . and immediately recognizes students who are in proper uniform. . . . [Next] students learn how to stand properly in line—silently and with a book in their hand. They are taught that lines should be SILENT, STRAIGHT, AND SERIOUS. . . . Students then learn silent hand signals for yes and no, [and] the clap that teachers use to get students' attention. ... Working hard, being nice, and following directions are constantly promoted as values that will get [students] into college.

(pp. 160–161; caps in original)

In SAC classes at Douglass, students were not expected to stand in line silently with books. They sat in a circle together, shared their lives through storytelling, and authored books together. Finally, KIPP emphasizes college going, with an emphasis on *going*. The assumption here is that students' communities are places to be left behind and forgotten. Whitman (2008) shares the poem of a KIPP sixth grader from the South Bronx, which epitomizes the values underlying KIPP culture:

> They say you can take the girl out the ghetto
> But you can't take the ghetto out of the girl
> The ghetto is leaving this girl
> Let me fly
> Give me wings ...
> 'Cause I'm leaving and I ain't coming back.

(p. 174)

Many SAC students at Douglass attended college (and graduate school), but they returned to the community to teach and organize for social justice. It is also worth noting that KIPP schools use a "paycheck" system to reward and punish students; virtual cash is acquired for good behavior and obedience (Whitman, 2008). Students are thus inducted into a market-based culture where motivation is linked to economic self-interest and commercial transactions. At Douglass, SAC students were invested in education for liberation, not education for marketization. There is a world of difference.

Elite plans to remake Douglass did not exist in a vacuum. Just blocks away, another project was being planned to reinvent the Bywater area. Once again, this project did not appear to be intended for existing students and residents.

Reinventing the Crescent City

Along the bank of the Mississippi River, not far from KIPP Renaissance, six miles of riverfront is to be developed as part of a $294 million dollar public–private venture to "Reinvent the Crescent [City]."[2] The project is partly funded through a $30 million Disaster Community Development Block Grant (Reinventing the Crescent, 2008b). Investment on the riverfront between 2008 and 2016 is meant to "encourage an augmented housing stock," "revitalize existing neighborhoods for renovation and redevelopment," "promote a more active tourist industry," "attract new residents" and capture "new industry and entrepreneurial capital" (Nagin, Fielkow, & Cummings, 2008, p. 14; see also Reinventing the Crescent, 2008a). Planning documents mention that new residents are to be members of a *professional creative class* (Reinventing the Crescent, 2008a). It seems that the contributions of longtime Bywater residents do not qualify as creative or sophisticated—no small irony since the commercialization of black cultural forms is the heart of the tourist industry in New Orleans. Development goals include a waterside park, performance venue, housing, cruise ship terminal, and a hotel (Nagin et al., 2008; Richardson & Heidelberg, 2008). Clearly, there is an affinity between the RSD's School Facilities Master Plan and developers' efforts to reconstruct the city's urban space economy. It will be important to map the effects of this on the historic Bywater neighborhood in the years to come.

Conclusion

Randels, Salaam, and Douglass students know well the effects of this ongoing assault. But they also continue to recognize that they have the voices and traditions of ancestors and the bonds of community to sustain them during the "long ride," including the struggle for equitable public schools in New Orleans. One of SAC's (2007b) digital videos, entitled "Writing with Light," shows Douglass students reading essays on how SAC enriched their lives and communities. One particular image from the video stands out: Salaam is seated on the periphery of the SAC circle, while Gabrielle Turner, SAC graduate-turned-teacher, assists a current SAC student who is filming the event. Captured here is a visual representation of SAC's genealogy and the collaborative exchanges that enable students to become teachers and teachers to become students. At the conclusion of the video, both Randels and Salaam reenter the process and are seen offering guidance on film-making techniques. All of this powerfully demonstrates what SAC has called "completing the circle of education" (SAC, 2007b).

Douglass' closure surely undermined the community's efforts to determine its future and to complete the circle of education. So did the mass firing of New Orleans black veteran teachers in early 2006. They would be replaced by mostly white, inexperienced recruits from outside the community; many KIPP teachers are Teach for America alumni. Just as the interests of black working-class communities would not be served by closing open-access neighborhood schools, such as Douglass, they would be equally undermined by firing veteran teachers indigenous to the community. This was another way that policymakers hoped to "reinvent" the Crescent City. As I discuss in the next chapter, Teach for America was a willing participant in the process of displacement.

Notes

1 A substantial number of the earliest charter schools were part of the Algiers Charter School Association, mentioned in chapter 1.
2 New Orleans is also known as the Crescent City based on its location where the Mississippi bends like a crescent and heads toward the Gulf of Mexico.

References

Allain, D. A. (1954, June 4). Message to graduates. *Rebel Yell, XXVI*(8), 4–5. Available: Orleans Parish School Board Collection, Francis T. Nicholls High School Series, Earl K. Long Library, Louisiana and Special Collections Department, University of New Orleans.

Anderson, K. (2005, September 20). It's a meaningful life. *Times-Picayune*. Retrieved from http://freepages.school-alumni.rootsweb.ancestry.com/~neworleans/nicholls/memorabilia/after/index.html

Apple, M. W., & Buras, K. L. (Eds.). (2006). *The subaltern speak: Curriculum, power, and educational struggles*. New York, NY: Routledge.

Baum, D. (2007, February 6). After-School conference. *The New Yorker*. Retrieved from http://freepages.school-alumni.rootsweb.ancestry.com/~neworleans/nicholls/memorabilia/after/future/new_yorker/index.html

Bobcat Yearbook. (1983). More to "Blackness" than the boogie [Box 7]. Available: Orleans Parish School Board Collection, Francis T. Nicholls High School Series, Earl K. Long Library, Louisiana and Special Collections Department, University of New Orleans.

Bobcat Journal. (1987, November). Russell S. Constanza retires as principal. *Bobcat Journal, 1*(1), 1. Available: Orleans Parish School Board Collection, Francis T. Nicholls High School Series, Earl K. Long Library, Louisiana and Special Collections Department, University of New Orleans.

Breunlin, R. (n.d.). The legacy of the Free Southern Theater in New Orleans: Interviews with Karen-Kaia Livers and Chakula Cha Jua. *Chicken Bones: A Journal for Literary and Artistic African–American Themes*. Available: www.nathanielturner.com/legacyfreesout theater.htm

Bring New Orleans Back Commission. (2006). Rebuilding and transforming: A plan for world- class public education in New Orleans. New Orleans, LA: Author.

Buras, K. L., Randels, J., Salaam, K. Y., & Students at the Center (2010). *Pedagogy, policy, and the privatized city: Stories of dispossession and defiance from New Orleans*. New York, NY: Teachers College Press.

Bywater Neighborhood Association. (2013). About Bywater: History [Webpage]. Available: www.bywaterneighbors.com/

Carr, S. (2008, September 21). Limits of resilience. *Times-Picayune*. Available: www.nola.com

Chapter 1 Application. (1982–1983). Document [Box 1: School profiles, 1983–1984, Division of Planning, Testing, and Evaluation]. Available: Orleans Parish School Board Collection, Francis T. Nicholls High School Series, Earl K. Long Library, Louisiana and Special Collections Department, University of New Orleans.

Common Ground. (2006). New Orleans in numbers: Pre- and Post-Hurricane Katrina snapshot [Pamphlet]. New Orleans, LA: Author.

Crossroads Project. (2006). Students at the Center [Digital video]. New Orleans, LA: Author.

daLuz, Z. (2008, May 13). Letter to Paul Pastorek. Retrieved from www.savefrederickdouglass.com

Delgado, R. (2000). Storytelling for oppositionalists and others: A plea for narrative. In R. Delgado & J. Stefancic (Eds.), *Critical race theory: The cutting edge* (pp. 60–70). Philadelphia, PA: Temple University Press.

Ehlinger & Associates. (1998, Third Quarter). School sited on 280 years of history [*Architecture* newsletter article]. Metairie, LA: Author. Retrieved from http://freepages.school-alumni.rootsweb.ancestry.com/~neworleans/nicholls/ memorabilia/after/index.html

Fagan, O. M. (1952, July 29). A follow-up study of the graduates of Francis T. Nicholls High School from 1940 through 1950 with the view of evaluating the educational program and the guidance services of the school [Box 1, Guidance and Counseling Department]. Available: Orleans Parish School Board Collection, Francis T. Nicholls High School Series, Earl K. Long Library, Louisiana and Special Collections Department, University of New Orleans.

Frederick Douglass Community Coalition. (2008, May 20). Meeting minutes. Retrieved from www.savefrederickdouglass.com

Free Southern Theater. (1963–). Free Southern Theater Collection. New Orleans, LA: The Amistad Research Center.

Freire, P. (1993). *Pedagogy of the oppressed.* New York, NY: Continuum.

Harris, C. I. (1995). Whiteness as property. In K. Crenshaw, N. Gotanda, G. Peller, & K. Thomas (Eds.), *Critical race theory: The key writings that formed the movement* (pp. 276–291). New York, NY: New Press.

Harvey, D. (2006). *Spaces of global capitalism: Towards a theory of uneven geographic development.* New York, NY: Verso.

Jackson, W. (2005). *What would the world be without women: Stories from the 9th Ward.* New Orleans, LA: Neighborhood Story Project.

Juvenile Justice Project of Louisiana (JJPL). (2013a, September). Suspensions matter: 2011–2012 year in review [Report]. New Orleans, LA: Author. Available: http://jjpl.org/2013/news/jjpl-releases-suspensions-matter-2011–2012-year-review/

Juvenile Justice Project of Louisiana (JJPL). (2013b). Suspensions matter: By the numbers, 2012–2013 [Flyer]. New Orleans, LA: Author.

KIPP New Orleans Schools. (2012–2013). Student code of conduct, 2012–2013. New Orleans, LA: Author.

KIPP Renaissance. (2010). Building Renaissance [Digital video]. Available: http://vimeo.com/16454087?ab

KIPP Renaissance. (2012, November 20). Homepage [Results]. Available: www.kipprenaissance.org/

Mathews, J. (2009). *Word hard, be nice: How two inspired teachers created the most promising schools in America.* Chapel Hill, NC: Algonquin Books of Chapel Hill.

Miron, G., Urschel, J. L., & Saxton, N. (2011, March). What makes KIPP work? A study of student characteristics, attrition, and school finance [Paper jointly released by National Center for the Study of Privatization in Education, Teachers College, Columbia University, and Study Group on Education Management Organizations, Western Michigan University]. Available: www.edweek.org/media/kippstudy.pdf

Myers, L. (2007, January 31). Did Iraq contractor fleece American taxpayers? [Article] NBC. Available: www.msnbc.msn.com

Nagin, C. R., Fielkow, A., & Cummings, S. (2008, February 27). Reinventing the Crescent: Six miles of riverfront development [entire plan]. Retrieved December 1, 2009 from: www.neworiverfront.com/ ThePlan.html

Orleans Parish School Board. (1995, March 27). Meeting minutes. Orleans Parish School Board Minutes [Vol. 1, Book No. 98]. Available: Orleans Parish School Board Collection, Francis T. Nicholls High School Series, Earl K. Long Library, Louisiana and Special Collections Department, University of New Orleans.

Pastorek, P. (2008, May 19). Letter to Ze' daLuz. Retrieved from www.savefrederickdouglass.com

Rebel Yell. (1955, November 23). 383 make first 1955–1956 honor roll; 163 lead with 90 average and above. *Rebel Yell, XXVI*(2), 1, 3. Available: Orleans Parish School Board Collection, Francis T. Nicholls High School Series, Earl K. Long Library, Louisiana and Special Collections Department, University of New Orleans.

Rebel Yell. (1956, June 1). 95 Confederates hold perfect attendance mark. *Rebel Yell, XXVI*(8), 5. Available: Orleans Parish School Board Collection, Francis T. Nicholls High School Series, Earl K. Long Library, Louisiana and Special Collections Department, University of New Orleans.

Rebel Yell. (1960, April 1). "Melting pot" theme set for annual spring fair. *Rebel Yell, XXIX*(5), 3. Available: Orleans Parish School Board Collection, Francis T. Nicholls High School Series, Earl K. Long Library, Louisiana and Special Collections Department, University of New Orleans.

Rebel Yell. (1963, March 11). Top scholars prepare for annual state rally. *Rebel Yell, XXXII*(5), 1, 4. Available: Orleans Parish School Board Collection, Francis T. Nicholls High School Series, Earl K. Long Library, Louisiana and Special Collections Department, University of New Orleans.

Rebel Yell. (1966, January 21). Southland observes Gen. Lee's birthday. *Rebel Yell, XXV*(4), 2. Available: Orleans Parish School Board Collection, Francis T. Nicholls High School Series, Earl K. Long Library, Louisiana and Special Collections Department, University of New Orleans.

Rebel Yell. (1966, June 2). Heroics recalled on Memorial Day. *Rebel Yell, XXV*(8), 10 (Section 1), 18 (Section 2). Available: Orleans Parish School Board Collection, Francis T. Nicholls High School Series, Earl K. Long Library, Louisiana and Special Collections Department, University of New Orleans.

Reinventing the Crescent. (2008a). Economic impact presentation. Retrieved May 1, 2008 from www. neworiverfront.com/documents/EconomicImpact_002.pdf

Reinventing the Crescent. (2008b). Homepage. Retrieved December 1, 2009 from: http:// reinventingthecrescent.org/about

Recovery School District (RSD), & New Orleans Public Schools (NOPS). (2008, August). *School facilities master plan for Orleans Parish.* New Orleans: Authors.

Richardson, J., & Heidelberg, R. L. (2008, January). New Orleans riverfront: Reinventing the Crescent—An economic perspective [Prepared for New Orleans Building Corporation]. Baton Rouge, LA: Louisiana State University.

Ruth, D. (2011, January). KIPP-New Orleans Education: An educational Camelot. *New Orleans Magazine.* Available: www.myneworleans.com/New-Orleans-Magazine/January-2011/An-Educational-Camelot/

Simon, D. (2009, February 20). RSD to phase out two high schools. *Times-Picayune.* Available: www.nola.com

Smith, H. (2005, October 5). KIPP: Making schools work [Digital video]. Arlington, VA: Public Broadcasting Service.

Students at the Center (SAC). (2005). *The long ride: A collection of student writings for the New Orleans Civil Rights Park* (1st ed.). New Orleans, LA: Author.

Students at the Center (SAC). (2007a). *Katrina and me.* New Orleans, LA: Author.

Students at the Center (SAC). (2007b). Writing with light [Digital video]. New Orleans, LA: Author.

Students at the Center (SAC). (2008, April 18). Vallas claims no community involvement [Blog]. *Education Week.* Available: http://blogs.edweek.org/edweek/nola_voices/

Thevenot, B. (2009, July 24). New Orleans charter school operator plans expansion. *Times-Picayune.* Available: www.nola.com

Times-Picayune. (1919, November 9). To commemorate services of men who served in war [Section 3, page 3]. New Orleans, LA: New Orleans Public Library.

Times-Picayune. (2007a, December 15). Protesters block HUD offices downtown. *Times-Picayune.* Available: www.nola.com

Times-Picayune. (2007b, December 19). Live updates on demolition vote from council chambers. *Times-Picayune.* Available: www.nola.com

United Teachers of New Orleans (UTNO), Louisiana Federation of Teachers (LFT), and American Federation of Teachers (AFT). (2006, November). "National model" or flawed approach?: The post-Katrina New Orleans Public Schools. New Orleans, LA: Author.

Vallas, P. (2008, April 14). Recovery school district status report. New Orleans, LA: Recovery School District.

Vasquez Heilig, J., Williams, A., McNeil, L. M., & Lee, Christopher. (2011). Is choice a panacea? An analysis of black secondary student attrition from KIPP, other private charter schools, and urban districts. *Berkeley Review of Education, 2*(2), 153–178.

Weaving the Web Collaborators. (2003, October 1). Weaving the web of community [Project report]. New Orleans, Louisiana: Author.

Whitman, D. (2008). *Sweating the small stuff: Inner-City schools and the new paternalism.* Washington, DC: Thomas B. Fordham Institute.

Willoughby, J. (1941, October). Rebel yell inspired men in Civil War. *Rebel Yell, 2*(1), 1. Available: Orleans Parish School Board Collection, Francis T. Nicholls High School Series, Earl K. Long Library, Louisiana and Special Collections Department, University of New Orleans.

Yosso, T. J. (2006). *Critical race counterstories along the Chicana/Chicano educational pipeline.* New York, NY: Routledge.

5

THE CULTURE OF THE EDUCATION MARKET

Teach for America, Union Busting, and the Displacement of Black Veteran Teachers

The phrase *closing the achievement gap* is the cornerstone of TFA's general philosophy, public-relations marketing, and training sessions. ... I was told immediately and often that 1) the achievement gap is a pervasive example of inequality in America, and 2) it is our personal responsibility to close the achievement gap within our classrooms. ...

But between these two messages lies the unspoken logic that current, non-TFA teachers and schools are failing at the task of closing the achievement gap, through some combination of apathy or incompetence. ... The subtext is clear: Only you can fix what others [traditional teachers] have screwed up. ...

Although I felt bad that TFA had created a system that caused a rift between corps members and traditional teachers, I didn't have much time to worry about it. The truth was, my five-week training program had not prepared me adequately. ...

[T]he time ha[d] come to send TFA an email announcing that I am leaving the program. ... [B]y showing I don't believe that American education can be saved by youthful enthusiasm, I feel more like a leader than I ever did in the corps.
                              —Olivia Blanchard, 2011 corps member who left Teach for
                                     America after her first year in the classroom (2013)

The struggle over public schools in New Orleans is not limited to where schools will be reconstructed or who will operate and govern them. It is likewise over who will teach in them. Three months after the storm, Orleans Parish School Board (OPSB) announced the district's teachers and school employees would be fired *en masse* in early 2006. Prompted by takeover of nearly all the city's public schools by the state-run Recovery School District (RSD) and plans by local and state officials to charter the schools and recruit new teachers, this action involved 7,500 veteran educators and support staff, many of them tenured and most of them African

American. In 2005, black veteran teachers constituted approximately 75 percent of New Orleans public school teachers and a substantial portion of the city's black middle class. Moreover, they were unionized and represented by United Teachers of New Orleans (Local 527 of the American Federation of Teachers) through a collective bargaining agreement with OPSB. The mass firing of black veteran teachers and their strategic displacement by inexperienced, transient white teachers from outside the community cannot be separated from these facts.

Human capital edu-businesses, such as TFA, have played a pivotal role in the racial-spatial reconstruction of New Orleans. While black veteran teachers were being fired and the union's contract nullified, TFA was signing a contract with the Louisiana Board of Elementary and Secondary Education (BESE) to supply new teachers. None of this was accidental or inevitable. In fact, the termination of veteran educators was deemed illegal by the Civil District Court for Orleans Parish in 2012. Although black veteran teachers were demonized and singularly blamed for the problems in New Orleans public schools, providing state officials and education entrepreneurs with a much-needed justification for their displacement, the truth was more complex.

The unlawful treatment of New Orleans' black veteran teachers has been part of a racially inspired project of *accumulation by dispossession*—one premised on purposeful renovation of the city's urban space economy, including displacement of indigenous black teachers, abrogation of their property rights, and disregard for the place-based knowledge, cultural contributions, and racial justice activism that informed their work for more than a century. In mid-2005, OPSB controlled more than 100 public schools and a budget of approximately $419 million—monies that state officials and education entrepreneurs said could be used more efficiently and effectively after the storm. The question remained: Used by whom and for whom?

To provide context for my analysis, I highlight the proclamations of state officials who wrongly cast veteran teachers and the union as the "problem" in public education and then provide an alternative history of black teacher associations in New Orleans (and Louisiana) to document their struggle for educational equity. One key point I emphasize is that historic state neglect of black public schools by white leadership generated the dire conditions under which black teachers have taught and against which they have fought for at least 100 years. The "crisis" that education entrepreneurs, including TFA, sought to resolve resulted from racism, not deficiencies of the city's black teachers. With this history in mind, I examine the findings of *Eddy Oliver et al. vs. Orleans Parish School Board et al.*, a class action lawsuit on the wrongful termination of veteran teachers (Civil District Court, 2012). These findings expose a strategic project to alter the governance structure of New Orleans public schools and, consequentially, the city's racial geography. Thus I follow by analyzing alternative teacher recruitment via human capital edu-businesses such as TFA and chart the demographic transformation of the city's teachers. I also discuss research on TFA and concerns regarding new recruits' lack of teaching experience and short-term commitment to the schools and communities in which they are placed. In addition, I consider the testimony of black veteran teachers, who shared with me through interviews their own analysis of school reform in New Orleans and the politics behind their displacement.

Ultimately, I argue, there are serious tensions between the *culture of the education market* and the *culture of the community*, with the former premised on an ahistorical and de-territorialized approach to education and the latter rooted in history and place-based consciousness or what King (2009) calls heritage knowledge. To render my point, I highlight indigenous educational programs developed by veteran teachers, with an emphasis on New Orleans' jazz tradition, and argue that such work should guide education reform, rather than seeking "talent" and "innovation" elsewhere. Finally, by contrast, I critique the racial understandings of many TFA recruits in New Orleans, who evidence a gross lack of the place-based knowledge that enables veteran teachers to teach with cultural awareness and competence.

The "Problem" with Veteran Teachers and the Union

Most charter schools in New Orleans have not hired black veteran teachers and none have a contract with United Teachers of New Orleans (UTNO), the city's teacher union (Carr, 2009; Nelson, 2010). This is a cost-saving mechanism or an attempt to decrease labor expenses for businesses that privately manage charter schools. New and transient teachers are less likely to demand laddered pay, benefits, and pensions. Paul Vallas praised temporary recruits and non-unionized charter schools when he was RSD superintendent:

> I don't want the majority of my teaching staff to work more than 10 years. The cost of sustaining those individuals becomes so enormous. Between retirement and healthcare and things like that, it means that you are constantly increasing class sizes and cutting programs in order to sustain the cost of a veteran workforce.
>
> (Conway, 2010, para. 21–22)

John Ayers, former head of the National Association of Charter School Authorizers, which held a contract in Louisiana to review charter school applications, shared similar sentiments: "In the urban setting, the unions add so little value, it's shocking" (Tisserand, 2007, para. 27).

However, the move to hire new teachers—most of them white and from outside the community—is not motivated by economics alone. It is connected to a low cultural valuation of black veteran teachers. In the wake of the storm, state officials and education entrepreneurs blamed black veteran teachers for the problems that plagued New Orleans public schools. BESE member Chas Roemer stated that "Charter schools are now a threat to a jobs program called public education"

(Sentell, 2009, para. 2). Roemer's reference to a "jobs program" called "public education" aligns with wider discourses that characterize African Americans as shiftless and dependent on state welfare, and implies that lazy and incompetent veteran teachers, who once relied on public schools for employment, can no longer count on collecting a salary in exchange for their alleged failure to perform. Louisiana Senator Mary Landrieu (2011) was more pointed during an address at the Center for American Progress in Washington, DC, where she discussed reform in New Orleans: "If the traditional teachers and principals in a school can rally themselves and admit that they failed ... they can be part of the turnaround. If not, [they] can leave." Her comments make clear that veteran educators are viewed as the primary cause of the challenges faced by New Orleans public schools before 2005. Along similar lines, Sarah Usdin, founder of the charter school and human capital incubator New Schools for New Orleans, lamented, "There seems to be incredible amnesia in this community about what we had before" (Tisserand, 2007, para. 14).

In actuality, veteran teachers and community members recollect with great clarity what they confronted before 2005—racism and a history of state neglect of black public schools. At Martin Luther King Elementary, three veteran teachers with 18, 32, and 33 years of experience, respectively, explained feeling "bitter" and "disappointed" about the blame placed on New Orleans' educators, even though they labored in schools "not fit for habitation" and in "total disrepair" (Interview, 2008). Not without irony, entrepreneurs and their state allies fault black teachers for conditions they have spent their lives challenging. A history of black teacher associations in New Orleans is instructive and suggests that entrepreneurs, not veteran teachers, have failed to remember. Black teacher associations have a long history of fighting racial inequities in New Orleans and throughout Louisiana.

A History of Black Teacher Associations in New Orleans

In 1901, the Louisiana Colored Teachers Association (LCTA) was formed when black educators were denied membership in the white Louisiana Teachers Association. Over the next three decades, LCTA sought to support black teacher preparation, publish an education journal, create libraries in black schools, review textbooks for racially distorted representations, equalize teacher salaries and school facilities, provide teacher pensions, train community leaders, and challenge white supremacist legislation (Middleton, 1984). During the early 1930s, Fanny C. Williams of New Orleans, president of the National Association of Teachers in Colored Schools, called on LCTA to develop a research committee that would conduct "a survey of the educational conditions in Louisiana" and provide "constructive recommendations" based on the findings. One of several actions that resulted from LCTA's research was the establishment of literacy workshops for more than 25,000 adults denied the chance to attend school. By the end of the decade, 2,000 of Louisiana's 3,800 black public school teachers were LCTA members. In early

1940, W. E. B. Du Bois rightly praised LCTA's program, which advanced despite the harsh conditions of segregation (Middleton, 1984).

A black teacher union likewise developed in New Orleans during the late 1930s: Local 527 of the American Federation of Teachers (AFT), which would become United Teachers of New Orleans through a merger in the 1970s. The AFT first suggested that Sarah Towles Reed, a well-known white public school teacher and legislative activist in New Orleans, establish a teacher union; she had founded two professional teacher associations in the city, including the New Orleans Classroom Teachers Federation (NOCTF). In 1935, NOCTF became AFT Local 353, representing white teachers and immediately demanding the restoration of salaries to pre-Depression standards. OPSB granted a raise in 1937, but it applied only to white teachers (although Reed did not oppose raises for black teachers). Frustrated by perpetually unequal salary schedules for black and white teachers and now denied a raise, black teachers formed a union of their own in 1938—AFT Local 527 or the New Orleans League of Classroom Teachers (Ambrose, 1999). Local 527's cofounder and past president, Veronica Hill, recollected during an interview in 1990: "When this [announcement of white teachers' raises] came out in the newspaper ... everybody rose up" (Hill, 1990). Hill went on to describe the union's effort to obtain raises from the school board:

> One of the things I'll always remember was the board ... the white and the black teachers coming together ... and [we] were adamant. They would not let us in, they locked the door. So, when we got there [board meeting] we couldn't get in, and somebody said "oh look, there's a fire escape" and got the cooperation of the janitor to open the window, and [the whole delegation] climbed through the window. ... We got in ... and slipped the petition under the door.
>
> (Hill, 1990)

As a result, the board granted the increase to white and black teachers. "Both got increases," Hill explained:

> But then we decided that we cannot wait any more time for us to file [in court] for equalization of salaries. ... It wasn't an easy thing to do because many of [the teachers] were rather skeptical about having their names involved when we filed. ... A group of men ... paid Thurgood Marshall, then [an attorney] for the NAACP, to come down and lay strategy for filing.
>
> (Hill, 1990)

Despite apprehension about white retaliation, the struggle for equalizing black teachers' pay in New Orleans (and ultimately Louisiana) proceeded.

Even with the increase from OPSB, black teachers still earned far less than white teachers, and they were not rewarded for experience or advanced degrees.

In 1938, for example, a black teacher with a master's degree would have earned $915 during her first year—or $65 less than a white teacher with *no* degree and *no* experience (Cassimere, 1999). Thurgood Marshall traveled to New Orleans in 1939 to discuss legal strategy, emphasizing that salary equalization "would be the beginning of a drive to secure better schools for Negroes" (Cassimere, 1999, p. 434). He directed teachers to "organize a special committee, raise money, and find suitable plaintiffs" and agreed to work with A. P. Tureaud, one of only two black attorneys in Louisiana, who would handle the day-to-day work of the case (p. 434). Teachers organized the New Orleans Citizens' Committee for Equalizing Educational Opportunities, which included "a local Negro doctor, a dentist, a Negro restaurant owner, two clergymen and several black teachers" (p. 434). The committee raised money with substantial contributions from teachers.

Tureaud filed a petition with OPSB in May 1941, with Joseph McKelpin and other black teachers demanding equalization for fall term of the same year. The board did not respond and Tureaud therefore filed suit in federal district court in New Orleans (Cassimere, 1999). The trial occurred in June 1942 and the judge determined black teachers were entitled to equal salaries. The NAACP demanded immediate equalization and the board suggested equalization over a five-year period, a plan the teachers rejected. Ultimately, the court ordered the board to increase black teachers' pay by 50 percent of the difference in fall 1942 and then to fully equalize in fall 1943. Notably, some teachers' salaries in 1943 were as much as $1,300 more than they had been before the legal battle (Cassimere, 1999). Prompted by Local 527's victory in New Orleans, LCTA (renamed the Louisiana Education Association in 1947) formed the Statewide Citizens' Committee on Equal Education and, by 1948, was pursuing eight cases for salary equalization, with Tureaud as legal counsel. Under pressure, the state legislature passed Act 155 in 1948, equalizing teacher salaries by race throughout Louisiana (Middleton, 1984). It was a hard-won victory.

Soon the battle would begin for equalization of school facilities, appointment of black representatives to the state education board, and voter registration (Middleton, 1984). By the early 1950s, the Louisiana Education Association (LEA) had 26 cases either in court or ready to be filed on issues such as teacher-tenure violations, elementary and secondary school integration, and access to higher education. In fact, on September 4, 1952, a petition to desegregate New Orleans public schools was filed by the LEA with support from the NAACP Legal Defense Fund. With *Brown v. Board of Education* underway in the Supreme Court, however, legal action was put on hold until a decision was issued (Middleton, 1984).

Massive resistance by whites after *Brown* is documented in chapter 1. Here it is important to note that the LEA and NAACP were in close contact with Federal Judge Skelly Wright, who intervened to stop Louisiana's governor and state legislature from obstructing desegregation and closing New Orleans public schools (DeVore & Logsdon, 1991; Middleton, 1984). LEA even committed to provide $100,000 in interest-free loans to Orleans Parish if the governor and legislature terminated black teachers' pay (Middleton, 1984). Throughout Louisiana in the 1960s, rural black teachers were displaced as a result of desegregation, school consolidation, and school closings. They were deemed incompetent; as well, it was said they were unable to pass the National Teachers Examination and graduated from substandard black southern colleges (Butler, 1999). A black lawyer who dealt with displacement cases described the racial dynamics:

> The whites have got the power. The power to call black teachers what they want to call them. And in a lot of cases they call them incompetent. So it is simply the power to define. Now I'm not saying that 100% of black teachers who come through this office are competent. But it sure is strange that I haven't heard of any white teachers being displaced because of incompetency.
>
> (Butler, 1999, p. 538)

Black principals in Louisiana likewise suffered demotion and displacement, although not without legal challenges (Butler, 1999). These dynamics were not as strong in urban New Orleans, where the volume of black teachers enabled greater pressure on the superintendent of schools and where public school faculty desegregation in the late 1960s accelerated the pace of white flight (Butler, 1999; DeVore & Logsdon, 1991).

In the first school strike in the South, black teachers with Local 527 picketed for three days in 1966 for salary improvement, but without success. In 1969, an 11-day strike was organized and included a procession down Canal Street in New Orleans (DeVore & Logsdon, 1991). The right to collectively bargain was a central component of both actions. Lamar Smith, a chemistry and physics teacher at G. W. Carver Senior High School and chairman of Local 527's Human Relations Committee, reflected on the meaning of the 1969 strike:

> The School Board was forced to give some token recognition to the Teacher Union. The strike witnessed a group of predominately black teachers starting at 1,200 and dwindling to [269], who for ten hectic days with sore feet, wet eyes, and fallen hopes courageously endured threats and fear tactics of every conceivable denomination. The question is: why did they persevere? Was this the beginning of something new—the prime step in demonstrating to the white power structure that black teachers are determined to solve their own problems and, moreover, plan, shape, and direct their own destiny?
>
> (Smith, circa 1970, p. 2)

Local 527 won board approval of the right to collectively bargain for teachers (DeVore & Logsdon, 1991). This was accomplished despite the absence of a public employee collective bargaining law in Louisiana.

This heightened sense of self-determination led to the formation of United Teachers of New Orleans (UTNO) in 1972. The largely black AFT Local 527 merged with the largely white Orleans Educators Association of the NEA (National Education Association) and designated Nat LaCour, a black science teacher and head of Local 527, as UTNO's president (Devore & Logsdon, 1991). In 1974, UTNO won its first contract and in 1977, it created a Health and Welfare Fund for teachers, partly through an agreement with OPSB to provide free vision and dental care, life insurance, and a free prescription drug program to union members; union members and OPSB contributed to the fund (McKendall, 1987). The fund also included a Teacher Center for professional development that became "the most stable avenue for improving teaching practices and sharing resources that black or white teachers in New Orleans have had for the last 30 or 40 years" (Randels, 2010, p. 102).

By this time, UTNO was the third largest union in New Orleans (DeVore & Logsdon, 1991). With greater power and ongoing concerns about salary and school conditions, another strike was planned in 1978 and lasted from August 31 to September 13 (Owsley, 1988). On the strike's first day, 67 percent of the teachers participated. The second day, despite threats to force teachers' return, 73 percent joined the strike and support remained steady. On September 1, a group of students at McDonogh No. 35, the city's first black public high school, wrote letters about the strike—many in support of teachers and some criticizing their absence (Treadway, 1978). Ultimately, however, a citywide coalition of students was formed to support striking teachers through a boycott of classes. Student leaders from high schools across New Orleans—Nicholls (later Frederick Douglass), Carver, Washington, Clark, Cohen, John McDonogh, Kennedy, McMain, and McDonogh No. 35— gathered at McDonogh No. 35 for a rally, chanting: "We Want Our Education, We Want Our Graduation" as well as "No Teachers, No School." They spoke with the school's principal about their concerns and were joined by 1,300 of the school's students who walked out. The campaign was supported by the Parent-Community Coalition, which stood ready to launch recall proceedings against several board members and issued a statement saying the board seemed concerned only "to force teachers back to school" and "prepared to use every demeaning tactic at their disposal to accomplish that goal" (Anderson, 1978). On September 11, a tentative agreement was negotiated—a 7 percent raise for teachers and an increased board contribution to teachers' health insurance, with the board opting to make cuts from other areas of the school budget (DeVore & Logsdon, 1991). A month later LaCour decried the "social and economic ills" that plagued New Orleans, criticized the "racial isolation" and "poverty" that many citizens endured, and urged support for "a strong [public] educational system." He also called on the city's black leadership to unify and organize against these problems (Times-Picayune, 1978). Both black teachers and students recognized that serious inequities remained.

Amid much tumult, the black LEA merged with the white Louisiana Teachers Association (LTA). The NEA passed a resolution in 1964 against racially segregated associations and called for complete integration of local and state affiliates. When the LTA refused, the LEA became the NEA state affiliate in Louisiana and continued to work against black teacher and principal displacement (Middleton, 1984). Circumstances were dire. Middleton (1984) reports that in some parishes, as black teachers were dismissed and black schools were closed, "trophies, pictures, and every symbol of their past achievement and school history were destroyed" (p. 111). Charles Johnson, a leader in the historic LEA (finally merged with the LTA in the late 1970s), reflected:

> LEA was more than a teacher organization: LEA was concerned with rights for black people regardless of education. The basic premise of the old LEA was that whatever help was needed in the black community throughout the state of Louisiana, you could depend on the LEA. ... For any civil rights movement or activity, any injustice in Louisiana, LEA was there.
>
> (Middleton, 1984, p. 115)

This history reveals that black teachers and their associations have been, and can be, a force for racial, economic, and social justice. They have defined their mission in broad terms exemplifying what Weiner (2012) calls *social movement unionism*. LCTA (later LEA) and Local 527 (later UTNO) recognized that teachers' interests were served by advocating justice on multiple fronts, including those that benefited students and communities. Black teacher associations have worked tirelessly to alter the conditions for which their members were blamed in 2005. This makes the mass displacement of veteran teachers, and attempts to bust the teacher union, even more troubling.

The Wrongful Termination of Veteran Teachers in 2005–2006

Despite their history as advocates of equitable public schools, black veteran teachers in New Orleans were fired *en masse* in early 2006.[1] This action occurred without due process and without regard for teachers' hard-won rights and contributions. When the state-run RSD took control and the school district in New Orleans was reorganized as a mere shadow of itself, veteran teachers of 20 and 30 years effectively lost all protections and entitlements guaranteed by UTNO's collective bargaining agreement. That is, the agreement was nullified because the district with which it was negotiated no longer controlled most public schools. The rights that teachers struggled to have recognized in previous decades were tossed to the wind. For policymakers, the legacy of Local 527 was best forgotten.

For veteran teachers, it was not so easy. They had not been paid since August 29, 2005. Another immediate issue was the cost of health insurance for teachers who remained in the revamped system. This escalation occurred because two school districts had emerged, with only a small number of schools under the locally controlled OPSB and the vast majority under the state-run RSD. As a result, teaching positions were limited with OPSB, which meant a small number of returning teachers and retirees constituted the pool of insured. Premiums rose to over $1,000 per month. Equally troubling, veteran teacher had no guarantee whatsoever of health insurance in the RSD, much less jobs. Veteran teachers hired in the RSD, including charter schools, were treated as first-year employees with respect to pension in the state teacher retirement system.

Once more, whiteness functioned as a form of property: Human capital edu-businesses and white TFA recruits leveraged public resources to their racial advantage, including positions once held by black veteran teachers. The state had no intention of rectifying these circumstances; the state had engineered them. In 2012, the Civil District Court for Orleans Parish would find the state had intentionally breached teachers' contracts.

Eddy Oliver et al. vs. Orleans Parish School Board et al.

On May 23, 2011, a class action lawsuit was initiated in the Civil District Court for Orleans Parish. In *Eddy Oliver et al. vs. Orleans Parish School Board et al.*, 7,000 tenured, certified teachers and school employees asserted they had been illegally fired, with teachers' due process and property rights violated by OPSB, Louisiana Department of Education (LDOE), BESE, and the RSD. Based on hundreds of documents and depositions, in fact, teachers claimed that local and state education officials "conspired to and committed wrongful conduct that included the wrongful termination of tenured employees and intentional interference with [their] employment contracts and/or property rights" (New Orleans Public School Employees Justice [NOPSE Justice], 2010). According to teachers, officials had not only enacted legislation to void property rights inhering in employment, but used the storm "as a once-in-a-lifetime opportunity to carry out an old political agenda to abolish the New Orleans Public School System … and replace it with quasi-private Charter Schools using public funds" (NOPSE Justice, 2007). A ruling in favor of teachers was issued by Judge Ethel Julien on June 20, 2012 (Civil District Court, 2012).[2] It should be noted that OPSB filed a cross-claim against the state defendants, arguing that state control over the city's schools through the RSD prevented the local school board from placing teachers in positions held before the storm. State officials would have to respond to both suits.

Court findings in *Oliver* provide a disturbing account of the strategic racial-spatial reconstruction of the city's public schools by white leadership in Louisiana. As discussed earlier, state officials faulted veteran teachers for public school problems (and OPSB for inefficiency and corruption). The court, however, affirmed that fired teachers had no record or notice of unsatisfactory performance prior to state takeover; in 2005, all were in "good standing" and "met or exceeded state requirements" (Civil District Court, 2012, p. 8). Additionally, OPSB was "making documented progress" with 88 of more than 120 schools meeting or exceeding the state's requirements for adequate yearly progress; in 2005, 93 schools showed academic growth (p. 14). OPSB's financial problems were being addressed as well and it "was on track to prudently manage and expend all federal monies allocated" after the storm (p. 21).

Evidence surfaced by the trial was telling. On August 30, 2005, the day after the storm, a Call Center was set up by Alvarez & Marsal (A&M), a New York-based financial consulting firm hired by the state to oversee financial matters of OPSB before the storm. The Call Center was to locate New Orleans' public school teachers for OPSB and determine who planned to return when schools reopened (Civil District Court, 2012, pp. 8–9). By October 4, nearly 7,000 employees had been located and Intent-to-Return applications were being processed online (p. 11). None of this mattered to state officials, or their allies at local and national levels, who planned to seize control, charter the city's public schools, fire veteran teachers, and contract with TFA to replace them.

Cecil Picard, state superintendent of education at the time, wrote a letter in mid-September 2005 to U.S. Secretary of Education Margaret Spellings requesting $2.4 billion in federal funds to reopen public schools and pay out-of-work school teachers' salaries and benefits while schools remained closed. Picard also added language indicating that the *LDOE should receive all federal monies rather than local school districts* affected by the storm (Civil District Court, 2012, pp. 8–9). Around the same time that Picard requested federal funds, he sought to replace OPSB's acting superintendent, Dr. Ora Watson, with William Roberti, lead financial consultant from A&M (p. 9). According to court records: "When Dr. Watson did not comply with this request, [State] Superintendent Picard indicated he had the power or authority to make major changes to the New Orleans public school system" (p. 9). Next, several members of OPSB placed an item on the board's agenda to replace Watson with Roberti (who would work in tandem with Rod Paige, President George Bush's former secretary of education) (p. 9). During the same meeting, Watson presented a detailed plan to reopen 13 of the city's public schools in Algiers, where storm damage was minimal. OPSB did not approve Watson's plan. Instead, OPSB placed all of the city's teachers on "Disaster Leave without Pay," which the court determined to be a *fictional employment status* (p. 10). In late September, Picard—this time joined by BESE's president—wrote another letter to federal authorities. Addressing the director of charter schools at the U.S. Department of Education, they requested several federal policy waivers related to charter schools and monies for ten charter schools that Picard said could be "up and running" by January 2006 (p. 10).

In short, although veteran teachers had been located and intended to return, and although the superintendent of public schools in New Orleans had a plan to reopen schools under OPSB, veteran teachers were placed on leave without pay while the state superintendent attempted to remove the local district's superintendent. The state superintendent also asked federal authorities to provide funds for teacher salaries and charter schools to the state, thereby disempowering OPSB. It became clear that state actions were meant to dispossess veteran teachers and students in New Orleans. Waiving state and federal education laws would be the next crucial intervention.

In early October, Governor Kathleen Blanco's legal counsel faxed Picard a draft Executive Order for the "Emergency Suspension of Education Laws." Blanco next signed the executive order, suspending the requirement for teachers and parents to approve charter school conversions and accelerating timelines for charter school applications and approval (Civil District Court, 2012, p. 11). By the minute, black veteran teachers and families were losing the right to control local public schools. Immediately following Blanco's executive order, a member of the OPSB representing Algiers proposed that all 13 of its public schools be converted to charters; these were the same schools Watson earlier proposed to reopen with veteran teachers, but without support from various OPSB members (p. 12). Betraying deeper motives, veteran teachers "were not allowed to transfer into jobs at the 13 new charter schools" (p. 12). Nonetheless, startup funds for the charter schools would be drawn from OPSB's revenue stream (pp. 12–13). One move set the stage for the next. Picard revised A&M's contract to give Roberti the *power to hire and fire OPSB employees, control OPSB money,* and *override the authority of the local district's superintendent* (p. 13). These actions, wrote the judge, "contributed to the mass termination" of veteran teachers (p. 13).

Governor Blanco called a special legislative session in November and Act 35 was passed, the mechanism for transferring "failing" schools into the state-run RSD, which readily took over more than 100 public schools in New Orleans (Civil District Court, 2012, p. 14). This abuse of power did not escape the court. The judge noted:

> Prior to November ... A&M worked with the [local] School Board to locate certified, highly qualified, and experienced teachers who were available to re-open schools. Also, the [local] School Board planned to open 52 public schools for 2005–2006 school year. However, *state officials did not support these plans.*
>
> (p. 13; italics added)

Once the state assumed control of the majority of public schools in Orleans Parish, "assigning work to all former OPSB employees became burdensome, especially since the [local] School Board no longer had authority to assign work at schools taken over by the [RSD]" (p. 14). None of this was by chance. Testimony provided during the trial revealed that legislation, such as Act 35, was "specifically designed to have the State take over the New Orleans public schools" (p. 22). Remarkably, the state "analyzed school performance scores in Orleans Parish to provide a listing of the scores to be used in drafting the legislation so that the highest number of OPSB schools could be taken over" (p. 23).

Before Act 35, OPSB's budget was over $400 million; the district's budget was approximately 40 million by 2011–2012. The bottom line is that 90 percent of

the local board's financial resources have been distributed to the RSD and charter schools (Civil District Court, 2012, p. 15). In part, the diverted "resources"
included black veteran teachers' jobs, soon handed over to novice white teachers through TFA and the like. On November 30—the same day that Act 35
was passed—a press release was prepared by A&M to notify all employees they
would be terminated and that their health insurance would be eliminated on
January 31, 2006 (pp. 16–17). Meanwhile, OPSB passed a resolution and asked
the state-run RSD "to support the rebuilding of New Orleans and the lives of
its displaced citizens by providing preferential employment opportunities to the
former employees of the New Orleans Public Schools" (p. 17). This would not
occur. On December 22, 2005, the press release on termination was disseminated
to employees, with termination letters officially mailed on February 8, 2006; the
final date of termination would be March 24 (p. 18). OPSB teachers had not
been paid since August 29, 2005, the day that the storm struck New Orleans.
To further cement teachers' dispossession—and in a move that is difficult to
believe—updated contact information collected by the Call Center was not used
to mail teachers' termination letters; they were sent to vacated addresses. Before
the storm, it was policy to send termination letters by certified mail, registered
mail, or to hand deliver them to ensure receipt (p. 20). Additionally, the ten-day
period for appeal noted in the termination letter was completely unreasonable
because the address specified in the letter, where appeals were to be sent, was
incorrect as well. OPSB's pre-storm address was listed, even though the board's
office had moved due to storm damage (p. 20). In sum, the entire process ensured
that termination letters and appeals would not be received in a timely way. This
was a violation of Louisiana statutes as well as OPSB policy, not to mention any
reasonable ethical standard (p. 20).

Despite the fact that veteran teachers had been located and expressed their
intent to return; despite OPSB's request that veterans be given preferential opportunity for employment in the RSD; and despite teachers' legal rights, the LDOE
and OPSB next asserted there was a *shortage of teachers* and proceeded to *advertise
nationwide* for teacher positions in the RSD. Even more telling, "although there
were thousands of certified, experienced OPSB teachers available for employment,
BESE approved, on April 20, 2006, a *contract with Teach for America*" (Civil District
Court, 2012, p. 20; italics added). This was nearly simultaneous with the mass
firing of veteran teachers. Perhaps most shocking, despite Picard's representation
to federal authorities that monies would be used to pay the salaries and benefits
of out-of-work teachers, state officials "did not ensure that any of this money
was used to pay [them]." Rather, "the State diverted [over $500 million] to the
RSD," offering *signing bonuses* and *housing allowances* to out-of-state recruits, some
as high as $17,500 (p. 22). The judge concluded that the state violated teachers
by contracting "with Teach for America to hire inexperienced and non-certified
college graduates, thereby preventing the [teachers] from exercising their legally
protected property rights" (p. 46). No words were minced. The judge determined

the state "intentionally" rendered the performance of teachers' contracts impossible or more burdensome (p. 22).

In fact, the judge recognized the state's treatment of public schools in Orleans Parish was "unique" when compared to similarly affected districts (Civil District Court, 2012, p. 23). One damning piece of evidence related to public schools in largely white St. Tammany Parish. Although St. Tammany had 5,600 public school employees and its schools were substantially damaged by the storm, state education officials were described by Gayle Sloan, the district's superintendent, as "very supportive." All public schools had reopened by October 3, 2005. Not a single employee was terminated and all were paid while schools remained closed. By contrast, when the superintendent of New Orleans proposed to reopen schools, the request was ignored and teachers were put on leave without pay (p. 23). The judge noted:

> Ms. Sloan also testified that she discussed with Picard the decision to continue paying employees while they were not working and that he was pleased with it. She added that she enjoyed a great deal of support from the LDOE and Picard manifested by the LDOE providing the [St. Tammany] School Board with both office space and a telephone number, encouragement, and assistance with getting the district operational.

This included a "hurricane buddy" to serve as a liaison with other agencies (pp. 37–38).

The mass termination of black veteran teachers in New Orleans is one of the most striking instances to date of accumulation by dispossession. It underscores how edu-businesses, such as TFA, assist state and local education officials in leveraging whiteness to secure particular privileges and powers. Meanwhile, the property rights of black teachers are violated willfully through displacement and teacher union busting.

Teach for America, Race, and the Remaking of New Orleans' Urban Space Economy

Harvey (2006) views the city as a built environment or space organized to facilitate economic profit. State and local policymakers certainly created the conditions for a new urban space economy to emerge in New Orleans, one in which TFA and new recruits would be paid to repopulate classrooms at the expense of veteran educators and students.

The proportion of new and veteran teachers in New Orleans has important implications for black student identity and achievement. The Southern Education Foundation (2009) reported:

> In Recovery School District schools... 47 percent of all teachers were entering the classroom for the first time in 2007. ... Experience does not

assure excellence in teaching, but it is well-established that students are often ill-served when most teachers in a school have little or no teaching experience.

(p. 16)

Like TFA, teachNOLA, a recruitment initiative organized by the RSD and New Schools for New Orleans in alliance with The New Teacher Project, assumed a "no experience necessary" posture for hiring (Robelen, 2007; United Teachers of New Orleans et al., 2007). Before 2005, only 10 percent of the city's teachers were in their first or second year of teaching; in 2008, 33 percent were (Nelson, 2010; United Teachers of New Orleans, 2010). In 2007–2008, 60 percent of teachers in direct-run RSD schools had one year of experience or less (only 1 percent had 25 or more years). By contrast, 4 percent of teachers in direct-run schools under OPSB had one year or less (48 percent had 25 years or more). RSD charters also had a higher percentage of inexperienced teachers than charters under OPSB (41 percent had 0–3 years of experience versus 29 percent, respectively) (Cowen Institute, 2009; Nelson, 2010).

As time proceeded, the assault by TFA became more strident. In 2007–2008 and 2008–2009, veteran teachers declined in percentage, especially in the RSD where their presence plummeted to 46 percent (Nelson, 2010, p. 10; see also Carr, 2009). In his study on teacher quality and distribution in New Orleans, Nelson (2010) reports, "Both the RSD and many charters decided to hire new teachers enrolled in alternative certification [programs] and some teachers with no certification at all" (p. 11). He goes on to explain that "New Orleans' low-achieving poor and minority students attend schools with the least experienced teachers" (p. 12).

RSD charter schools, especially those that subcontracted with private management companies, barely hired any veteran teachers (Nelson, 2010, p. 8). New teachers on temporary licenses have been largely affiliated with TFA, teachNOLA, and The New Teacher Project (p. 20). While traditional schools under RSD and OPSB had substantial portions of African American teachers (roughly 70 percent), Nelson explains that "Charter school governance is associated with a disproportionately white teacher population" (p. 19). In 2004–2005, approximately 75 percent of the city's teachers were black. By 2009–2010, in both RSD and OPSB charter schools, less than 50 percent of the teachers were black (Nelson, pp. 18–19; see also Zubrzycki, 2013). In 2010–2011, nearly 40 percent of the city's teachers had been teaching for three years or less and the percentage of white teachers had nearly doubled since the storm from 24 percent to 46 percent (Zubrzycki, 2013).

The RSD's human capital strategy presents some real concerns. The National Academy of Education (2009) issued an education policy white paper on "Teacher Quality" reporting that the empirical evidence on the knowledge and performance of teachers recruited through alternative certification programs is mixed at best. Generally, recruits are not trained to teach and a number of the recruitment programs have high attrition rates, meaning that those recruited do not remain in the teaching profession.

Over the course of a decade, Veltri (2010) taught, observed, and interviewed hundreds of TFA teachers in Arizona and documented inadequate pedagogic preparation, teaching out-of-field (including special education), class and race incongruence with students, high turnover, and many other challenges. Approximately 90 percent departed after three years. Concerns about the effects of teacher inexperience and turnover on student achievement have been well documented.

In a comprehensive review of the research on TFA, Vasquez Heilig and Jez (2010) found that TFA teachers perform better only when compared with other uncertified new teachers in the same school. When compared with traditionally prepared beginning and veteran teachers, they perform worse, with students of novice TFA teachers receiving lower reading and math scores. TFA teachers only compare in performance if they remain long enough to become certified and experienced, but, Heilig and Jez affirm, more than 50 percent leave in two years and more than 80 percent depart after three years.

Turnover affects student achievement as well as school climate more generally. Ronfeldt, Loeb, and Wyckoff (2013) studied teacher turnover in New York City for almost a decade and found that students in grades with high turnover score lower in language arts and math, especially in schools with low-performing African American students. They also discovered negative consequences beyond those experienced by students of departing teachers; students of teachers who remained in schools with high turnover performed worse as well, especially in already low-performing schools. On the whole, they affirm, turnover is harmful.

Despite the negative effects of poor preparation and teacher turnover for low-income students and students of color, TFA recruits reap a host of benefits. Veltri (2010) explains that TFA teachers use their short-term experience in urban schools to polish their résumés; qualify for in-state tuition at regional universities; collect thousands of dollars through AmeriCorps to cover past and future educational costs after two years of service; and receive special consideration by law and medical schools that value TFA service. Some TFA recruits even go on to secure entrepreneurial and leadership positions in public education—pathways facilitated and accelerated by TFA's emerging leadership initiative. Trujillo, Scott, and Rivera (2013) explore how TFA networks provide a "yellow brick road" to career success and private entrepreneurship. Most concerning, they point out, is the fact that recruits with only two to four years of experience quickly acquire leadership positions in schools and educational organizations.

This trend is exemplified in a video produced by 4.0 Schools and Idea Village (2012), networks in New Orleans that provide consulting services and resources to entrepreneurs. In the video, a young white woman in her 20s declares that New Orleans stands at the "intersection of a vibrant entrepreneurial community." In a revealing biographic note, she discloses, "I was teaching ninth grade math and now I run a company. I'm CEO of a company." She runs an ed-tech startup and sells data management software to public schools. Interspersed throughout the video are typical scenes from New Orleans' French Quarter, where newcomers exclaim: "There's a rhythm to living here!" Others say they enjoy the delicious food, weather, and awesome bands. One says he fell in love with the city's people, but only whites are shown in the background shot. An entrepreneurial brainstorming session is also featured, as nearly all-white 20-somethings sit around and ponder innovation in the public education market. The video fades with jazz music playing. This is the culture of the education market, where the line between tourist, teacher, innovator, and profiteer is thin. It seems there is little need to know students or schools, except to sell something. "Find who your user is and build what they need," concludes one entrepreneurial leader in the video.

Knowingly or unknowingly, inexperienced white recruits with TFA undermine the best interests of black working-class students and veteran teachers to leverage a more financially stable and promising future for themselves. TFA's 2008 annual report boasted: "By 2010, one in three students in Greater New Orleans will be taught by a Teach for America corps member" (p. 6). The report also noted TFA's efforts to "expand [the] alumni footprint" in New Orleans, where over 200 alumni were working as education leaders (TFA, 2008, p. 17). Delpit (2012) discusses how veteran teachers across the nation, many of whom are black, have been displaced by TFA recruits in Charlotte, Chicago, Dallas, Houston, Kansas City, Las Vegas, New York City, Washington, DC, and elsewhere.

This reality has not gone unnoticed by veteran teachers in New Orleans. Their mass termination, unfortunately, provided the blueprint for other cities.

Veteran Teachers and Charter Schools in New Orleans: Experiences on the Ground

After mass termination, many veteran teachers in New Orleans sought positions in the newly reconstructed system. Yet again, they were systematically dismissed as traditional public schools were taken over by or closed as a result of charter school operators. This was a near-universal experience shared during group interviews I completed with veteran teachers and members of UTNO.

One veteran teacher shared the following account regarding one of the RSD's "transformation" schools, where a newly chartered school was set to push out grade-by-grade an existing traditional school: "Evidently, there's an unwritten memo that says 'Anyone making over $50,000, don't hire them.' I have an excellent teaching record. I've been teaching for 30 years. And no one would hire me." This included the incoming charter school that made hiring promises to veteran teachers (Group Interview c, 2009).

In so many words, a fellow veteran pondered the racial dynamics of New Orleans' urban space economy:

> It's all about the dollars. … Our rights as teachers have been trampled upon. … They are saying that they are revamping the schools or whatever. They get rid of everyone … and they rehire whoever they want to rehire. In many cases, they replace veteran teachers with first, second, and third year teachers.
>
> (Group Interview c, 2009)

The teacher continued:

> It's been across the board. It's a pattern. Every time they close a school, [veteran teachers] lose their jobs. They don't have bad evaluations. It has nothing to do with their evaluations. It has nothing to do with their teaching ability and skill. It has nothing to do with their years of experience.
>
> (Group Interview c, 2009)

The gross injustice of the circumstances is palpable.

Another veteran teacher describes the entrepreneurial emphasis on accumulation and profit, all to the detriment of teachers and students:

> In charter schools, it's test scores and checkbooks. It's no longer people. And [although] I really felt like there was a somewhat similar problem before the storm ... now in the charter schools, it [testing] is held over your head every breathing moment—that you have to do this or we're not going to exist. ...
>
> [In charter schools, it's now,] "Oh, where's the money going to come from? We don't have money to do this." Out of one side of their mouth they're bragging that we have four million dollars in the bank and the other side of their mouth they're saying we don't have enough money to pay our veteran teachers, so we'll get rid of these two veteran teachers and then we can hire four young teachers in their place for the same money.
>
> (Group Interview b, 2009)

In the final analysis, she warns that test scores and checkbooks are numbers, "not people." "When you stop treating teachers and students like people," she concludes, "you have an ultimate breakdown in your education system" (Group Interview b, 2009). Her critique is a shared one. The president of the Louisiana Federation of Teachers pronounced, "If [the] idea is to lower the wages for educators, to deprive them of benefits, then we are definitely going to oppose those kinds of initiatives" (Sentell, 2009, para.16).

If veteran teachers are hired in RSD schools, including charters, they are treated as first-year teachers in terms of vestment. Despite 20 or 30 years of teaching, they start all over in accumulating long-term health insurance benefits. A veteran teacher explains:

> In order to be vested, to be able enjoy the payment of your insurance premium, you have to be employed for ten years. So now that they've acquired and rehired you as a state employee, you start back at year one. ... We didn't have any tenure with RSD.
>
> (Group Interview c, 2009)

All the while, novice white teachers assume jobs that many evacuate within several years and do not demand laddered pay or health and retirement benefits. Reflecting on Vallas, master planners, charter school operators and those they represent, a veteran educator and affiliate of UTNO deemed them "functionaries of privatization," indicating they spoke for "white men and all that entails, probably in its nastiest forms" (Group Interview a, 2009).

TFA's culpability is glaring, even as it presents its efforts as salutary. For example, take George Washington Carver High School. In 2013, TFA's alumni magazine (Yu, 2013) highlighted Carver, at first praising its rich history as an all-black school serving New Orleans' 9th Ward. Its marching band was one of the "jewels of the community," the article reads, and one graduate of the 1960s reports the school played a formative role in shaping her racial identity (p. 28). By 2005, reports TFA, "the shining community beacon that had been Carver had long since dimmed" (p. 30). Not surprisingly, Carver would be phased out while two other charter schools were co-located on its campus. The takeover provoked former graduates to protest outside the school. "Nowhere is this mistrust starker than in New Orleans," the article continues, "where 7,500 school employees…the majority of whom were African American, were dismissed" (p. 32). Despite this seemingly sympathetic acknowledgment, the article takes a self-congratulatory turn. Since this time, "Teach For America has been a driving force behind much of the progress, fueling the influx of human capital" (p. 32). TFA's regional director, Kira Orange-Jones, also explains that progress was possible because reforms "dismantled perceived democratic institutions like school boards and collective bargaining" (p. 32). The system is now run by "people who are not from here," acknowledges Orange-Jones, which suggests the question: "What do we [TFA] do with that power?" (p. 32).

TFA asserts it is "pioneering" something new on Carver's campus—a conversation around the possibility of shared governance between charter operators, TFA, and a segment of alumni who originally protested takeover. The charter schools have no black decision makers, lack black teachers, and have stringent discipline codes, all concerns for Carver alumni. TFA, however, does not seem concerned. The president of the charter management organization (CMO) operating at Carver reflects on the notion of shared governance and asks: "Is it worth the value-added?" (Yu, 2013, p. 35). She shields the schools' principals from laborious exchanges with community members "so they can focus on the arduous task of founding new schools" (p. 35). Never mind that they are founding schools in the absence of community input and consent. The CMO's president continues: "This whole concept of shared governance, I mean it's scary. I'm trying to look at this from a perspective of us having 20 schools, 50 schools someday, in multiple markets across the country" (p. 35). Put simply, expanding the CMO's market share takes precedent over the concerns of the community presumably being served. TFA does not appear to understand or care about the contradictions or the anti-democratic consequences of the "progress" it brings. Despite a nod to working with communities rather than imposing reforms, the article basically concludes: "When the futures of children are at stake, many overtaxed school leaders feel they simply can't prioritize the difficult and slow process of winning over resistant communities. Instead they focus on boosting student achievement as quickly as possible" (p. 37). In the end, black students are to be rescued by white TFA recruits and the education marketplace that motivates CMO leadership.

All of this has cultural and racial implications for African American school-children who make up 95 percent of public school enrollment in New Orleans (Nelson, 2010). It is black veteran teachers who possess intimate knowledge of the city's history, culture, and communities, not those supplied from elsewhere by TFA.

The Culture of the Education Market *Versus* the Culture of the Community

Entrepreneurs portray the market as a neutral and cultureless arbiter of educational goods and services. This simply is not so. Education markets are characterized by a host of cultural presumptions and outcomes, revealing that present strategies to "recruit new talent" and "replace lazy teachers" (the word *place* is crucial here) protected by the union are part of New Orleans' racial-spatial reconstruction. All of this demonstrates a complete disregard for place-based consciousness and community knowledge in the education of black students, the kind of knowledge veteran teachers indigenous to the community are most likely to possess. The same problem pertains to charter management organizations that operate schools without regard for community input and hire new recruits in record numbers. Entrepreneurs have little sense, if any, of how culture and place have shaped black education or how white power and state neglect have necessitated the creation of school and neighborhood networks for survival. Instead, they seek to impose racialized management principles ("discipline," "high standards," and "efficiency") on a community they perceive to be culturally deficient. And they make a profit in the process.

The ahistorical and de-territorialized approach of education markets is challenged by longstanding initiatives of veteran teachers to preserve black cultural forms and knowledge. The analysis below centers on historic school- and community-based programs that build on the legacy of Native American and African American resistance in New Orleans, teach literacy and history, and uphold the city's distinct cultural and indigenous arts traditions, including jazz, brass bands, and multigenerational masking as Mardi Gras Indians. Earlier chapters highlighted programs of veteran teachers that recognize the import of culture, place, and race to black education—Mos Chukma Institute, Wetland Warriors, the Creole Cottage Program, and Students at the Center (see also Buras 2009; Buras et al., 2010). Similarly, veteran teachers have mentored generations of students by linking music to the wider curriculum and community (Kennedy, 2005, 2010). Perhaps this history will illuminate what is at stake when TFA provides recruits who displace veteran teachers and have little to no knowledge of the culture that teachers and students have guarded for centuries.

Veteran Teachers, the Geography of Racial Identity, and All That Jazz

Historically, black teachers in New Orleans public schools have endeavored to connect education and community through jazz and other indigenous cultural traditions. The meaning of these traditions often escapes those beyond the local neighborhood, who too often perceive them to be nothing more than commercialized "festivities" associated with the French Quarter. In black working-class communities, these traditions certainly have brought pleasure to many, but they are tied as well to issues of identity, intergenerational knowledge, community cohesion, resistance, survival, and self-determination (Burns, 2006; Harrison-Nelson, 2013; Kennedy, 2005, 2010; Nine Times, 2006).

In the case of jazz, black teachers infused this musical culture into the curriculum as early as the 1920s. Kennedy (2005) explains: "Because so many teachers were linked to the music and musicians of the city through their performance networks or through their kinship networks, their presence in the schools brought the schools into [a] complex, multifaceted network ... within the community" (p. xxiii). It is essential to note, as Kennedy does, that teachers generally taught subjects other than music, although they wove music into their teaching or taught music in after-school programs. For example, James McNeal, vice principal of Fisk School in the early 1900s, was a member of Onward Brass Band in New Orleans; Louis Armstrong attended Fisk. William Nickerson also trained the first generation of jazz students; he gave lessons to Jelly Roll Morton and ultimately taught public school at Thomy Lafon Elementary. So important was Nickerson's work that parents petitioned OPSB to permit him to lead an after-school orchestra (Kennedy, 2005). His daughter, Camille Lucie Nickerson, born in 1888, later graduated from a teacher-training program at Southern University and taught at two different New Orleans public schools. She established the B-Sharp Music Club in 1917 and it still exists today. "B-Sharp membership became an extended cultural, social, and educational network that promoted music in the community and in the schools," writes Kennedy (2005, p. 11). Many public school teachers and principals were members. Not without significance, music supported learning in other areas. During B-Sharp musical performances, principals would "present readings or give short talks between selections" (p. 11).

Valmore Victor taught at Lafon and Ricard Elementary Schools from 1928 to 1953; Ellis Marsalis, now an internationally recognized jazz master, was a student in his band. Earl Turbinton, another highly respected jazz musician, recollected taking lessons at Victor's home:

> He had a house which must have had a thousand instruments; tuba, maybe twenty or thirty saxophones, twenty or thirty trumpets and trombones. You'd

> bring your own mouthpiece and Professor Victor would say, "Go in there
> and get an alto 'til you find one that feels good to you. Play all these horns."
>
> (Kennedy, 2005, p. 15)

In short, his home and his classroom were a wellspring of resources for students.
At Lafon, Victor organized what was probably the first elementary public school
brass band, which played at funerals and community gatherings. His music pedagogy permeated school culture:

> In the mornings, the children marched into Lafon to the lively accompa-
> niment of Victor's band. It was an upbeat way to start the day, with Vic-
> tor's students playing fast-paced numbers, including spirituals, while "all
> the little boys would be trying to make little fancy turns, and the little girls
> would be strutting."
>
> (Kennedy, 2005, p. 15)

Children in the band were revered like athletes, indicating the status of music in
the schools.

Osceola Blanchet, a science teacher at McDonogh No. 35, was a jazz musician
who taught for almost 50 years. With little support from OPSB, Blanchet developed a thriving music program; he also provided music lessons during lunch and
after school. He taught more than music to students, however:

> He was always trying to open up the whole spectrum of arts to them.
> Although African American students were seldom invited to the Delgado
> Arts Museum, Blanchet took his students there anyway. He made sure
> McDonogh 35 students visited the Cabildo and many other places of his-
> torical and cultural interest. He introduced them to different philosophies,
> and he challenged them with discussions about world religions. For years
> he painstakingly prepared a weekly bulletin that was posted throughout the
> school. In addition to regular school announcements in the bulletin, Blan-
> chet would use the front page to inform students about famous paintings,
> definitions of unfamiliar words, notes about operas, lists of poems, and sug-
> gestions of books for students to read.
>
> (Kennedy, 2005, p. 18)

The relationships that Blanchet built through music instruction were part of a
larger pedagogic project. Students developed a sense of place in the community
(and the world) and expanded the bounds of knowledge to the arts, religion, literature, and history (Kennedy, 2005).

Born in 1929, Yvonne Busch ultimately inspired generations of public school
students in New Orleans. She spent part of her childhood near the historic Congo
Square in Tremé, perhaps the longest-standing black neighborhood in the nation.

"Everything came through there," Busch recollected, "all the parades, the second-lines, and the jazz funerals" (Kennedy, 2005, p. 50). Busch relied on tubs and chairs to make music before moving to Mississippi for school, where she mastered the alto horn and trumpet and traveled with the International Sweethearts of Rhythm. Upon returning to New Orleans, she learned to play the drums, baritone horn, and trombone and attended a teacher-training and music program at Southern University from 1947 to 1951. Her first teaching position was at Booker T. Washington, opened in the early '40s as New Orleans' second black public high school. Relying on personal funds, she had instruments repaired and bought sheet music for students. Busch instilled discipline and pride in students, who relished the chance to be seen in band uniforms that signaled belonging and accomplishment. Busch's students won state competitions; Anthony Bazley, who learned drumming under Busch, contributed years later to poetry and jazz performances with Langston Hughes. When students could not afford music lessons, their teacher paid the bill. Later reassigned to Joseph Clark Senior High, McDonogh No. 41 Junior High, and Joseph Craig Elementary, Busch carried books and music stands daily from one school to another. Despite these challenges, her students thrived. Joseph "Smokey" Johnson, one of Busch's students, was Fats Domino's drummer. Others once under her tutelage reported: "Everything she did in her classroom was designed to encourage her students to go on to college" (Kennedy, 2005, p. 67). She even taught students to play the fight songs of top colleges. Another student said Busch taught him that he could "control his destiny through music" (p. 67). Like Blanchet and others, Busch taught students much more than music. Kennedy (2005) writes: "Although the students' course schedule might reflect 'band' or 'music,' once inside the band room, they were just as likely to get lectures on ... how to get along with their parents, or why they should be on time" (p. 68).

Although she retired after 32 years of teaching, Busch did not abandon students. Rather she continued to encourage them through phone calls and remembered the details of their lives (Kennedy, 2005). Many of Busch's students also went on to become doctors, lawyers, politicians, educators, engineers, athletes, and community leaders (Smith, 2009). It is difficult to fathom untrained, transient teachers who have no knowledge of students' history, culture, or community inspiring an entire generation toward excellence. It simply will not happen. Yet in the absence of resources, veteran teachers have been instrumental in sustaining culture and ensuring that students acquired a broad education despite state neglect.

Cherice Harrison-Nelson is a part of this honorable tradition, although she was fired with thousands of black veteran teachers in 2006. Harrison-Nelson's father, Big Chief Donald Harrison, was a revered member of the Mardi Gras Indian community. The Mardi Gras Indians go back more than a century and are known for their hand-beaded suits and ritualized neighborhood processions (or "masking") in honor of those who resisted racial oppression in colonial and antebellum Louisiana. Resistors included Native Americans who acted in solidarity with people of African descent, hence the melding of black and native cultural forms. It is essential to note that Mardi Gras Indian culture is not reserved for a single day of the year (Mardi Gras), but instead consists of cultural and educational practices that constitute a way of life.

Chief Harrison, an avid reader who was self-taught, made certain his children were immersed in jazz and literature as well as the oral history, song, and artistry of Mardi Gras Indians. "The house on Orleans Avenue became a headquarters for beading patches, wrapping feathers, and sewing suits. Whether they would go on to mask or not, all of the Harrison children absorbed the culture that, literally, was stitched together in their presence" (Kennedy, 2010, p. 114). Herreast Harrison, Cherice's mother, similarly contributed to the education of her children and those in the community. In the late 1960s, she opened a nursery school that operated for 32 years and helped pay her children's way through college; Cherice's father stopped masking for a number of years to reserve financial resources for his children's education. Cherice recollects her mother's commitment to education generally: "There always was someone who was not paying tuition [at the nursery school]. My mother always felt that if they didn't have a place to bring their children that was safe during the day, what was their option?" (Kennedy, 2010, p. 182).

FIGURE 5.1 Cherice Harrison-Nelson poses in hand-beaded Mardi Gras Indian headdress

A former student of Yvonne Busch, Cherice's mother would play jazz at the nursery and "developed new and innovative ways to incorporate New Orleans into her curriculum" (p. 183). Place-based consciousness factored heavily in Cherice and her peers' education. Of Donald Harrison, Kennedy (2010) notes: "[He] and jazz came from the same place—not just the geographic location of New Orleans but a place of freedom and energy" (p. 237). This spirit and knowledge are things Harrison shared with the younger generation. In 1989, he resumed masking and founded Guardians of the Flame, a multigenerational Mardi Gras Indian group. The group's chosen name pretty much says it all. Children would be taught to honor the heritage knowledge (King, 2009) passed down over the centuries.

Cherice Harrison-Nelson taught in New Orleans public schools for almost 25 years. She established the Young Guardians of the Flame to enable more children to be involved in learning and contributing to the city's cultural traditions. At Charles Gayarre Elementary School (later renamed Oretha Castle Haley Elementary School), Harrison-Nelson, with support from Principal Rosalyn Smith, developed a cultural studies curriculum that included jazz, brass bands, and the Mardi Gras Indians (Kennedy, 2005, 2010). Materials that Harrison-Nelson developed for Jazz Awareness Month moved beyond Gayarre to over 100 schools across Louisiana. Lessons involved language arts, history, art, and musical appreciation. Students read the biographies of jazz musicians, were encouraged to author narratives of their own ("If I were a saxophone ..."), write reviews of jazz recordings, build musical instruments and second-line umbrellas, and even apply math and geography to understanding jazz (Harrison-Nelson, n.d.; Kennedy, 2005).

Harrison-Nelson "understood that children bring their culture into the classroom where their teachers either teach them how to see it and appreciate it, or, by omission, cause the culture to be suppressed or dismissed" (Kennedy, 2005, p. 138). This culture was connected to learning across the curriculum as well as Louisiana's educational standards. For example, Kennedy (2005) explained:

> She starts with biographical sketches of various musicians and Mardi Gras Indians, a collection of readings filled with new words relating to different musical styles, insights into New Orleans history, and information about New Orleans neighborhoods. She describes the areas of the city where musicians lived or performed....
>
> Then Harrison-Nelson brings in the loose feathers used on the Mardi Gras Indian suits, and her class discusses places in the world where the feathers were obtained. She shows students copies of her father's invoices from a New York company that supplies beads and stones ... for the patches on the suit. Using the per-unit cost on the invoice, Harrison-Nelson has the students find a total price. ... The children learn the sacrifices participants make to perpetuate the traditions [as well as math and history].
>
> (pp. 142–143)

FIGURE 5.2 Artist's rendering of New Orleans brass band for Jazz Studies curriculum guide

Many community elders and musicians were invited to Gayarre as well, including Chief Harrison and Cherice's brother, Donald Harrison, Jr., a legendary jazz musician who played with Art Blakey and the Jazz Messengers. From this work grew the Mardi Gras Indian Hall of Fame in 1999. It first developed at the school and is located now in Harrison-Nelson's home as an archive that chronicles and preserves the history and culture of the community.

The Guardians Institute was founded by the Harrison family in the late 1980s and its work continues today through Harrison-Nelson and others. Its work is too extensive to document here, but a few illustrations will demonstrate the difference between managerial and indigenous models of schooling. Partnering with local groups, Guardians Institute supports *Sankofa Saturdays*, providing time for community elders to educate youth in the traditions of the Mardi Gras Indians. This involves careful study of history, art, song, music, and performance. Additionally, *Big Chief Donald Harrison Book Club* provides culturally relevant literature to children free of charge in classroom and community settings. Art and literacy activities, including presentations and performances by community members, accompany the ceremonious distribution and reading of books. With little financial support, 33,000 books valued at over $400,000 have been placed in the hands of children in New Orleans (Guardians Institute, n.d.; Woods, 2009).

FIGURE 5.3 Multigenerational gathering organized by Harrison-Nelson in Congo Square

It is nothing short of an assault on the dignity and epistemology of black communities in New Orleans to assume that talented teachers, innovative leaders, and educational institutions need to be "incubated" from without, especially when there are such rich cultural traditions from within. Herreast Harrison donated land she owns in New Orleans' 9th Ward for construction of a facility that houses a museum, classroom, library, and performance space. The facility was being considered as a possible United Nations Educational, Scientific, and Cultural Organization (UNESCO) site (Guardians Institute, n.d.).

In an interview several years after she was unlawfully terminated, Harrison-Nelson reflected on the onslaught of new recruits:

> Many nonprofits are operated by people of European descent who are not from New Orleans. … Ultimately, or when you get to the root of it, it's really not about community but how they are able to maintain their status quo and image as "the great savior."
>
> (Woods, 2009, pp. 639–640)

She also expressed concern about the replacement of neighborhood public schools by charter schools across the city. "Neighborhood schools build community cohesiveness," she emphasized. Along these lines, she spoke on the meaning of place to the Mardi Gras Indian tradition, sharing: "We have a legacy of ritualized processions in our neighborhoods. The tradition is largely transmitted by direct contact and communication with the elders" (p. 642). Guardians' work in schools, Harrison-Nelson explains, is "a form of civic engagement" for elders, who are "community heroes and leaders" (p. 644). When they encourage children to read and learn, it means something. The influence of the culture and the elders cannot be overstated. In a recent book edited by Harrison-Nelson (2013) to document the Mardi Gras Indian tradition, Eldon Harris, who admired the traditions as a young boy and later came to participate, credited the culture with saving his life and many others:

> If you are true to it, it will help you out. If I wouldn't have been learning to sew, learning the culture, I would probably have wound up dead or in jail. New Orleans is a city where trouble is easy to get into, but hard to get out of.
> (p. 28)

Harris says the culture gave his life "discipline" and "focus" (p. 28). When he masks as a Mardi Gras Indian, he feels a sense of "accomplishment" that he has crafted a suit worthy of admiration. Most important, he knows he is "trying to keep something alive that I saw when I was a kid, something that's been in the neighborhood since the 1800s" (Harrison-Nelson, 2013, p. 28).

Teach for America and the Culture of the Market

TFA's venture in New Orleans has more than economic consequences. By displacing veteran teachers, this human capital edu-business threatens to destroy a culture, one that is fundamental to the education and survival of black youth in New Orleans' neighborhoods. Of course, TFA is engaged in its own cultural project: poor black students are to be "rescued" from an ostensibly negative social environment by new teachers promising discipline and a compass leading someplace better.

In her study of TFA recruits in New Orleans charter schools, Sondel (2013) learned that despite how recruits perceived the purpose of their work, there was homogeneity in terms of their teaching. Most relied on what she called the *pedagogy of compliance* focused on rules, punishment, and narrowly defined learning objectives disconnected from students' lives. For many TFA recruits, this pedagogic approach resulted not only from a lack of teaching experience and thus an inordinate emphasis on discipline. It also emanated from notions of racial and cultural deficiency held by recruits about the students they taught. Dave, a 26-year-old white recruit from the Northeast, illustrates this orientation. He explained:

I'm trying to raise a responsible citizen. I'm trying to raise someone that is informed, a citizen that's polite, that has manners. ... It doesn't mean replacing everything that the parents did. But there are things in the culture that need to be changed.

(Sondel, 2013)

In exchange for what? Dave continued:

A term we use a lot in Teach for America ... is the *locus of control*. ... I can't control what happens when [students] go home and on the weekend. But I can control what happens from 7:30 in the morning until 4:00 in the afternoon. And I can do my best to instill *my values.*

(Sondel, 2013; italics added)

Dave believes that students lack access to any meaningful cultural capital in their own communities and that his own background, perceived as responsible, intelligent, and mannered (presumably the antithesis of students' culture), should be imposed. In a meager attempt to incorporate popular New Orleans culture into his classroom, Dave uses king cake, a local pastry associated with Mardi Gras, as a classroom reward and has students read passages about Mardi Gras parades to teach writing concepts. When one considers the rich cultural legacy sustained by veteran teachers and the sophisticated ways that many used students' culture across the curriculum, it becomes evident that what is deficient is Dave's knowledge of local history and teaching. While Cherice Harrison-Nelson invites students to guard the flame, Dave fails to see it.

Another TFA recruit, Jonathan, likewise hopes he can teach students who will "no longer be a drain on society" (Sondel, 2013). Like the allusions of state officials about lazy veteran teachers on the public dole, Jonathan reflects: "If you teach [students] responsibility, they will be productive and be able to have a family and save money and eventually maybe their kid won't be on government assistance" (Sondel, 2013). As before, there is no sense of history and the role that white supremacy has played in maintaining racial and economic disadvantage. There is also the inaccurate perception that low-income families do not work for a living. Jonathan and Dave believe their role is to provide students with a strong work ethic, like theirs. There is little understanding that veteran teachers and students hold high aspirations; the discipline, hard work, and accomplishments of Yvonne Busch's students are forgotten. Instead of the place-based knowledge that undergirded veteran teachers' pedagogy, Jonathan relies on a decontextualized command-and-control model of curriculum:

I have a curriculum captain who tells me weeks in advance, plans out my calendar, tells me exactly what is going to be on the benchmark, exactly the facts the kids need to know, gives me about 40 key points to teach and as long as they know the key points, I know they will get the answers right. ... That is a good system.

(Sondel, 2013)

When compared to the organic connections that veteran teachers built with students and the school and neighborhood networks in which they participated, this model of teaching seems hopelessly impoverished. The parameters of Jonathan's knowledge are most evident when he complains about black parents and their alleged failure to wisely navigate the education market in New Orleans:

Consumer choice only works with an educated consumer base. And the consumer base is not educated. ... [Parents] don't even know if academics are important. A lot of them want their kids to go to a school because they have a good band. ... Without even thinking about: Will my kid go to college for band?

(Sondel, 2013)

The basis of black parents' decision making escapes TFA recruits like Jonathan. They do not understand, or take the time to learn, that community traditions, such as music, were the foundation of a much broader education, certainly much broader than the one distributed by the curriculum captain. Blanchet's weekly bulletin and Harrison-Nelson's jazz studies program were much richer.

Only one TFA recruit in Sondel's (2013) study exemplified a social justice orientation rooted in knowledge of race, place, and community history. Caroline, the recruit, reached out to community members to learn more about their concerns and culture and aimed to "make my classroom a less oppressive place" (Sondel, 2013). Yet even Caroline found it difficult to supersede the mandates of the charter school in which she taught. She also reached out to UTNO and New Teachers' Roundtable, a group of ex-TFA members critical of TFA's efforts, to develop stronger teaching skills and anti-racist understandings. She described education reform in New Orleans, including TFA's effort, as an act of white supremacy and historical annihilation: "If you think about the whole city, I can't contain my rage. ... [They're] creating this militant punishing judgmental environment for students' culture and intellect" (Sondel, 2013). Notably, when Caroline spoke out regarding concerns about the KIPP charter school in which she was working and her desire to affiliate with the teacher union, she was told she would not be rehired the next year. She was no longer considered a "good fit" (Sondel, 2013).

Ultimately, claims made by TFA about the need to import "human capital" and "innovative models" of education are deeply troubling. Cultural capital already exists within the community. There are indigenous models upon which we can and should build. The intrusion of TFA and development of privately managed charter schools threaten to restructure public education as a business, with indigenous traditions and place-based curricula giving way to management practices that have little connection to students and what they need to thrive. The market is not a neutral culture—it is an ahistorical and de-territorialized regime based on racialized management principles and profit-making.

The Culture of the Market and the Problem with Ed-Ventures

In an attempt to reengineer the city's middle class more generally, Leslie Jacobs (2010) founded 504ward—New Orleans' area code is 504—a social networking initiative to keep newly recruited twenty- and thirty-somethings living in New Orleans. Jacobs' other initiative, Educate Now, which promotes market-based education reform, sent out word on a workshop called "NOLA: A Haven for Ed Startups." The description of the workshop demonstrates the problem with the culture of the market. I quote most of the call below to illustrate the raw language of edu-business:

> Finding the right place to launch and grow your company is one of the most important decisions an entrepreneur can make early on. In the last few years, there has been an explosion in ed tech ecosystems. ... With so many options, it can be difficult for entrepreneurs to accurately assess what different ... communities, and ultimately cities offer. New Orleans, recognized as a leader in the ed reform movement, is coming into its own as an excellent place for education entrepreneurs to launch their ventures, gain early market traction, and grow. Come hear from a diverse group of people from the New Orleans ed ecosystem about what the city can offer your startup.
>
> (Edtech NOLA, 2013)

The questions at the heart of the event—ones deemed important to education entrepreneurs—were:

1. Why is the ed market in New Orleans the best place to launch a new product?
2. What is life like in New Orleans as an ed entrepreneur?
3. What supports does the city offer entrepreneurs as you look to launch, validate, and grow your company? (Edtech NOLA, 2013)

One of the event's speakers, CEO of an ed-tech company noted earlier, is an alumna of TFA.

The ecosystem described by entrepreneurs is strikingly different from the place-based consciousness of the city's black veteran teachers, who were removed to make room for such ventures. While edu-businesses speak of launching products and gaining early market traction, veteran teachers speak of producing children who contribute to the community and gain traction in terms of achievement and equity long denied.

It is instructive to recall the words of a veteran teacher and UTNO representative who declared: "If this [New Orleans model] is the panacea for education, please visit this city and take a look at what's going on. Take a visit to these schools. Talk to the [veteran] educators in this city … because it's not all peaches and cream that you're reading about or hearing about" (Group Interview d, 2009).

Notes

1 White veteran teachers were fired as well, but black veteran teachers constituted the vast majority of the city's educators and were the primary target of racially motivated education policies.
2 The case was under appeal at the time of writing. If Judge Julien's decision is upheld, the case can be converted from seven plaintiffs, awarded $1.3 million, to a class action lawsuit that covers thousands of terminated employees, with damages estimated at $1.5 billion. These damages would be paid by either the LDOE or BESE (Dreilinger, 2013). Ultimately, the terminated teachers won the appeal.

References

4.0 Schools, & Idea Village. (2013). NOLA: A haven for ed startups [Video]. Available: http://vimeo.com/56775955

Ambrose, E. R. (1999). Sarah Towles Reed: Teacher and activist. In M. G. Wade (Ed.), *The Louisiana Purchase Bicentennial Series in Louisiana History: Education in Louisiana* [Vol. XVIII] (pp. 383–405). Lafayette, LA: Center for Louisiana Studies at University of Southwestern Louisiana.

Anderson, E. (1978). Student coalition calls for walkouts, picketing [*Times-Picayune* article]. In United Teachers of New Orleans, Local 527 Collection (Container 135–18). New Orleans, LA: Earl K. Long Library, Louisiana and Special Collections Department, University of New Orleans.

Blanchard, O. (2013, September). I quit Teach for America. *The Atlantic.* Available: www.theatlantic.com/education/archive/2013/09/i-quit-teach-for-america/279724/

Buras K. L. (2009). "We have to tell our story": Neo-Griots, racial resistance, and schooling in the other South. *Race Ethnicity and Education, 12*(4), 427–453.

Buras K. L. Randels, J., Salaam, K. Y., & Students at the Center. (2010). *Pedagogy, policy, and the privatized city: Stories of dispossession and defiance from New Orleans.* New York, NY: Teachers College Press.

Burns, M. (2006). *Keeping the beat on the street: The New Orleans brass band renaissance.* Baton Rouge, LA: Louisiana State University Press.

Butler, J. S. (1999). Black educators in Louisiana—A question of survival. In M. G. Wade (Ed.), *The Louisiana Purchase Bicentennial Series in Louisiana History: Education in Louisiana* [Vol. XVIII] (pp. 529–543). Lafayette, LA: Center for Louisiana Studies at University of Southwestern Louisiana.

Carr, S. (2009, February 14). Many New Orleans school have lack of veteran teachers. *Times-Picayune.* Available: www.nola.com

Cassimere, R. (1999). Equalizing teachers' pay in Louisiana. In M. G. Wade (Ed.), *The Louisiana Purchase Bicentennial Series in Louisiana History: Education in Louisiana* [Vol. XVIII] (pp. 429–440). Lafayette, LA: Center for Louisiana Studies at University of Southwestern Louisiana.

Civil District Court for the Parish of Orleans. (2012, June 20). *Eddy Oliver et al. v. Orleans Parish School Board et al.* [Reasons for judgment]. New Orleans, LA: Author.

Conway, Z. (2010, April 8). Education "revolution" in New Orleans. BBC News. Retrieved on March 13, 2012 from http://new.bbc.co.uk/go/pr/fr/-/2/hi/ameicas/8608960.stm

Cowen Institute. (2009, October). Is education reform in New Orleans working? A few facts swimming in a sea of unknowns [PowerPoint presentation]. New Orleans, LA: Author.

Delpit, L. (2012). *"Multiplication is for white people": Raising expectations for other people's children.* New York, NY: The New Press.

DeVore, D. E., & Logsdon, J. (1991). *Crescent City schools: Public education in New Orleans, 1841–1991.* Lafayette, LA: Center for Louisiana Studies at the University of Southwestern Louisiana.

Dreilinger, D. (2013, May 30). Appeal argued in $1.5 billion Hurricane Katrina teacher termination case. *Times-Picayune.* Available: www.nola.com

EdTech NOLA. (2013). NOLA: A haven for ed startups. Retrieved on August 21, 2013, from http://panelpicker.sxsw.com/vote/23233

Guardians Institute. (n.d.). Background [Brochure]. New Orleans, LA: Author.

Harrison-Nelson, C. (Ed.). (2013). Mardi Gras Indian Hall of Fame: Spy Boy yearbook. New Orleans, LA: Author.

Harrison-Nelson, C. (n.d.). Jazz awareness month: The Haley School model. [Curriculum guide]. New Orleans, LA: Author.

Harvey, D. (2006). *Spaces of global capitalism: Towards a theory of uneven geographical development.* New York, NY: Verso.

Hill, V. (1990, November 7). Veronica Hill interview by Edith Ambrose. In United Teachers of New Orleans, Local 527 Collection (Container 135–18). New Orleans, LA: Earl K. Long Library, Louisiana and Special Collections Department, University of New Orleans.

Kennedy, A. (2005). *Chord changes on the chalkboard: How public school teachers shaped jazz and the music of New Orleans.* Lanham, MD: Scarecrow Press.

Kennedy, A. (2010). *Big Chief Harrison and the Mardi Gras Indians.* Gretna, LA: Pelican Publishing Company.

King, J. E. (Ed.). (2009). *Black education: A transformative research and action agenda for the new century.* New York, NY: Routledge.

Landrieu, M. (2011, June 30). School turnaround 2.0: How federal policy can support school turnaround [Video]. Washington, DC: Center for American Progress. Available: federal-policy-can-support-school-turnaround/

McKendall, R. (1987, May 28). Teachers group opposes diversion of money [*Times-Picayune* article]. In United Teachers of New Orleans, Local 527 Collection (Container 135–18). New Orleans, LA: Earl K. Long Library, Louisiana and Special Collections Department, University of New Orleans.

Middleton, E. J. (1984). *History of the Louisiana Education Association.* Washington, DC: National Education Association.

National Academy of Education. (2009). Teacher quality [Education policy white paper]. Washington, DC: Author.

Nelson, F. H. (2010, September). *Teacher quality and distribution in post-Katrina New Orleans.* Washington, DC: American Federation of Teachers.

New Orleans Public School Employees (NOPSE) Justice. (2007). About NOPSE Justice [Pre-Katrina political agenda]. Available:www.nopsejustice.com/about.htm

New Orleans Public School Employees (NOPSE) Justice. (2010, June 9). Frequently asked questions. Available: www.nopsejustice.com/faq.htm

Nine Times Social Aid and Pleasure Club. (2006). *Coming out the door for the Ninth Ward.* New Orleans, LA: Neighborhood Story Project.

Owsley, B. (1988, April 18). Interview with Nathaniel Hawthorne LaCour by Beatrice Owsley. [Interview guide]. In United Teachers of New Orleans, Local 527 Collection (Container 135–18). New Orleans, LA: Earl K. Long Library, Louisiana and Special Collections Department, University of New Orleans.

Randels, J. (2010). Passing on a torch. In K. L. Buras, J. Randels, K. Y. Salaam, and Students at the Center, *Pedagogy, policy, and the privatized city: Stories of dispossession and defiance from New Orleans* (pp. 101–103). New York, NY: Teachers College Press.

Robelen, E. W. (2007, November 12). New teachers are New Orleans norm. *Education Week, 27*(12), 26–28.

Ronfeldt, M., Loeb, S., & Wyckoff, J. (2013). How teacher turnover harms student achievement. *American Educational Research Journal, 50*(1), 4–36.

Sentell, W. (2009, September 12). Charter schools praised. *The Advocate.* Retrieved August 12, 2009 from http://theadvocate.com

Smith, L. (circa 1970). The plight of the black teacher. In United Teachers of New Orleans, Local 527 Collection (Container 135–15). New Orleans, LA: Earl K. Long Library, Louisiana and Special Collections Department, University of New Orleans.

Smith, L. (2009). A legend in the classroom: The life story of Ms. Yvonne Busch [Film trailer]. Available: http://vimeo.com/3206947

Sondel, B. (2013). Raising citizens or raising test scores: Ideology and pedagogy in post-Katrina charter schools. Unpublished Dissertation, University of Wisconsin, Madison.

Southern Education Foundation. (2009, November). New Orleans schools four years after Katrina: A lingering federal responsibility. Atlanta, GA: Author.

Teach for America (TFA). (2008). Annual report. New York, NY: Author.

Times-Picayune. (1978, October 25). N.O. plagued with social, economic ills—LaCour [*Times Picayune* article]. In United Teachers of New Orleans, Local 527 Collection (Container 135–18). New Orleans, LA: Earl K. Long Library, Louisiana and Special Collections Department, University of New Orleans.

Tisserand, M. (2007, August 23). The charter school flood [Reprint]. *The Nation.* Available:www.civilrights.org/library/features/charter-school-flood-1.html

Treadway, J. (1978, September 1). Upset students write letters [*Times-Picayune* article]. In United Teachers of New Orleans, Local 527 Collection (Container 135–18). New Orleans, LA: Earl K. Long Library, Louisiana and Special Collections Department, University of New Orleans.

Trujillo, T., Scott, T., & Rivera, M. (2013, April). Follow the yellow brick road: Teach for America and the making of educational leaders. Presented at the annual meeting of the American Educational Research Association, San Francisco, California.

United Teachers of New Orleans (UTNO). (2010). The New Orleans model: All our students deserve more [Issue brief]. New Orleans, LA: Author.

United Teachers of New Orleans (UTNO). (2010, March). The New Orleans model: Shortchanging poor and minority student by over-relying on new teachers [Brief]. New Orleans, LA: Author.

United Teachers of New Orleans (UTNO), Louisiana Federation of Teachers (LFT), & American Federation Teachers (AFT). (2007, June). No experience necessary: How the New Orleans school takeover experiment devalues experienced teachers. New Orleans, LA: Author.

Vasquez Heilig, J., & Jez, S. J. (2010). Teach for America: A review of the evidence [Policy brief]. Boulder and Tempe: Education and the Public Interest Center and Education Policy Research Unit. Available: http://nepc.colorado.edu/publication/teach-for-america

Veltri, B. T. (2010). *Learning on other people's children: Becoming a Teach for America teacher.* Charlotte, NC: Information Age.

Weiner, L. (2012). *The future of our schools: Teachers unions and social justice.* Chicago, IL: Haymarket Books.

Woods, C. (2009). Upholding community tradition: An interview with Cherice Harrison-Nelson. *American Quarterly, 61*(3), 639–648.

Yu, T. (2013). One road to "One Day"? *One Day, XVII,* 28–38.

Zubrzycki, J. (2013, April 19). TFA alumni aid new teachers in New Orleans. *Education Week* [online]. Available: www.edweek.org/ew/articles/2013/04/19/29neworleans_ep.h32.html?tkn=TMZF%2BO0ozaBgLk0hzoPB7fjTQ1jAozaXOouD&cmp=ENL-EU-NEWS1

6

NEW ORLEANS—A GUIDE FOR CITIES OR A WARNING FOR COMMUNITIES?

Lessons Learned from the Bottom-Up

(with Urban South Grassroots Research Collective)

> Despite being the recipient of an $800,000 federal grant, John McDonogh Senior High School [in New Orleans] is having serious money problems. ...
>
> Future Is Now (FIN), the Charter Management Organization (CMO) running the school, sent an email to board members expressing concern that without additional funding, they would not be able to make payroll. ... FIN CEO Steve Barr announced a possible 20 percent salary cut across the board. And he said they may lose one of their principals. Principal Marvin Thompson makes an annual salary of $150,000. Angela Kinlaw was hired ... as the principal of the school's incoming freshman class with a salary of $115,000. Barr makes $250,000. ...
>
> The grant is part of the $28 million in federal funds awarded in 2010 to New Schools for New Orleans (NSNO), the Recovery School District, and the Achievement School District in Tennessee.
>
> John McDonogh was one of the recipients chosen by NSNO.
>
> Most of the grant money in New Orleans has been spent and is being spent on salaries and benefits—and not for teachers, but ... for upper management.
> —Excerpt from Kari Harden's *Louisiana Weekly* article,
> "Implementation of i3 education grants
> being questioned" (2013, p. 1)

Is education reform in New Orleans a model for urban school districts across the United States? Senator Mary Landrieu (Democrat–Louisiana) believes so. On March 1, 2012, Landrieu, co-chair of the Senate Public Charter School Caucus with Senator Lamar Alexander (Republican–Tennessee), hosted a forum for education policymakers in Washington, DC. The forum centered on *New Orleans-Style Education Reform: A Guide for Cities (Lessons Learned, 2004–2010)*, a report published by the charter school incubator New Schools for New Orleans (Brinson, Boast, Hassel, & Kingsland, 2012). Landrieu proclaimed:

> With its *Guide for Cities*, New Schools for New Orleans is doing the important work of sharing lessons learned throughout the transformation of New Orleans' public schools. Through relentless focus on accountability, human capital, and charter school development, New Orleans has become a national leader in education reform. ... I hope that this story and the *Guide for Cities* will inspire and equip other cities to follow New Orleans' lead.
>
> (Landrieu, 2012, para. 2)

Next to Landrieu was Neerav Kingsland, chief strategy officer for New Schools for New Orleans (NSNO) at the time; Kingsland is now CEO of NSNO because the organization's founder and former CEO, Sarah Usdin, was running for a seat on Orleans Parish School Board—a point taken up later. At the forum, Kingsland echoed Landrieu's remarks and added: "The New Orleans story is really one of transferring power back to educators and parents—to date, this had led to incredible gains in student learning" (Landrieu, 2012, para. 4).

In this chapter, I join members of Urban South Grassroots Research Collective, including longstanding educational and cultural organizations in New Orleans, to articulate a different perspective. Based on our experiential knowledge and qualitative research over a decade, we do not believe that New Orleans school reform represents a guide for cities. Instead we conclude that current reforms, including human capital and charter school development, have been immensely destructive to African American students, veteran teachers, and historically black neighborhoods in New Orleans. Ours is a warning for communities nationally. These "reforms" are not a guide for cities; they are a stark threat to the education, cultural integrity, and political-economic power of communities struggling for a semblance of justice.

To make our case, we draw on testimony from community-based education groups and scholarly research on the inequitable effects of New Orleans school reform for students, teachers, and schools targeted by organizations such as NSNO. Our focus will be on human capital and charter school development, and we will use the *Guide for Cities* as a sounding board for our concerns and critiques. However, we want to make clear that in responding to NSNO's *Guide*, we also are speaking back to a larger set of reports that have been written since 2005 about education reform in New Orleans and distributed nationally (Hill et al., 2009; Hill & Hannaway, 2006; Meese, Butler, & Holmes, 2005; Mind Trust, 2011; Osborne, 2012; Smith, 2012). All have highlighted New Orleans as a site of innovation and a model for replication. We firmly disagree and our disagreement is based on an evidentiary record rooted in community experience and almost a decade of research rather than the ungrounded assertions that characterize the aforementioned reports.

Before directly addressing the *Guide* and analyzing its claims, we first describe the critical race methodology that we employed and introduce Urban South

Grassroots Research Collective. Next some background on NSNO is provided, but only briefly since detailed background appeared in chapter 2. Following this, the *Guide's* policy recommendations on human capital and charter school development are examined and the concerns community groups have about these policies are considered through testimonies and primary source documents. Finally, we position NSNO within a wider policy network that includes elite actors at the local, state, and national levels, revealing its pivotal role in a circuit of education entrepreneurs who seek to transform urban public schools through market-based reforms. Like preceding chapters, we argue these reforms serve the interests of entrepreneurs rather than the communities at the center of their efforts. In conclusion, we offer principles of educational reform rooted in a more democratic and critically conscious tradition. These principles are informed not only by concerns over the *Guide*, but follow as well from the problems explored in this book.

Critical Race Methodology and Urban South Grassroots Research Collective

Critical race theorists have established testimonies by communities of color as an evidentiary record that challenges dominant narratives in law and education (Dixson & Rousseau, 2006; Lawrence, 1995; Solórzano & Yosso, 2009). Legal scholar Charles Lawrence (1995) explains that "in the white male academy, narrative is valued primarily as an instrument of private expression" and viewed "as a source of distortion rather than as a resource for understanding" (pp. 345–346). To the contrary, he argues narrative is an invaluable text "because it is dense in the detailed and moving articulation of the teller's ... life experience" (p. 346). In order to adequately appraise social conditions, it is imperative to consider the experiential knowledge of those most intimately involved in navigating them. Lawrence (1995) gets to the heart of the matter when he writes:

> Stories always refer to a particular context, place, and moment. The historical and cultural setting is critical to the readers' interpretation of facts, feelings, and understandings. ... Human problems considered and resolved in the absence of context are often misperceived, misinterpreted, and mishandled. ... Blacks and others whose stories have been and are excluded from the dominant discourse are more likely to be injured by the error of noncontextual methodology. This is because the reader considering facts and abstract argument without context will inevitably provide a setting of his or her own. This imaginary, though often unacknowledged, contextualization will be based on his or her own experiences or upon stories that he or she has heard.
>
> (p. 345)

He explains that the "imagined context often directly contradicts" the experiences and stories of racially oppressed groups affected by circumstances and policies

(p. 345). For these reasons, *counterstories* expose, analyze, and challenge majoritarian stories that depict the world from the viewpoint of racially dominant groups (Solórzano & Yosso, 2009, p. 138; see also Buras, 2013a). As Lawrence (1995) stresses, "Giving narrative form to experience creates a rich evidentiary record for analysis and assessment of complex social processes" (p. 345).

In this chapter, we draw heavily on narrative testimony to provide thick description of how education reforms have been experienced by those actually navigating the newly chartered landscape. This is crucial since these voices have been left out of discussions on school reform in New Orleans. The *Guide for Cities* excluded them as well. In fact, it is our contention that NSNO's *Guide* represents the abstract arguments and decontextualized claims that Lawrence (1995) warns against. The *Guide* is a majoritarian story about education reform in New Orleans told by those who are imposing the reform and stand to benefit the most. The picture looks very different when marginalized groups participate in assessing the reforms. We also draw attention to research literature—some of which appears in this book—that readers may consult on the racial politics and inequities that characterize the New Orleans education model. However, this chapter prioritizes firsthand accounts and the details they provide for analysis; these accounts are confluent with research findings cited throughout the chapter and should not be considered anomalies or anecdotes.

A word on Urban South Grassroots Research Collective (USGRC) is essential before proceeding. USGRC was cofounded by education scholars and longstanding grassroots organizations in New Orleans in the wake of experimental education reforms implemented in 2005. Based on a commitment to engaged educational research, scholars, veteran teachers, students, parents, and grassroots organizers affiliated with USGRC: (1) collaborate in developing questions focused on governmental transparency and integrity in public education; (2) engage in grassroots research that highlights the voices, experiences, and concerns of racially and economically marginalized communities; and (3) disseminate research findings locally and nationally in an effort to reinvigorate a public education system that serves *all* communities.

For this chapter, the following grassroots members of USGRC contributed writings and documents relevant to NSNO's *Guide for Cities*, and these were used alongside existing scholarship to illuminate concerns about education reform in New Orleans. Some may be familiar from preceding chapters:

- *Students at the Center*—a 20-year-old writing and digital media program cofounded by veteran teachers and students, which is based in New Orleans public schools and informed by civil rights struggles in New Orleans (see Buras, 2009; Buras et al., 2010);
- *Guardians Institute*—a school and community-based youth program founded in 1988 that builds on the legacy of Native American and African American resistance in New Orleans, promotes literacy, and upholds the city's cultural and indigenous arts traditions;

- *Mos Chukma Institute*—an indigenous healing arts program, housed in a Lower 9th Ward public elementary school founded two decades ago, which draws on Native, African, and African American traditions to develop place-based education, student resiliency, and community agency;
- *Pyramid Community Parent Resource Center*—an organization founded more than two decades ago by parents of two sons with Autism Spectrum disorders, which provides support and assistance to families of children with disabilities in New Orleans;
- *Lower 9 School Development Group*—a coalition of Lower 9th Ward community groups organized to fight for rebuilding a neighborhood high school amid master planners' efforts to construct schools elsewhere in the city and undermine the restoration of black working-class communities (Buras, 2011a, 2013b);
- *New Teachers' Roundtable*—a group in which early career educators engage in critical dialogue about racial, cultural, and economic justice in New Orleans and take action with their students' communities to build a more liberatory education system; and
- *United Teachers of New Orleans*—the local teacher union that has represented the city's educators for decades, with a long history of supporting equal pay among black and white teachers, equitable resources for public schools, and social justice activism in the community.

Thus, the evidentiary record that we draw upon grows out of decades—even centuries—of accumulated knowledge about cultural politics, racial inequities, and struggles for equitable public education in New Orleans.

Around the same time the *Guide* was released, Kristen Buras, author of this book and director of USGRC, participated in a forum sponsored by Harvard University's Graduate School of Education entitled "New Orleans Education Reform: Pass or Fail?". Usdin, NSNO's founder and former CEO, was the other participant. The two issues at the center of this chapter—human capital and charter school development—were vigorously debated (for video recorded forum, see Buras 2012b). Usdin, like many of those who advocate these reforms, ignored the viewpoints and experiences of those on the ground. This now familiar dynamic sets the stage for the analysis we will present.

In the *Guide's* foreword, Kingsland and Usdin acknowledge, "Tens of thousands of students, families, teachers, and leaders make up the New Orleans system, and we are in no position to speak for all of them" (Brinson et al., 2012, p. 11). We could not agree more. In fact, we have grave concerns that the stakeholders who were consulted for the *Guide* included only advocates of current reforms, such as state and district officials, charter school leaders, support organization leaders, education reformers, and philanthropists (p. 9). It is empirically unsound to make claims about the effects of reforms without consulting the communities most intimately affected by those reforms. This is where we enter, building on testimony and documentation provided by those who historically have worked in and had children attend the public schools of New Orleans. Our concern rests with communities across this nation that stand to lose, and to lose dearly, if the reforms in New Orleans are "taken to scale" in their own backyards.

A quick paragraph on NSNO's background will be helpful.

Background on New Schools for New Orleans

Founded in early 2006, NSNO is committed to human capital and charter school development. It seeks founders to *start* charter schools, principals to *lead* charter schools, teachers to *teach* in charter schools, members to *serve* on charter school boards, and investors and philanthropists to *contribute* to these efforts (NSNO 2008a, 2008b, 2008c). NSNO has partnered with the national organization New Leaders for New Schools (NLNS) to recruit, train, and place principals and other school leaders in the public schools of New Orleans (NSNO, 2010). An additional human capital initiative is teachNOLA, a teacher recruitment collaboration with the RSD and The New Teacher Project (TNTP), a national organization that "works with clients on a fee-for-service basis" to place "alternate route teachers" in "high-need schools" (TNTP, 2010). NSNO has received millions from nationally recognized, market-oriented venture philanthropies and from the federal government as part of its Investing in Innovation program (i3) through Race to the Top (Chang, 2010b; Maxwell, 2007; NSNO, 2012c). In fact, the *Guide* was written "to meet the [i3] requirement that grantees disseminate the lessons of their work" (Brinson et al., 2012, p. 9). In sum, NSNO has been at the forefront of human capital recruitment and the incubation of charter schools and charter school management organizations (NSNO, 2010, 2011).

In the *Guide's* foreword, Kingsland and Usdin stress: "If numerous cities undertook this course, our urban education landscape could be transformed over the next decade. ... We hope this guide will serve cities who wish to begin this difficult work" (Brinson et al., 2012, p. 11).

It would be wrong to assume that reforms have proceeded without resistance from affected communities. We now turn to the testimonies of longstanding community groups and relevant policy scholarship to raise questions about the *Guide* and warn education scholars, policymakers, and urban communities across the nation about the destructive reforms that education entrepreneurs hope to spread. What follows are some of the lessons we have learned since 2005.[1]

Human Capital Development

First Lesson: Marginalization of indigenous veteran teachers and leaders is viewed as innovative by education entrepreneurs, who recruit inexperienced staff to teach in charter schools at the expense of our children.

It helps to recall Kingsland's words at the Washington, DC, forum where Landrieu hailed the *Guide*. "The New Orleans story is really one of transferring power back to educators and parents," he proclaimed (Landrieu, 2012, para. 4). As we will show, this assertion is perverse in light of the evidence.

The *Guide* stresses that "charter growth requires high-quality teachers and leaders" and warns that "empowering underprepared educators is a dismal strategy." In our view, this is precisely what NSNO has done—empowered underprepared educators—through its human capital initiatives. While the *Guide* emphasizes that it is important to "empower existing talent," meaning local veteran teachers, the larger focus is on "recruiting new teachers and leaders" from beyond the city. "To effectively scale up a charter sector, cities must make themselves magnets for innovative talent," suggests the *Guide*. This is essential for attracting "national talent organizations," such as TFA or TNTP, and a city aspiring to replicate the New Orleans model should create a "buzz" and "market itself as one that embraces bold reforms" (Brinson et al., 2012, p. 24).

Short shrift is given to the role of veteran educators in an environment of bold reforms. In fact, the *Guide* explains, "Veteran educators may be skeptical of charter reforms." The reasons for this are not examined, although we explore them below. Instead the *Guide* indicates: "Effective, experienced teachers possess the knowledge and expertise honed through their years of teaching. They bring strong classroom management and deep experience in instruction, a *boon to a young charter staff*" (Brinson et al., 2012, p. 25; italics added). Here again, the emphasis is on young charter staff as the fulcrum for innovation and charter school development. The *Guide* provides the following advice:

> Cities should also use alternative certification organizations such as TFA or TNTP to staff their growing charter sector's schools. ... TFA is increasingly a market requirement. Many high-quality charter operators will not enter a market without a TFA presence, making clear the connection between human capital and charter growth.

In New Orleans, the *Guide* boasts, "30 percent of the city's teachers come from either TFA or TNTP."

The *Guide* does not examine what allegedly was wrong with the veteran teachers who were fired. It is implicitly assumed they were responsible for the failure of New Orleans public schools prior to 2005, thereby necessitating the recruitment of "new talent." There is no discussion of the history of racial inequity, white flight, and state disinvestment that contributed to the crisis in the city's public schools. This history is charted in previous chapters. It should suffice to underscore that black teachers with the same level of education and experience as white teachers were paid substantially less, while black students attended poorly maintained, overcrowded, and grossly underfunded schools. These were conditions challenged by black teachers. The era of desegregation brought massive resistance by whites.

From 1950–2000, New Orleans lost two-thirds of its white residents and state disinvestment in black education continued (Baker, 1996; DeVore & Logsdon, 1991). From the *Guide's* ahistorical standpoint, it appears black teachers somehow are responsible for the dire conditions they actually spent their lives fighting.

The *Guide* likewise fails to examine what precisely constitutes new teacher "talent" or why organizations such as TFA and TNTP should be considered "talent organizations." In one of the *Guide's* vignettes, entitled "Hire for Potential," readers learn about the efforts of Sean Gallagher to hire staff for Akili Academy of New Orleans, a charter school that Gallagher founded with support from NSNO. "The majority of teachers he ultimately hired," explains the *Guide*, "were inexperienced, nearly all from beyond New Orleans, and from Teach for America or other alternative routes." The vignette continues, "Despite his teachers' limited experience, Gallagher has been able to put together a staff that gets academic results for students." He hires those with the "necessary mission alignment and work ethic," which is all that seemingly is required to teach well. Yet Gallagher himself concedes that hiring such a high proportion of first-year teachers (who are uncertified) has required "an intentional focus on lesson planning." However, he goes on to note, "Our teachers write lesson plans that are 50 times better than the ones I wrote in my tenth year of teaching. So even if they are *not yet excellent at the execution of those plans* because they're new to teaching, their lessons are *still going somewhere* and students are learning" (Brinson et al., 2012, p. 26; italics added). This begs the question: If human capital initiatives are truly about recruiting the best and most "talented" teachers, shouldn't these teachers be excellent in the execution of their lessons?

Our own experiences and those documented by education researchers tell us that talent and excellence are not the most accurate descriptors of inexperienced teachers recruited through organizations such as TFA and TNTP. Over the course of a decade, for example, Veltri (2010) taught, observed, and interviewed hundreds of TFA teachers in urban schools and documented high turnover, inadequate pedagogic preparation, teaching out-of-field (including special education), class and race incongruence with students, and many other challenges. Speaking of TFA teachers, an experienced teacher in one school shared with Veltri: "They're smart; they're dedicated; but they haven't got a clue. . . . It's like they're playing like they're a teacher" (pp. 109–110). Indeed, many relied on a "trial and error" approach and "fillers" to get through the day and often the years, with 90 percent departing after three years. "The first year they try to figure out what they're doing," another veteran teacher explained, "and the second year they figure out where they're going" (p. 37). The effects of teacher inexperience and turnover on student achievement are documented in chapter 5 (see also Heilig & Jez, 2010; Wilson, 2009).

New Teachers' Roundtable (NTR) was founded by former TFA teachers in New Orleans who left TFA due to concerns about the effects of new teacher recruitment on the city's public schools. NTR works with early career teachers to become more informed about racial and educational injustice in New Orleans.

Reflecting on "new talent coming to the rescue" in New Orleans, one member of NTR discloses:

> TFA seemed like it would be a way to get started in teaching. I assumed based on their advertising that their summer training, while short, was state of the art and that I would have opportunities to observe great teaching and be mentored by seasoned veterans with impressive records. While at training for a total of five weeks, I team taught maybe ten 45-minute periods of math and reading to a group of 15 third graders. While our five weeks had been grueling, I couldn't say the time was well spent. What I remember is lots of busy work and pep rallies.

Even worse, he reports, a significant amount of time at summer training "was spent practicing how to justify our position as white middle-class teachers of mostly poor children of color." The response was made clear: TFA teachers would "overcome all possible cultural conflict" through "relentless work" and "high expectations." But what did these things mean exactly?

"For all their talk of holding children to high academic standards," writes this former TFA teacher, "I felt completely confined by the draconian structure of the lessons that were modeled for us." He reports:

> There was no room for critical thinking. Opportunities to speak were mainly restricted to reading the objectives or "key points" from a piece of butcher paper next to the "teacher." There was no open-ended group work. The proper answer to every question was utterly clear, visible from your desk on the butcher paper, or drilled incessantly through the "lesson."

Needless to say, when this TFA recruit was assigned to teach in New Orleans, he "felt like an impostor." "I hadn't even taught before," he reflects, "not to mention the fact that I had never before stood alone in a classroom full of students." What is more, although now responsible for students' learning, he still had not been connected with a veteran teacher for much-needed mentorship. He likens his experience to a fatally flawed rescue mission with students suffering the dire consequences:

> I was considered "new talent" and sent to New Orleans to rescue poor black children from a failing public school system. The reinforcements sent to rescue the children were unprepared and untrained. It was like being dropped from a helicopter to rescue the stranded and wounded with no tools and no capacity to give them access to what they needed. All this occurred while experienced, professional rescuers, veteran teachers, were essentially being asked to keep out.

He laments that the space for new teachers was created when the state-controlled Orleans Parish School Board illegally fired all of its employees in early 2006 (see also Nelson, 2010; UTNO et al., 2006, 2007).

Another TFA teacher, one affiliated with NTR and United Teachers of New Orleans, expressed grave concerns about the misinformation propagated by TFA:

> Having studied Sociology and Africana Studies in college, clearly I was equipped to enter a public school system and classroom of all students of color, wasn't I? That's what TFA told me anyway. I (and hundreds of others pretty similar to me) was just the person to touch a few lives and potentially be a "transformational teacher." I would later find out this was not true. Despite what TFA says, teaching is actually very hard.

This recruit questions whether or not TFA and other human capital providers are prepared to deliver on their promises. In the end, aspirations alone do not produce high performance, especially in a profession as complex as teaching (Ladson-Billings, 2009; Wilson, 2009).

A TFA teacher with like affiliations ponders difficult lessons from what she symbolically calls "Super Charter School," indicating that her experiences are similar to those of other new recruits in New Orleans' charters. She recollects how the principal of Super Charter "evaluated the effectiveness of our teaching by the extent to which we were all at the same place, at the same time, in the same pre-approved, administration-sanctioned, standardized lesson." Sadly, in Super Charter, it was standard procedure to treat teachers "as replaceable, mechanized parts within a well-oiled, so-called 'ed-reform-movement'" and students "as passive, empty vessels, desperately needing to be filled by our unimaginative, over-scripted lesson plans." The language that pervaded the school was most telling: noise level zero; eyes tracking the speaker; hold your bodies still—your voices are off, your eyes are on me; sit in scholar position; hands down, I am speaking. "As the months passed," she admits, "the system began to break me, too." This TFA teacher's analysis disrupts the notion that new teachers and charter schools bring innovation and excellence—a lesson to be heeded by communities seen as the next "market" for human capital and charter school development.

The consequences of all of this are made brutally clear through the story of one veteran teacher and union member in New Orleans. Her story is not completely unique and sheds light on the tragic face of human capital development. Returning to the city after the storm, this veteran teacher hoped to assist in reopening the public high school where she had taught for 30 years; she was heartbroken to return and find that her cherished collection of yearbooks going back to the 1970s had been destroyed. She welcomed the chance to spend the next summer enrolling students, although it would be a "new" era in the school's history. The school now would be privately managed as a charter school. Her excitement was short-lived:

> Daily, I realize that this new school is not the old one. It is not the family atmosphere that we had built through tradition. It has become a business venture, with the focus on dollar signs and test scores. Time and again, I

remember a colleague's words of distrust about charter schools. I begin to understand his mistrust and to develop my own.

Teaching, she feared, was taking a back seat to entrepreneurial considerations.

Several years before the storm, this veteran teacher developed a college writing course that she taught with stellar results. "Almost every student who took the class was placed in regular college English rather than remedial," she explains. The school's new operator said it could not afford to offer the class. At the end of her third year at her newly chartered high school, she was chosen by faculty for a teaching award. Nonetheless, she received news that her contract would not be renewed because, as she was told, "her value did not outweigh her liability." In short, the school could hire two-and-one-half teachers for the same cost as an experienced teacher.

The next year she taught at another charter high school in New Orleans. She regretfully shares, "It is not long before I realize that their promises of support are theoretical at best." She discovered that her "tried and true methods of teaching are not respected" and that she is expected to "teach according to the instructions of a woman who has never been in the classroom as a teacher." She is once again told at the end of the year that her contract will not be renewed, but refused to accept the decision this time. After much pressing, she was offered a part-time position as community service coordinator for $17,000 rather than the $56,000 she was earning. To the administration's surprise, she accepted. Meanwhile, they hired several more "inexpensive, uncertified, recent college graduates" to teach in her place. As she worked on various projects in her new role, she saw "a parade of English teachers" come through. In fact:

> Four different first-year teachers took a turn teaching the class I had taught for a lifetime. After each one is fired or resigns, students ask why I am not their teacher. After all, I am right there in the building. But instead of returning me to the classroom, another inexperienced young person is hired to give it a whirl.

Over December break, the existing principal was fired and the new principal fired the veteran teacher. This teacher reports:

> I refuse to leave and tell her that I will work for free until she can find the funds to pay me. The faculty is shocked by my boldness, but I must stand up for what I believe in. This school has no band, no choir, no football, baseball, or soccer team…only a basketball team, about which the administration complains incessantly because it costs money. How can we rebuild New Orleans if we do not rebuild its youth?

Meager funds were found to pay the teacher and she continued her work the next year—this time teaching a class on community service.

Meanwhile, the constant turnover of new teachers continues and the faculty of this largely black high school is more than 90 percent white and mostly from other states. Ultimately, this veteran teacher concludes, "The teaching profession cannot survive when the majority of those in classrooms are not there because they want to teach." Instead, she asserts, many come because loans will be forgiven through sponsoring programs. What about the pipeline of talent that TFA and other human capital initiatives were supposed to deliver?

In the *Guide's* foreword, Kingsland and Usdin mention that after the storm, "the district laid off every teacher, which led to a lawsuit that remains in court" (Brinson et al., 2012, p. 10). At the very least, this would suggest the claim that New Orleans-style reform has empowered educators is contested. This is never acknowledged. Rather, the *Guide's* history of reform in New Orleans states: "Without a student body to serve, Orleans Parish School Board was forced to terminate contracts with all teachers, effectively disbanding the teachers' union" (Brinson et al., p. 15). This account fails to square with the facts. The mass firing of veteran teachers was far from inevitable.

Less than six months after the *Guide* was released, the Civil District Court for Orleans Parish ruled that state education officials had used the storm as an excuse for the illegal mass firing of teachers, and that their actions were part of a political strategy to take over and charter New Orleans public schools (Civil District Court, 2012). As discussed in chapter 5, the court found the following:

- The Louisiana Department of Education and Orleans Parish School Board asserted that there was a shortage of teachers to hire. By October 2005, however, education officials had located nearly all Orleans Parish School Board employees, including thousands of certified teachers who had provided updated contact information and intent to return forms. Rather than hiring these teachers, the Louisiana Department of Education advertised nationwide for teacher positions with the RSD.
- Although there were thousands of certified, experienced Orleans Parish School Board teachers, the state Board of Elementary and Secondary Education approved a contract with TFA on April 20, 2006.
- Although the Louisiana Department of Education received over $500 million from the U.S. Department of Education based on the representation that it needed to pay the salaries and benefits of out-of-work school employees, it did not ensure that any of this money was used in such a manner. Rather, the money was diverted to the RSD and used in part to offer signing bonuses and housing allowances to teachers recruited from out of state. (pp. 20–22)

The tenured teachers who were fired illegally were not empowered by current reforms. Veteran teachers, a substantial portion of New Orleans' black middle class, suffered great harm.

Recruiting human capital is not NSNO's sole priority. Charter school development is another closely related initiative.

Charter School Development

Second Lesson: The development and expansion of privately managed charter schools threaten to restructure public education as a business, with indigenous traditions and place-based curricula giving way to management practices that have little connection to students and what they need to achieve and thrive.

The *Guide* delineates three strategies for taking the charter school market to scale in cities nationwide: converting existing traditional schools into charter schools; incubating new charter schools; and supporting the development of CMOs. In the first case, entrepreneurs are advised, "A city's charter market can take time to develop if charter growth relies solely on new-start schools or focuses solely on the takeover of the lowest performing schools" (Brinson et al., 2012, p. 28). The most ideal strategy, according to the *Guide,* is "converting a portion of a city's best schools early in the process," which "can quickly open the local market and increase the performance of already-successful educators" (pp. 28–29).

We find the recommendation to charter a city's best public schools remarkable. Education entrepreneurs have argued that privately managed charter schools are necessary because of the failure of government-run public schools. These bureaucratic entities, the argument goes, have no impetus to innovate or improve (Brinson et al., 2012; Broad Foundation, 2012b). Yet the *Guide* advocates chartering the "best schools" in order to open the local market and enhance existing achievement. In short, the *Guide* proposes that education entrepreneurs leverage the success of public education as their own, thereby justifying further penetration of public education by market forces, which are presented as the solution. This is ironic to say the least.

The story of a New Orleans high school student is relevant here. Writing for Students at the Center—a literacy program that builds on the voices and experiences of young people—this student reflects on the conversion of his public elementary school into a charter school after Katrina. He expresses pride in his academic performance prior to 2005, sharing: "When I began school, I immediately became attached to the environment. Whenever my first grade teacher asked students to read, I would always raise my hand high in the air." By the time he entered second grade, he was reading several grade levels ahead. By fifth grade, he had decided that he wanted to be a teacher when he grew up. This public elementary school in New Orleans was working—his reading and his aspirations were a testimony to this. Returning after the storm, he attended this same school, only this time it had been chartered. In fact, it was a charter school supported by NSNO. His experiences are illuminating:

My first day of 7th grade was a total shock to me—it was no longer my school. It was foreign to me: new paint, new teachers, new principal. Practically everything was new, except for some familiar faces of students I knew. The school was heavily promoted during orientation, which took place at some fancy hall. The people who ran our school showed us a video of how successful charter schools were run across the country. I couldn't believe my eyes as I watched these perfect kids on the big projector with their perfect smiles as if they were receiving the perfect education.

However, my school was nothing like that. One of the odd things I noticed most at school were the teachers. They were all young, very young. I still remember my 7th grade teacher. She was supposedly just my math teacher (the only subject she was qualified to teach), but then she discovered that she had to teach my class all core subjects. I began to realize that something was wrong when she spent more of her time burying her face in lesson plans than acknowledging the curious faces of students. I began to hate school. My classmates began to feel the same way too.

In his preexisting public elementary school, this student developed a passion for reading and even aspired to be a teacher. In his newly chartered school, one that was supposed to be much improved, he "began to hate school."

This student's account is not unique. Many students in New Orleans have expressed concerns about the conversion of their schools to charters (see Buras et al., 2010). As highlighted later, Dixson, Bigard, and student activists (2013) discuss a walkout—one that occurred when an NSNO-supported CMO planned to take over a historic high school. Such concerns, in fact, have led to the development of a group called United Students of New Orleans, a coalition of students organizing for equity and justice in the city's public schools (Ravitch, 2013b).

The *Guide* also suggests incubating new charter schools rather than solely converting existing public schools into charter schools. Once more, the recommendations provided are worrisome. After selecting a leader or entrepreneur to start a charter school, the process is described as follows:

> Incubators often run fellowship programs, providing a salary for a year or more while offering intensive training in *leadership, management, and finance.* ... [School leaders] *learn what works,* and visit or work in successful schools. In the year before the school opens, leaders identify and hire *management teams* that can plan together.
>
> (Brinson et al., 2012, p. 29; italics added)

Not a single word is dedicated to culturally relevant pedagogy, curriculum, or community involvement. Education is understood in financial and managerial terms, and apparently those who open charter schools can "learn what works" without doing much more than visiting or working in other schools for a limited period. What is more, the *Guide* underscores the importance of providing support services for "school founders who lack local community connections" (p. 29). Of course, this suggests a very serious question: Should anyone who lacks community connections actually start or lead a school attended by our children? This seems more than troublesome in our view.

Mos Chukma Institute, an indigenous arts program based in Martin Luther King Elementary School in New Orleans' Lower 9th Ward, illuminates why such reform is problematic. In its program, by contrast, students "connect with their culture, community, and personal inner resiliency." Essential to this work is:

> integrating Native, African, and African American teaching stories. The stories and songs are also correlated with indigenous science and local eco-systems: the wetlands, the bayou, the river. These teachings, these ways, of place-based education bring connection and engagement to our students; they reveal the science of the natural world and our place within it.

A majority of the school's teachers are veteran educators who were born and raised in New Orleans and have more than 25 years of experience in the classroom. Artist-educators with Mos Chukma Institute explain:

> Students do not question the commitment of their teachers. The teachers are sophisticated, master teachers whose dedication goes beyond the classroom. The children can feel this—they understand the difference between a community member and a visitor; someone who has one foot out the door, someone who does not try to understand them or may have another agenda entirely.

They stress, "We enjoy pursuing and answering our own questions, not out-of-life-context questions posed by folks who don't even know us." That is to say, the incubation of schools by those outside the community, and by those who view education as a business enterprise, is an affront to the cultural identity and integrity of students. These artist-educators warn:

> In the new charter school model being imposed on our schools, we see a reflection of a world riddled with crime as our students are treated like inmates prepared for death row, made to wear uniforms like Wal-Mart employees, and subjected to remedial tasks such as penciling in boxes and walking on taped lines in the hallway.

Contrary to this model, Mos Chukma Institute "teaches its students culturally relevant history and gives them the freedom to create their own."

In a similar way, the Guardians Institute in New Orleans builds on centuries-old traditions of racial resistance, ensuring that historic cultural practices are connected to youth development and education (Guardians Institute, n.d.; Kennedy, 2010; Woods, 2009; see also chapter 5). There are many other educational initiatives indigenous to city that could be mentioned. The point remains the same: It is an assault on the dignity and epistemology of black communities in New Orleans to assume that talented teachers, innovative leaders, and educational institutions need to be "incubated" from without, especially when there are such rich cultural traditions from within.

Lastly, the *Guide* suggests that taking charter schools to scale through the development of charter management organizations (CMOs) is a priority. "Starting a CMO poses additional challenges," states the *Guide*. CMO leaders manage multiple facilities, have more extensive back-office and legal requirements, and must orchestrate instructional and human capital efforts across schools in the network. If stand-alone charter school operators are akin to "small business owners," then "CMO leaders must manage the difficulties of operating a high-growth corporation" (Brinson et al., 2012, p. 31). To imagine and reconstruct schools in this manner is to alter in fundamental ways what it means to educate children, who we are asked to entrust to a corporation.

This is not a promising model to follow, especially when scholars have documented that charter schools do not outperform traditional public schools and often enough perform worse (Fabricant & Fine, 2012; Lubienski & Weitzel, 2010). Miron (2010) examined and synthesized the findings on student achievement in charter schools from a wide range of studies—ones varying by design and quality—and found that the general conclusion that could be drawn ten years ago remains the same today. "The overall picture," he writes, "indicates that charter schools perform at levels similar to those of traditional public schools." Notably, the inclusion of lower-quality studies "did little to change the overall findings" and studies done by independent researchers "tended to have a wide array of outcomes, with some positive, but most with mixed or slightly negative findings" (pp. 86–87).

Charter school performance in New Orleans has been disappointing, if not dismal (see Box 6.1). In sum, it is evident that the charter school model is not serving our children's best interests (see also Buras, 2012a, 2012b, 2012c; Hatfield, 2012; UTNO, 2011).

Special Education and the New Orleans Model

Third Lesson: Rather than universally respecting students' rights to learn, charter schools focus on cost containment in special education and may fail to adequately serve or exclude students based on such concerns.

NSNO's *Guide* sets forth a number of suggestions on special education. These are important to consider because charter schools in the RSD have significantly fewer special education students than direct-run public schools in the RSD, 8 and 13 percent, respectively (Cowen Institute, 2011, p. 7). The *Guide* acknowledges,

BOX 6.1   A NOTE ON ACHIEVEMENT IN NEW ORLEANS: INCREDIBLE GAINS IN STUDENT LEARNING?

At the forum in Washington, DC, Kingsland stated that charter school development in New Orleans has produced "incredible gains in student learning" (Landrieu, 2012, para. 4). Despite his and the *Guide's* claims about increased student achievement, charter schools in New Orleans are failing. Drawing on School Performance Scores (SPS) and letter grades provided by the RSD in 2011–2012, *Research on Reforms* offers the following summary:

- 100 percent of the 15 state-run RSD schools assigned a letter grade received a D or F;
- 79 percent of the 42 charter RSD schools assigned a letter grade received a D or F; and
- RSD schools that have been open for less than three years were not assigned a letter grade. (Hatfield, 2012)

Table 6.1 shows the cut points from 2004–2013. Note the cut point in 2004–2005 (and at the time Hurricane Katrina struck in August 2005) was SPS 60. Act 35, passed in November 2005, *raised* the definition of school failure from SPS 60 to SPS 87.4 to increase the number of "failing" public schools in Orleans Parish, allowing them to be taken over by the RSD and chartered (for more on Act 35, see chapter 2). In 2005–2006, the state *lowered* the SPS cut point back to 60—the pre-Act 35 SPS cut point—and it remained there until 2009–2010. The cut point never again approximated SPS 87.4, the standard used by the state to judge and take over New Orleans public schools in November 2005; it was 65 in 2010–2011 and 75 in 2011–2012. In 2012–2013, the cut point was set at SPS 50, *below* the previous year's standard of SPS 75; the scale was also changed from a 200-point scale to a 150-point scale; attendance and dropout figures were no longer counted as part of the SPS calculation; and a "bonus system" was created to reward schools serving low-performing students for progress on state-mandated assessments. Taken together, these changes translated into low-performing schools receiving higher letter grades without substantially changing their performance (see Table 6.2 for letter grade scales).

In 2012–2013, therefore, school performance in New Orleans "increased." State education superintendent John White (formerly RSD superintendent) betrayed the politics at work when he commented, "Changes made to the formula have led to real increases in student achievement" (LDOE, 2013, p. 1). The state declared in its annual letter grade release for 2012–2013:

- In 2004–2005, 78 public schools in New Orleans... were failing on the state's standards. Today, only 9 schools in the city... are failing.

TABLE 6.1 Louisiana School Performance Score (SPS) Cut Point, 2004–2013

School Year	Louisiana School Performance Score (SPS) Cut Point	Scale
2004–Nov. 2005	60	**0–200**
Nov. 2005 **(Act 35)**	**87.4** (retroactively applied to 2004–2005 performance data for takeover by RSD)	
2005–2006	60	0–200
2006–2007	60	0–200
2007–2008	60	0–200
2008–2009	60	0–200
2009–2010	60	0–200
2010–2011	65	0–200
2011–2012	75	0–200
2012–2013	**50** (formula for calculating SPS changed as well: bonus points, etc.)	**0–150**

TABLE 6.2 School Letter Grades by Scale, 2004–2013

2004–2012 0–200	A 120–200	B 105–119.9	C 90–104.9	D 75–89.9	F 0–74.9
2012–2013 0–150	A 100–150	B 85–99.9	C 70–84.9	D 50–69.9	F 0–49.9

- In New Orleans, only 5.7 percent of students now attend a failing school—down from 65 percent in 2005.
- 67 percent of students in New Orleans attend A, B, or C schools—up from 20 percent in 2005. (p. 2)

In its declaration, the state did not acknowledge or make explicit the fact that the standard used prior to November 2005 was more stringent than the current standard, among other differences that presently benefit charter schools (e.g., bonus points, selective entry and exit of students without consequence for performance calculations). The local *Times-Picayune* newspaper also reported on 2012–2013 gains in letter grades:

> Some long-subpar schools saw absolutely jaw-dropping gains. Of the 67 schools that had 2012 letter grades, 12 jumped two or more grades. Eight elementary schools climbed from F to C. ... [Two elementary schools] shot from F to B.

> Only six schools saw their letter grades drop. However, five [of those] are considered among the city's top schools.
>
> (Dreilinger, 2013, paras. 12, 14)

It also points out that schools in the "early stages of a turnaround effort" received a T from the state; in short, they were exempt and did not receive a performance evaluation. In New Orleans, the gains are more than incredible, they are *unbelievable*—literally.

In the final analysis, performance increases have been *legislatively contrived* by altering the cut point (as well as the formula by adding bonus points, etc.) to advantage charter schools. A higher standard was used to judge traditional schools in Orleans Parish in 2005, and a much lower standard has been used since that time to judge the city's charter schools.

NSNO and other groups advocating New Orleans as a model often present data on *percentage increases* and *growth in proficiency*, without addressing that the cut point and formula for calculating school performance have been altered by the Louisiana state legislature to advantage charter schools (Buras, 2012c; Nelson, 2013). For exactly these reasons, Nelson (2013) stresses that the research literature "is replete with warnings and detailed expositions of these measures' [percentage increases] limitations" (p. 7). Every valid study to date—ones that do not rely on such measures—shows that New Orleans charter schools have had no impact on achievement or, worse, have widened the gap between black and white students (Nelson, 2013). "The New Orleans miracle," writes Nelson, "appears to be the product of misleading accountability data" (p. 1).

Many other issues could be raised that pertain to performance data provided in NSNO's *Guide* (pp. 13–14). There is only space to mention two final concerns. Market advocates often aggregate data from charter schools in the Recovery School District and those under Orleans Parish School Board (OPSB). As explained in chapter 2, OPSB only retained a handful of the highest-performing schools after Act 35 was passed. As a result, inclusion of those schools artificially shifts charter school performance measures upward (Hatfield, 2012).

Finally, there is the issue, not a minor one, of "cherry picking" by New Orleans charter schools. Suspension rates in some charter schools are higher than 60 percent (JJPL, 2013a, 2013b). Data on dropout rates and graduation rates is strikingly inconsistent, which raises questions (Deshotels, 2011). Charter schools in New Orleans also have substantially fewer special education students, which can shift school performance upward. Traditional public schools in New Orleans served all students, including students with disabilities (Ferguson & Royal, 2010).

"Nationally, questions have been raised about charter schools' ability to provide adequate special education services or, worse, whether schools actively discourage students with disabilities from attending their school" (Brinson et al., 2012, p. 37). The *Guide* fails to mention that the same questions have been raised about charter schools in New Orleans, an issue addressed by Pyramid Community Parent Resource Center below.

It is distressing to read through the *Guide's* suggestions on special education. Cities adopting the New Orleans model are encouraged to do some of the following:

*   Allow charters to develop specialized programs for certain disabilities so that parents have choices that include programs tailored to their children's needs, and so that economies of scale can be captured in program delivery; and
*   Create risk pools that individual schools can participate in to cover the potential costs of serving students with high needs. (Brinson et al., 2012, p. 37)

For those families, educators, and scholars with an intimate knowledge of the rights of special education students, a number of problems are apparent here (e.g., see Welner & Howe, 2005). The notion that each charter school should develop a specialized program for certain disabilities sounds like segregation. This defies the principal of mainstreaming in the Individuals with Disabilities Education Act (IDEA) and sets charter schools down a path of potentially violating federal law. Moreover, there is the distinct impression that such suggestions address charter schools' concerns about the financial costs of serving special education students, rather than concerns directly associated with students' right to learn. In the *Guide,* special education appears to be a matter of cost containment for charter schools. It certainly should not be.

Pyramid Community Parent Resource Center was established in New Orleans in the early 1990s by parents of children with disabilities and supports families with special needs children in the city's public schools. Pyramid has "worked through placement and due process issues as well as behavioral challenges at school and mediations" for over 20 years. Advocates with Pyramid warn:

> Stepping back into New Orleans to deal with the redevelopment of the educational system after the storm was traumatic on multiple levels. The families we worked with had evacuated, schools were destroyed in many parts of the city, and the networks of people working for quality public education were obliterated. From this point forward the forces that represented privatization of public education, destruction of unions and the undermining of democratic control of schools became the driving force for educational change.

The climate in which NSNO issued its *Guide* is described as "one characterized by misinformation and disregard for truth." Part of this disregard relates to special education students and is evidenced in the *Guide's* recommendations. Advocates with Pyramid are aghast:

> Not once are the concepts of inclusion, Individualized Education Planning (IEP) and Least Restrictive Environment (LRE) mentioned as foundational aspects of the provision of services to children with disabilities. There is also no mention of connection with federally funded parent organizations that have a documented history of advocating for and supporting families of children with disabilities. Even after their experience with special education over the past seven years, the so-called reformers fail to grasp that there is a body of rights about which they should be aware. These protections do not need to be reinvented or edited for charter schools.

Needless to say, terminology such as "economies of scale" and "risk pools" does not sit well with special education advocates, those who respect federal law, or those who are concerned that inclusion "will be supplanted in favor of some form of segregation of children with disabilities."

Unfortunately, these worries are not unfounded. In October 2010, a federal civil rights lawsuit (*P.B. et al. v. Pastorek*) documenting violations of IDEA in more than 30 schools in the RSD was filed by the Southern Poverty Law Center (2010a). This class action lawsuit represents 4,500 students with disabilities who assert that they were denied appropriate services and/or access to public schools in New Orleans, the majority of them charters. In one case, for example, an eight-year-old student who is blind and developmentally delayed applied to eight different charter schools. Five said they would take the application but could not accommodate him; a sixth said it would accept him but was stretched thin; and a seventh said it had a solid program but access was not guaranteed due to a selective application process. The eighth school, which he attended, "had no services, materials, or support staff to help him" (Southern Poverty Law Center, 2010b). The lawsuit is ongoing, but the evidence appears compelling (Dreilinger, 2013; Southern Poverty Law Center, 2013).[2] We question whether or not such actions are a guide for cities, especially when reformers legitimize their efforts by claiming to serve those students most in need, even as they are excluded.

Top–Down Education Reform and the Paradox of Choice

Fourth Lesson: Human capital and charter school development are reforms imposed from above without genuine community engagement regarding how to improve local public schools.

There are serious concerns about whose decision it was to implement human capital and charter school development in New Orleans. "Failing to inform and engage communities can hobble citywide efforts to scale charters," reads the *Guide* (Brinson et al., 2012, p. 33). It is conceded that "the early stages of reform in New

Orleans were not—to the city's detriment—driven by grassroots efforts" (p. 34). This is not a minor point. It matters a great deal because it reveals that human capital and charter school development have been top-down reforms rather than bottom-up initiatives. This is also significant because education entrepreneurs claim support and authority for their alleged innovations under the banner of "school choice." By and large, however, communities in New Orleans have not "chosen" these reforms. Rather, these reforms most often have been rammed through against their will. The racial politics of charter school advocacy are relevant here. Scott (2013) argues that advocates of market-based school reform, many of them white and wealthy, have embraced the discourse of racial uplift to legitimize their efforts, even as they lack grassroots connections to communities they seek to transform. With this in mind, consider one last prompt offered in the *Guide*: "To increase community engagement and local support of charter schools, educational organizations and the government must implement a plan for closing schools and choosing new school sites that includes the community early in the process" (p. 34). Note the fact that school closings are not up for debate. The community is merely invited to participate in a process already determined by "reformers" to be in their best interest.

These dynamics are apparent in NSNO's 2008 operational plan, which predated the *Guide*. Under its advocacy objectives, specifically in relation to community leaders, the plan delineates the need to "map out which groups we need to build relationships with—both pro and anti-charter" and "create a strategy to influence all unaligned organizations" (Childress, Benson, & Tudryn, 2010, p. 408). Strategies premised on "influencing" community leaders rather than bringing them and their constituencies to the table to understand *their* concerns, needs and visions of education are not democratic. They are oppressive and make a mockery of genuine community engagement.

The experiences of the Lower 9 School Development Group (L9SDG) are relevant on this account (see chapter 3). Recall that L9SDG was organized to press the RSD and school facility master planners to fund and rebuild this historic neighborhood's only high school, which was destroyed in 2005. Despite the fact that the RSD received millions from the Federal Emergency Management Agency (FEMA) for damage to schools in the Lower 9th Ward, money was not allocated to rebuild schools there. It was instead put in a general fund to support school construction based on the vision of master planners, not community members (L9SDG, 2010, 2011; RSD & NOPS, 2008).

Adrienne Dixson has written with parent activist Ashana Bigard and students (2013) regarding the takeover and planned closure of Walter Cohen High School. In 2012, Future Is Now (FIN), a CMO supported by NSNO, signed a contract with the RSD to manage Cohen until its closure in 2014. Cohen College Prep High, a charter high school also supported by NSNO and part of the New Orleans College Prep network (NSNO, 2012a), occupies Cohen's second and third floors and is set to replace Cohen. On October 4, 2012, students were told about FIN's management contract, resulting in a protest by students, parents, and community members. They also issued a set of demands to RSD superintendent Patrick Dobard, including:

- Students cannot be bought and sold. [Our] opinions should have been considered, and [decisions] not done behind closed doors. Cohen students and parents demand real "CHOICE" to determine the governance of the school. Any previous decisions made determining the governance of Cohen should be reversed and required to go through a parent/student/teacher/administrator committee;
- ALL teachers and administrators must be retained. Any faculty member fired from school year 2012–2013 must be reinstated. We need written documentation demonstrating why any faculty members were dismissed. We need written documentation of any reprimands of faculty members. In the future, if a faculty member is to be dismissed, written documentation and a plan must be created and followed. ALL teachers and administrators must be fully certified by the state of Louisiana; and
- This type of hostile takeover did not just begin with Cohen—it has been going on since after Katrina. (Walter Cohen High School Students, 2012)

Cohen students were later joined by other high schools with similar concerns (see also Dixson, 2011). Sit-ins and walkouts at various high schools have continued, with students demanding books, "teachers they can relate to" and an end to "a strict discipline regimen that they feel is unfair and unyielding" (WDSU-News, 2013; WWL-TV, 2013).

Nonetheless, the inequitable dynamics surrounding top-down decisions about where to build schools, and who ultimately will teach in and lead those schools, continue to propel reform in New Orleans.

New Schools for New Orleans and a Growing Policy Network

If NSNO did not consult longstanding community-based groups, then who exactly was consulted regarding the "lessons" to be learned from New Orleans-style reform? The *Guide* provides a partial map of the elite policy network that has shaped human capital and charter school development in the city, with NSNO playing a central role. In closing, a sketch of this network or policy ecology (Ball & Junemann, 2012; Weaver-Hightower, 2008) is offered to render more transparent the self-serving and accumulative interests behind the New Orleans model. According to Weaver-Hightower (2008), policy ecology "consists of the policy itself along with all of the other texts, histories, peoples, places, groups, traditions, economic and political conditions, institutions, and relationships that affect it or that it affects" (p. 155). The *Guide* offers a glimpse into the people, institutions, and relationships supporting current reforms and reveals why our children were barely mentioned by NSNO, while words such as *human capital, labor costs, operating margins, market share, management,* and *portfolio* are used to describe the public schools in black working-class communities (Brinson et al., 2012). Close analysis of network relationships is revealing. A visual map is provided (Figure 6.1) to assist in following the complex interactions.

Usdin's work in education began in 1992 as a fifth-grade teacher in East Baton Rouge, Louisiana, where she taught for three years through TFA. From 1995 to 2000, she served as TFA's executive director in Louisiana, and from 2000 to 2005 she acted as founding partner for TNTP (Usdin, 2012).

In March 2006—just six months after the storm—Usdin founded NSNO. NSNO initially received $500,000 in seed money from the Greater New Orleans Foundation, which connects philanthropic donors with local organizations (Childress et al., 2010, p. 386). Anthony Recasner, a member of the foundation's board, would receive support from NSNO for charter schools he cofounded and operated through the CMO Firstline Schools, illustrating a tightknit circuit of power (Greater New Orleans Foundation, 2012; NSNO, 2012a). As Usdin's affiliations suggest, NSNO's founding and funding were not an accident, but were made possible by her and others' involvement in an elite policy network that stretches far beyond New Orleans.

Within weeks of the storm, Usdin rode in a National Guard helicopter alongside Walter Isaacson—native New Orleanian, president of the Aspen Institute (a think tank in Washington, DC), and chair of TFA's board at the time—to survey the city's destruction (Isaacson, 2007). Not only would the Aspen Institute become a hub for actors in a wider policy network supporting NSNO, but related philanthropies would provide financial resources. Isaacson (2007) explains:

> [Usdin's] work was supported by the NewSchools Venture Fund, a philanthropic investment fund started by two venture capitalists and Kim Smith, who launched it as her project when she had a fellowship at the Aspen Institute. … For the past three summers, fund members have convened a meeting in Aspen of educational entrepreneurs, and at the July 2006 gathering, they decided to make New Orleans a focus of their involvement.
>
> (para. 5)

NSNO received funding from NewSchools Venture Fund as well as the attention, human resources, and capital of education entrepreneurs throughout this policy network. Isaacson continues: "The attendees decided that they needed a 'harbor master' in New Orleans, someone who could coordinate the various organizations, funders and school operators. So one of the group, Matt Candler, was recruited to become [Usdin's] chief executive officer at [NSNO]" (para. 6). Indeed, Usdin reports, "There were many national players trying to figure out what to do, but there was not a logical place for them to go" (Childress et al., 2010, p. 386). NSNO would become a conduit for their influence.

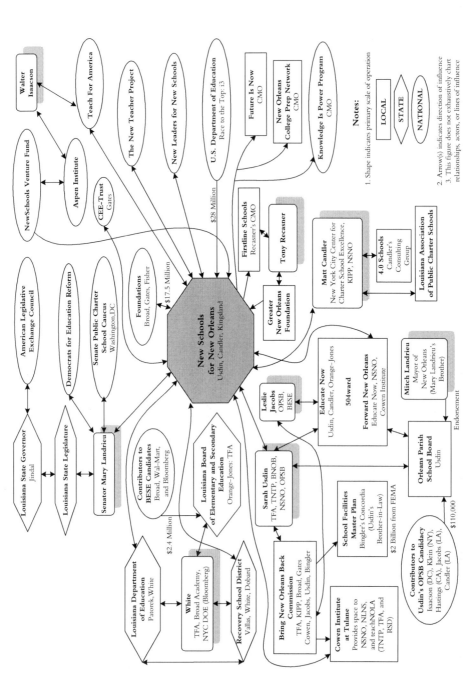

FIGURE 6.1 Policy ecology of New Schools for New Orleans

The following are the labels that appear in the figure:

Walter Isaacson

Teach For America

The New Teacher Project

New Leaders for New Schools

U.S. Department of Education
Race to the Top: 13

Future Is Now
CMO

New Orleans
College Prep Network
CMO

Knowledge Is Power Program
CMO

NewSchools Venture Fund

Aspen Institute

CEE-Trust
Gates

Foundations
Broad, Gates, Fisher

$17.5 Million

$28 Million

American Legislative Exchange Council

Democrats for Education Reform

Senate Public Charter School Caucus
Washington, DC

New Schools for New Orleans
Usdin, Candler, Kingsland

Firstline Schools
Recasner's CMO

Tony Recasner

Matt Candler
New York City Center for Charter School Excellence,
KIPP, NSNO

4.0 Schools
Candler's Consulting Group

Louisiana Association of Public Charter Schools

Greater New Orleans Foundation

Louisiana State Governor
Jindal

Louisiana State Legislature

Senator Mary Landrieu

Contributors to BESE Candidates
Broad, Wal-Mart, and Bloomberg

Louisiana Board of Elementary and Secondary Education
Orange-Jones: TFA

$2.4 Million

Leslie Jacobs
OPSB, BESE

Educate Now
Usdin, Candler, Orange-Jones

504ward

Forward New Orleans
Educate Now, NSNO, Cowen Institute

Mitch Landrieu
Mayor of New Orleans
(Mary Landrieu's Brother)

Endorsement

Louisiana Department of Education
Patorek, White

White
TFA, Broad Academy, NYC DOE (Bloomberg)

Recovery School District
Vallas, White, Dobard

Sarah Usdin
TFA, TNTP, BNOB, NSNO, OPSB

Orleans Parish School Board
Usdin

Bring New Orleans Back Commission
TFA, KIPP, Broad, Gates Cowen, Jacobs, Usdin, Binger

School Facilities Master Plan
Bingler's Concordia
(Usdin's Brother-in-Law)
$2 Billion from FEMA

Cowen Institute at Tulane
Provides space to NSNO, NLNS, and teachNOLA
(TNTP, TFA, and RSD)

Contributors to Usdin's OPSB Candidacy
Isaacson (DC), Klein (NY), Hastings (CA), Jacobs (LA), Candler (LA)
$110,000

Notes:

1. Shape indicates primary scale of operation

LOCAL

STATE

NATIONAL

2. Arrow(s) indicates direction of influence
3. This figure does not exhaustively chart relationships, actors, or lines of influence

To understand the interpenetration of local, state, and national networks, consider Candler for a moment. Prior to becoming NSNO's CEO, Candler worked for the New York City Center for Charter School Excellence and acted even earlier as vice president of school development for the Knowledge is Power Program (KIPP), a nationally recognized CMO that developed a network of schools in New Orleans with funding from NSNO (Childress et al., 2010). Within several years, Candler would develop his own consulting group in New Orleans called 4.0 Schools (2012), and also serve as chair of the Louisiana Association of Public Charter Schools (LAPCS). NSNO's *Guide* says LAPCS has been "instrumental in eliminating the charter cap, maintaining supportive finance laws, and generally protecting charter autonomy" (Brinson et al., 2012, p. 22).

By December 2007, Usdin and staff "fielded countless congratulatory phone calls from education reform leaders around the country" (Childress et al., 2010, p. 384). The Eli and Edythe Broad, Bill and Melinda Gates, and Doris and Donald Fisher Foundations had awarded $17.5 million jointly to NSNO, TFA, and NLNS to recruit new teachers and principals and open new charter schools in New Orleans (Maxwell, 2007). These national foundations—all created and financed by wealthy white philanthropists—clearly grasped that New Orleans was a malleable and opportune place for implementing the market-based reforms they hope to spread (e.g., see Saltman, 2010, for more on Broad).

The *Guide* acknowledges some of "the following people for sharing their time and insights." The list includes a cofounder of the CMO Firstline Schools; executive director of KIPP New Orleans Schools; partner of NewSchools Venture Fund; and executive director of the Louisiana Association of Public Charter Schools, Caroline Roemer Shirley. The report's external reviewers are also positively acknowledged, including Candler of 4.0 Schools; director of the Broad Foundation; and chief program officer of the Fisher Foundation (Brinson et al., 2012, p. 3). TFA and TNTP are mentioned throughout the *Guide* for their efforts in New Orleans.

Much of NSNO's early funding was based on its 2008 operational plan (Childress et al., 2010). The plan included advocacy objectives for building relationships with the Louisiana State Legislature, Louisiana Department of Education, Louisiana Board of Elementary and Secondary Education (BESE), and the state-run RSD. A few illustrations will demonstrate how state officials have embraced charter school reform to NSNO's benefit (see also Buras, 2011b, 2012a).

Senator Landrieu and her colleagues have played a major role in providing the legislative infrastructure necessary for the proliferation of charter schools in New Orleans. In the wake of Katrina, Landrieu became a darling of Democrats for Education Reform (2010), a political action committee with a market-based agenda nearly indistinguishable from Republicans. Her touting of the *Guide* in Washington, DC, is emblematic of her ongoing legislative work. John White, former RSD superintendent and current state superintendent of education in Louisiana, has been a big supporter of charter school expansion. White is a former TFA teacher and a graduate of the Broad Superintendents Academy, and was deputy chancellor for the New York City Department of Education under Michael Bloomberg, who closed public schools and replaced them with charters (Cunningham-Cook, 2012; Simon, 2012). Much like NSNO's ascendancy in New Orleans, White's climb up Louisiana's political ladder was not by chance. A number of now familiar billionaires, such as Eli Broad, Wal-Mart heiress Carrie Walton Penner, and Michael Bloomberg, contributed $2.4 million to support the campaigns of market-oriented candidates to BESE. By comparison, teacher union-endorsed candidates had only $200,000. BESE must approve the governor's nominee for state superintendent of education and the state superintendent plays a role in deciding which charter schools can operate in Louisiana (Cunningham-Cook, 2012). Ensuring White's approval by a like-minded state education board was essential. Not surprisingly, White and Paul Pastorek, the state superintendent previous to White, are acknowledged in the *Guide*, and Pastorek was appointed to the board of the Broad Center for the Management of School Systems (Brinson et al., 2012, p. 3; Broad Foundation, 2012a).

One of the above BESE candidates, Kira Orange-Jones, is executive director of TFA for Louisiana—the position that Usdin once held—and was bankrolled during her campaign with $472,000 compared to a meager $14,000 by the teacher union-endorsed candidate (Cunningham-Cook, 2012). An ethics investigation surrounding Orange-Jones' seat on BESE revolved around potential conflict of interest, since she simultaneously heads TFA in Louisiana and sits on a state board responsible for approving million-dollar contracts with TFA (Adelson, 2012).

Louisiana Governor Bobby Jindal is also a part of this policy network. Jindal advocated and signed anti-teacher union, pro-charter school legislation that is perhaps the most radical in the nation (Barrow, 2012a, 2012b), creating a hospitable operating environment for NSNO. Jindal received an award from the American Legislative Exchange Council (ALEC), a corporate front group that drafts model legislation for states. Between 2001 and 2010, ALEC companies spent over $3 million in Louisiana political campaigns, with Jindal receiving approximately $132,000 (Picard, 2013). ALEC, which met in New Orleans in 2011, has had a startling influence on Louisiana's legislation (Center for Media and Democracy, 2012; Picard, 2013; Pocan, 2011; Underwood & Mead, 2012).

Locally, the Education Committee of the Bring New Orleans Back Commission, which formed after the storm, had similar players. Its landmark report advocated the nation's first charter school district and touted the consultation of "top education experts," including Wendy Kopp, founder of TFA; Mike Feinberg, founder of KIPP; and Usdin. The Broad and Gates foundations were also consulted. Usdin's brother-in-law, Steven Bingler, owner of Concordia architects, sat on the stakeholder advisory committee (BNOB, 2006). Concordia later emerged as one of only two consulting firms that helped develop New Orleans' School Facilities Master Plan. It determined which schools would remain open, be closed, or be rebuilt. Ultimately, the plan was backed by $2 billion (billion, not million) from FEMA, a settlement partly negotiated by Landrieu (Chang, 2010a). The

Usdin–Bingler connection is important because most charter schools in New Orleans are given free access to facilities, which Bingler had a hand in shuttering, renovating, or building and Usdin in filling with charter operators.

Perhaps most revealing was the membership of the BNOB Education Committee. It included Tulane University President Scott Cowen, who headed the BNOB, and Leslie Jacobs, a wealthy New Orleans business woman whose role in charter school advocacy cannot be overstated (see below) (BNOB, 2006). The Cowen Institute for Public Education Initiatives, an action-oriented think tank at Tulane, provides free room and board to NSNO, NLNS, and teachNOLA (Buras, 2011b). Landrieu's former legislative aide worked for its public policy arm. Landrieu's brother, Mitch Landrieu, is mayor of New Orleans and endorsed Usdin during her school board campaign (Vanacore, 2012a).

Jacobs is a case study of policy networking. While an insurance executive and member of the Orleans Parish School Board, she sold insurance to the school district. She also sat on BESE and had a hand in shaping legislation that created the RSD. Since 2005, Jacobs has used her political influence to push charter schools and alternative teacher recruitment (New Orleans Independent Media Center, 2009). She developed *Educate Now* (2012), an advocacy group focused on market-based education reform in New Orleans. Its advisory board includes Usdin, Candler, Orange-Jones, and Roemer Shirley as well as associates from the Cowen Institute. Jacobs likewise founded *504ward* (504 is New Orleans' area code). 504ward (2012) provides social networking opportunities for "new talent" in the city, with the goal of retaining young entrepreneurial newcomers. The synergy with NSNO is obvious enough and it continues to build.

Usdin stepped down as NSNO's CEO to run for a seat on Orleans Parish School Board in November 2012 (Vanacore, 2012b). A group calling itself *Forward New Orleans for Public Schools*, which has Jacob's imprint, asked candidates in the election to sign on to its guiding principles (Forward New Orleans, 2012). There is growing recognition by education entrepreneurs that the state-run RSD will need to return schools to governance by the locally elected Orleans Parish School Board, and thus a board guided by principles of charter school autonomy and development is priority one. Organizations affiliated with Forward New Orleans include NSNO, Educate Now, and Cowen Institute, among others (Forward New Orleans, 2012).

The financing of Usdin's race for school board in November 2012 reflected network relationships. Usdin raised $110,000, an amount unheard of in local school board campaigns (Vanacore, 2012b). Campaign finance reports from the state reveal noteworthy contributors, including Candler, Jacobs and her husband, and Jacobs' brother Stephen Rosenthal, who is chair of NSNO's board; Isaacson; former New York City schools chancellor Joel Klein; and Reed Hastings of Netflix (Louisiana Ethics Administration Program, 2012).[3] By comparison, Karran Harper Royal, a public school parent and community-based education activist running for school board, registered $5,500 (Vanacore, 2012b). The local paper writes, "The list of contributors for Usdin stands as another testament to the national spotlight that has shined on New Orleans since the city began its controversial experiment with a system of autonomous charter schools" (Vanacore, para. 6). Jacobs and her brother are among the luminaries thanked in the *Guide* (Brinson et al., 2012, p. 3).

Aside from venture philanthropies, NSNO's other major funding stream is the federal Investing in Innovation program (i3), a component of Race to the Top. In 2010, NSNO received a $28 million grant to turn around schools in New Orleans and to extend its work to Memphis and Nashville; this was topped by $5.6 million in private funds, totaling $33.6 million (Brinson et al., 2012; Chang, 2010b). In fact, the *Guide* was written "to meet the Investing in Innovation (i3) requirement that grantees disseminate the lessons of their work" (Brinson et al., 2012, p. 9). The collaboration with Memphis and Nashville follows from Landrieu's affiliation with Senator Alexander from Tennessee, who co-chairs the Senate Public Charter School Caucus with her. In addition, NSNO has reached out to education entrepreneurs and policymakers in Denver, Detroit, Indianapolis, Seattle, and elsewhere, and participated on a panel in New Orleans for the Council of Chief State School Officers, which includes state and district superintendents from across the nation (NSNO, 2012b).

In a recent interview, Kingsland explained the following about the significance of this policy network:

> At the end of the day, we are morally accountable to the students of New Orleans and that's what motivates our staff. More practically speaking, we're accountable to where we get money from. That's the only reason we operate, is because other folks invest in us. ... So, just like anybody else we have to prove our worth and every couple of years we have to go back to the folks who have invested in us and show them results for them to continue investing.
>
> (Hess, 2012, p. 3)

This raises questions about whose interests matter most. When it comes to competing loyalties—one ethical and the other monetary—the danger is that financiers win out, especially when they are the "only reason" for NSNO's ongoing operation. It is clear who was consulted for the *Guide*: venture philanthropists, education entrepreneurs, and state allies. Kingsland's claim that reforms in New Orleans "empower parents and educators" falls flat. He who pays holds sway.

The monies flowing through NSNO's network are substantial and the priorities set for using financial resources, some of which come from federal tax dollars, have been questioned. In the excerpt that opened this chapter, we highlighted John McDonogh High School and the executive salaries paid to administrators of FIN, the CMO running McDonogh, through federal i3 grant monies distributed by NSNO. Around 55 percent of the grant monies from NSNO were designated for FIN salaries and benefits. In addition to the administrators already mentioned, grant monies paid 45 percent of the following FIN salaries: $130,000 for the director of community outreach; $150,000 for the president; $150,000 for the chief financial officer; and $135,000 for the director of policy development (Harden, 2013). Only $250,000 of the grant was allocated for a summer program attended by McDonogh students. In this case, due to "a delay in the preparation of the building," 45 teachers were paid for five 40-hour weeks, three of which were spent on faculty preparation. The remaining two weeks included a morning program for 280 students and afternoon planning time for teachers (Harden, 2013). In sum, for $250,000, students received summer programming for ten mornings; FIN teachers, mostly out of state recruits, were paid full-time for four weeks to prepare for ten mornings. In 2012–2013, McDonogh's SPS was 9.3 on a scale of 150.

Other CMOs in New Orleans have spent federal i3 grant monies from NSNO in a similar manner. Firstline divided $1 million during its first year among 20 different positions. Collegiate Academies spent 70 percent of $1.8 million on CMO salaries and benefits for employees working outside the schools in its network. Meanwhile, Firstline and Collegiate Academies are among the CMOs with the highest out-of-school suspension rates in New Orleans, alongside KIPP. Some NSNO board members also serve on CMO boards receiving i3 monies (Harden, 2013). Raynard Sanders, a past principal at John McDonogh and a longtime public education advocate in New Orleans, is concerned that the needs of students come last. Sanders concludes that NSNO and the CMOs it funds "act like private companies that don't have to answer to the public" and "are ripping off these communities" (Harden, 2013, p. 7). Unfortunately, the New Orleans model is spreading despite its ill effects.

BOX 6.2 CITIES FOLLOWING THE NEW ORLEANS MODEL

Look to New Orleans for a troubled schools turnaround model.
—Editorial Board of *St. Louis Post-Dispatch* (2013)

NSNO is a member of Cities for Education Entrepreneurship Trust (CEE-Trust), an undertaking to create the "ecosystem" necessary for charter school incubation and related reforms (Gray, Ableidinger, & Barrett, 2012). CEE-Trust is funded by the Gates Foundation, and policy partners include Mind Trust (CEE-Trust's founder), Center for Reinventing Public Education, and Fordham Institute—think tanks that authored the reports on New Orleans mentioned at the beginning of this chapter. CEE-Trust queries (2012): "Think you're...a 'flyover' city with no realistic possibility of attracting sufficient charter leaders and teaching talent?" As part of its 2012 meeting in Boulder, Colorado, the Trust gathered leaders from various cities to "make you think again" about the potential to attract like-minded reformers. It works with partners in cities across the nation to support the growth of entrepreneurial education initiatives.

From Chicago and Philadelphia to New York City, Detroit, Minneapolis, St. Paul, Milwaukee, Newark, Cleveland, Indianapolis, St. Louis, Memphis, Nashville, Atlanta, Denver, and Seattle, cities nationwide have implemented charter school and human capital development, building on the model established in New Orleans. Dixson, Royal, and Henry (2013) write: "An interesting commonality between Philadelphia, Chicago, and New Orleans... has been the leadership of Paul Vallas.... That Vallas used Philadelphia and Chicago as test runs for his complete dismantling of public education in New Orleans is obvious" (pp. 491–492). In Chicago, Lipman (2013) explains:

> The Chicago Board of Education has closed 105 public schools in African-American and Latino working-class low-income communities since 2001, while it has expanded its "portfolio" of charter and selective enrollment schools. ... Public hearings prior to the decision have become notorious for their mockery of democracy. ... Rallies, marches, pickets, petitions, candlelight vigils, and more have spared only a handful of schools.
>
> (pp. 11–12)

In Detroit, Michigan's governor appointed an Emergency Manager to run the city's public schools; 125 public schools have been closed in the last five years. By the end of 2011–2012, Detroit will not have a single neighborhood public high school (Lipman, 2013). "Public high schools are either selective enrollment or are part of the new state-run 'recovery district' á la New Orleans," writes Lipman (2013, p. 11). Pedroni (2011) notes that Detroit's mayor has a vision to remake urban space by:

> "clearcutting" and then mothballing "vacant" areas of the city for future development, with current residents of those areas enticed to leave through federally-subsidized purchase offers, and, for the more determined holdouts, through the discontinuation of vital services such as utilities and police and fire protection.
>
> (p. 207)

Closing schools in these areas has been a central part of the master plan. "The forced removal of those who remain in designated neighborhoods are cleared through a process... reminiscent of post-Katrina New Orleans" (Pedroni, p. 212). Once the land is cleared, investors and new public investment will flow in, with white urban "pioneers" reaping the benefits (Pedroni, 2013).

In New York City, the mayor closed over 117 schools since 2002. Picower (2013) reflects, "These closures and subsequent colocations of charters within closed or existing public school buildings force local communities brought together through their neighborhood schools to compete via lottery for coveted spots in charters" (p. 45). She regrets that hearings on New York City school closing have been described as a "sporting event" in which parents take sides, with one segment defending the neighborhood school and the other segment pushing for a charter school. Like USNO, students in Chicago formed the Chicago Student Union (CSU) to fight against school closings and charter schools (Burns, 2013; Stovall, 2013). Similarly, teacher activists in New York City have joined the Occupy the Department of Education (ODOE) movement, an educational outgrowth of the Occupy Wall Street movement, to battle market-based school reform (Picower, 2013).

As well, the New Orleans model has been borrowed globally. Toward the end of his tenure as RSD superintendent, Vallas traveled to Haiti and Chile to spread educational reforms piloted in New Orleans (Chang, 2011; Hagopian, 2011). "Vallas' scheme for Haitian education centers on maintaining a system in which 90 percent of schools are private—with the one modification that the Haitian government finance these private schools " (Hagopian, p. 2). Politicians from Honduras, where unionized teachers have been targeted and attacked for protesting privatization and leading democracy struggles, also visited New Orleans to learn some lessons (Martin, 2010).

In England, New Orleans has provided inspiration and guidance alongside market-based education reform in the United States more generally (Ball & Junemann, 2012). Absolute Return for Kids (ARK) operates a chain of academies, modeled on KIPP and US charter schools. ARK hired Jay Altman, cofounder of New Orleans' Firstline charter school network, as its education director. Altman also cofounded Future Leaders, a UK program that accelerates new teachers' entry into school leadership positions. Teach First (TF), which recruits, trains, and places new teachers in some of England's most challenging schools, was an innovation borrowed from TFA. Like New Orleans, many TF recruits teach in academies. Finally, Teach for All is a collaboration of global scope between TFA and TF, with education initiatives in Brazil, Chile, Argentina, Israel, Lebanon, China, Germany, Estonia, Latvia, Lithuania, Bulgaria, and Australia (Ball & Junemann, 2012).

The racial inequities and problems of accumulation by dispossession documented in this book have national and global relevance (see also Ravitch, 2013a).

A Different Blueprint for the Future

The *Guide* states that its purpose is to "aid others' efforts to build on New Orleans' success by providing tools and resources to guide their initial thinking, early work, and longer-term planning" (Brinson et al., 2012, p. 9). We are concerned that short- and long-term planning in other cities will continue to be guided by the example of New Orleans, with entrepreneurial interests undermining what should be a process of democratic decision making that includes working-class communities of color at the center of urban school reform. From the beginning, the New Orleans model has been a means for dispossessing black teachers, students, and families of public education resources (Buras, 2005, 2007, 2009; Buras et al., 2010). This model has enabled human capital and charter school development to proceed by undermining veteran educators and the teacher union, installing inexperienced staff from outside the community, and advancing the interests of charter school operators at the expense of the children they claim to serve (Buras, 2011b, 2012a, 2012b). The voices of community members have been marginalized and ignored, even as they continue to be raised in opposition (Buras, 2012a). It is time to recognize that the New Orleans model is a guide for white education entrepreneurs (and select allies of color) to racially reconstruct the city, including its schools, for their profit (Buras, 2013a).

Yet a different model is possible. We suggest that there are democratic and collective principles to guide reform of schools in New Orleans and other cities. These include ensuring public schools that are:

- *neighborhood-based*, supporting the restoration and rebuilding of racially and economically oppressed communities along lines that are self-determined and inclusive;
- *open access*, without either formal or informal barriers to student enrollment and retention;
- *respectful of the contributions, rights, and benefits of veteran teachers* who have been subjected to the loss of assets accrued through decades of public service and are best positioned to offer a curriculum that is grounded in students' history and culture;
- *prepared to recognize the teacher union* in collectively representing the interests of veteran educators;
- *welcoming of substantive and democratic participation of grassroots communities in educational decision making*, including plans for building and governing schools throughout the city; and
- *born from governmental transparency and accountability* in the allocation and use of public monies based on legitimate, sustained, and widespread community input.

We hope the lessons that we have learned allow working-class communities of color to challenge expansion of the New Orleans model to other cities. In the meantime, grassroots resistance continues to build in New Orleans.

Notes

1 Because this chapter is coauthored with members of USGRC and the original handwritten testimonies upon which we draw are not publicly available, page numbers are not cited when members are quoted.

2 In 2013, Southern Poverty Law Center (2013) submitted a memorandum in support of seven discrete subclasses of disabled students that allege discrimination, and the court has been asked to certify them and extend the case beyond the initial plaintiffs. Among the subclasses are:

- Students who have requested a special education evaluation that was *never completed* because the move to another school required the process to begin anew;
- Students given a "Response to Intervention" (RTI) program rather than a special education evaluation, even though IDEA specified that RTI (interventions for students who fail to respond to traditional classroom instruction) cannot be used to delay or deny evaluations to students suspected of having a disability;
- Students who have been given a less expensive 504 plan, meant to ensure that disabled students receive the same treatment as abled ones, rather than a special education evaluation that qualifies the student for a level of services that may be costly;
- Students removed for more than ten days in a school year without the timely provision of the disciplinary safeguards or the educational services required by IDEA if they are removed from the classroom;
- Students not provided services contained in their IEPs because autonomous schools cannot provide them cost effectively;
- Students with disabilities who have been denied admission or instructed not to apply to a public school on the basis of their disabilities; and
- Students with mobility impairments who have been denied access to programs and services of public schools as a result of structural or architectural barriers.

3 Reed Hastings, founder of Netflix and former board member of Microsoft, is also the cofounder and CEO of Rocketship Education, a national CMO that relies heavily on computer–based instruction. Rocketship submitted an application in 2011 to operate eight charter schools in New Orleans and East Baton Rouge (Rocketship, 2011).

References

4.0 Schools. (2012). Management team [Web page]. Available: http://4pt0.org/?page_id=15

504ward. (2012). Homepage. Available: www.504ward.com/

Adelson, J. (2012, August 2012). Kira Orange-Jones will keep seat on state board of education. *Times-Picayune*. Available: www.nola.com

Baker, L. (1996). *The second battle of New Orleans: The hundred-year struggle to integrate the schools.* New York, NY: HarperCollins.

Ball, S. J., & Junemann, C. (2012). *Networks, new governance, and education.* Bristol, UK: Policy Press.

Barrow, B. (2012a, April 4). Louisiana Senate votes to expand vouchers, public charter schools. *Times-Picayune*. Available: www.nola.com

Barrow, B. (2012b, April 4). Senate approves teacher tenure restrictions, pay changes. *Times Picayune*. Available: www.nola.com

Bring New Orleans Back Commission. (2006, January 17). Rebuilding and transforming: A plan for world-class public education in New Orleans. New Orleans, LA: Author.

Brinson, D., Boast, L., Hassel, B. C., & Kingsland, N. (2012). New Orleans-style education reform: A guide for cities (Lessons learned, 2004–2010). New Orleans, LA: New Schools for New Orleans. Available: www.newschoolsforneworleans.org/guide.

Broad Foundation. (2012a). Broad Center for the Management of School Systems announces four new members of board of directors [News release]. Los Angeles, CA: Author.

Broad Foundation. (2012b). 75 examples of how bureaucracy stands in the way of America's students and teachers [Web page]. Available: www.broadeducation.org/about/bureaucracy.html

Buras, K. L. (2005). Katrina's early landfall: Exclusionary politics behind the restoration of New Orleans. *Z Magazine, 18*(12), 26–31.

Buras, K. L. (2007). Benign neglect? Drowning yellow buses, racism and disinvestment in the city that Bush forgot. In K. Saltman (Ed.), *Schooling and the politics of disaster* (pp. 103–122). New York, NY: Routledge.

Buras, K. L. (2009). "We have to tell our story": Neo-Griots, racial resistance, and schooling in the other South. *Race Ethnicity and Education, 12*(4), 427–453.

Buras, K. L. (2011a). Challenging the master's plan for the Lower Ninth Ward of New Orleans. *Z Magazine, 24*(5), 19–22.

Buras, K. L. (2011b). Race, charter schools, and conscious capitalism: On the spatial politics of whiteness as property (and the unconscionable assault on black New Orleans). *Harvard Educational Review, 81*(2), 296–330.

Buras, K. L. (2012a). "It's all about the dollars": Charter schools, educational policy, and the racial market in New Orleans. In W. H. Watkins (Ed.), *The assault on public education: Confronting the politics of corporate school reform* (pp. 160–188). New York, NY: Teachers College Press.

Buras, K. L. (2012b, April 26). New Orleans school reform: Pass or fail? [Askwith Forum]. Boston, MA: Harvard Graduate School of Education. Available: www.youtube.com/watch?v=xb-qlt3O0As

Buras, K. L. (2012c, March). Review of "The Louisiana Recovery School District: Lessons for the Buckeye State." Boulder, CO: National Education Policy Center.

Buras, K. L. (2013a). Let's be for real: Critical race theory, racial realism, and education policy analysis (Toward a new paradigm). In M. Lynn & A. D. Dixson (Eds.), *Handbook of critical race theory in education* (pp. 216–231). New York, NY: Routledge.

Buras, K. L. (2013b). "We're not going nowhere": Race, urban space, and the struggle for King Elementary School in New Orleans. *Critical Studies in Education, 54*(1), 73–86.

Buras, K. L., Randels, J., Salaam, K. Y., & Students at the Center. (2010). *Pedagogy, policy, and the privatized city: Stories of dispossession and defiance from New Orleans.* New York, NY: Teachers College Press.

Burns, R. (2013, October 23). Schoolyard syndicalists: From the Chicago public school closings, some students emerge radicalized. *In These Times.* Available: http://inthesetimes.com/article/15745/schoolyard_syndicalists/

Center for Media and Democracy. (2012). ALEC exposed [Website]. Available: www.alecexposed.org

Chang, C. (2010a, August 26). $1.8 billion from FEMA for Hurricane Katrina school rebuilding is "worth the wait," Sen. Mary Landrieu says. *Times-Picayune.* Available: www.nola.com

Chang, C. (2010b, August 7). Charter incubator to get grant: It will help turn around more schools. *Times-Picayune.* Available: www.nola.com

Chang, C. (2011, February 21). Recovery School District's Paul Vallas to help overhaul schools in Chile. *Times-Picayune.* Available: www.nola.com

Childress, S. M., Bensen, S., & Tudryn, S. (2010). New Schools for New Orleans 2008. In S. M. Childress (Ed.), *Transforming public education: Cases in education entrepreneurship* (pp. 384–410). Cambridge, MA: Harvard Education Press.

Cities for Education Entrepreneurship Trust. (2012, October 4–5). October CEETreat agenda with session descriptions [Meeting agenda]. Boulder, CO: Author.

Civil District Court for the Parish of Orleans. (2012, June 20). *Eddy Oliver et al. v. Orleans Parish School Board et al.* [Reasons for judgment]. New Orleans, LA: Author.

Cowen Institute. (2011). NOLA by the numbers: School enrollment and demographics, October 2011. New Orleans, LA: Author.

Cunningham-Cook, M. (2012, October 17). Why do some of America's wealthiest individuals have fingers in Louisiana's education system? *The Nation*. Available: www.thenation.com

Democrats for Education Reform. (2010, September 13). Bursting the dam: Why the next 24 months are critical for education reform politics [Brief]. Washington, DC: Author.

Deshotels, M. (2011). New Orleans school dropout figures questionable [Policy brief]. New Orleans, LA: Research on Reforms. Available: www.researchonreforms.org/html/documentreposit.html

DeVore, D. E., & Logsdon, J. (1991). *Crescent City schools: Public education in New Orleans, 1841–1991*. Lafayette, LA: Center for Louisiana Studies at the University of Southwestern Louisiana.

Dixson, A. D. (2011). Whose choice? A critical race perspective on charter schools. In C. Johnson (Ed.), *The neoliberal deluge: Hurricane Katrina, late capitalism, and the remaking of New Orleans* (pp. 130–151). Minneapolis, MN: University of Minnesota Press.

Dixson, A. D., Bigard, A., & Walter Cohen High School students. (2013). New Orleans students protest for quality education and the right to fairness and dignity [Postscript]. *Berkeley Review of Education, 4*(1), 158–160.

Dixson, A. D., & Rousseau, C. K. (Eds.). (2006). *Critical race theory in education: All God's children got a song*. New York, NY: Routledge.

Dixson, A. D., Royal, C., & Henry, K. L. (2013). School reform and school choice. In H. R. Milner & K. Lomotey (Eds.), *Handbook of urban education* (pp. 474–504). New York, NY: Routledge.

Dreilinger, D. (2013, August 3). Unrelenting New Orleans special education problems alleged in new court filings. *TimesPicayune*. Available: www.nola.com

Editorial Board. (2013, August 17). Look to Louisiana for troubled school turnaround model [Editorial]. *St. Louis Post-Dispatch*. Available:www.stltoday.com/news/opinion/columns/the-platform/editorial-look-to-louisiana fortroubledschoolsturnaroundmodel/article_8f3131eb-d305–51be-b440-604b4d0dcd63.html

Educate Now (2012). Homepage. Available: http://educatenow.net/

Fabricant, M., & Fine, M. (2012). *Charter schools and the corporate makeover of public education: What's at stake?* New York, NY: Teachers College Press.

Ferguson, B., & Royal, K. H. (2010, April). Fewer special education students in charter schools [Brief]. New Orleans, LA: Research on Reforms.

Forward New Orleans for Public Schools. (2012). Forward New Orleans for Public Schools [Pamphlet]. Available: www.Schools.ForwardNewOrleans.com

Gray, E., & Ableidinger, J., & Barrett, S. K. (2012, August). Kick-starting reform: Three city based organizations showing how to transform public education. Indianapolis, IN: Cities for Education Entrepreneurship Trust.

Greater New Orleans Foundation. (2012). Board of trustees. Available: www.gnof.org/about/who-we-are/board/

Guardians Institute. (n.d.). *Background* [Brochure]. New Orleans, LA: Author.

Hagopian, J. (2011, September 9). Shock–Doctrine schooling in Haiti: Neoliberalism off the richter scale. *Common Dreams*. Available: www.commondreams.org/view/2011/09/09 13

Harden, K. (2013, October 28). Implementation of i3 education grant being questioned. *Louisiana Weekly*. Available: www.louisianaweekly.com/inplementation-of-i3-education-grants-being-questioned/

Hatfield, C. J. (2012, November 5). National model for reform or district in academic crisis? [Brief] New Orleans, LA: Research on Reforms.

Heilig, J. V., & Jez, S. J. (2010). *Teach for America: A review of the evidence* [Policy brief]. Boulder, CO & Tempe, AZ: Education and the Public Interest Center and Education Policy Research Unit. Available: http://epicpolicy.org/publication/teach-for-america

Hess, R. (2012, May 21). Straight up conversation: New NSNO CEO Neerav Kingsland. *Education Week* [Blog]. Available: http://blogs.edweek.org/edweek/rick_hess_straight_up/2012/05/straight_up_conversation_new_nsno_ceo_neerav_kingsland.html

Hill, P., Campbell, C., Menefee-Libery, D., Dusseault, B., DeArmond, M., & Gross, B. (2009, October). *Portfolio school districts for big cities: An interim report*. Seattle, WA: Center on Reinventing Public Education.

Hill, P., & Hannaway, J. (2006, January). *The future of public education in New Orleans*. In M. A. Turner & S. R. Zedlewski (Eds.), *After Katrina: Rebuilding opportunity and equity into the new New Orleans* (pp. 27–35). Washington, DC: Urban Institute.

Isaacson, W. (2007, September 6). The greatest education lab. *Time Magazine*. Retrieved from www.time.com/time/magazine/0,9171,1659767,00.html

Juvenile Justice Project of Louisiana [JJPL]. (2013a, September). *Suspensions matter: 2011–2012 year in review* [Report]. New Orleans, LA: Author. Available: http://jjpl.org/2013/news/jjpl-releases-suspensions-matter-2011–2012-year-review/

Juvenile Justice Project of Louisiana [JJPL]. (2013b). Suspensions matter: By the numbers, 2012–2013 [Flyer]. New Orleans, LA: Author.

Kennedy, A. (2010). *Big Chief Harrison and the Mardi Gras Indians*. Gretna, LA: Pelican Publishing.

Ladson-Billings, G. (2009). *The dreamkeepers: Successful teachers of African American children* (2nd ed.). New York, NY: John Wiley & Sons.

Landrieu, M. L. (2012, March 1). Landrieu hosts education panel and launches New Orleans style education reform: A guide for cities [press release]. Baton Rouge, LA: Author.

Lawrence, C. (1995). The word and the river: Pedagogy as scholarship as struggle. In K. Crenshaw, N. Gotanda, G. Peller, & K. Thomas (Eds.), *Critical race theory: The key writings that formed the movement* (pp. 336–351). New York, NY: New Press.

Lipman, P. (2013). Economic crisis, accountability, and the state's coercive assault on public education in the USA. *Journal of Education Policy, 28*(5), 557–573.

Louisiana Department of Education [LDOE]. (2013, October 24). Students, schools gain in annual letter grade release [Press release]. Baton Rouge, LA: Author.

Louisiana Ethics Administration Program. (2012, October 9). Sarah Newell Usdin [Candidate's report]. Available: www.ethics.state.la.us/CampaignFinanceSearch/

Lower 9 School Development Group [L9SDG]. (2010, October). Letter to Congress [Document]. New Orleans, LA: Author.

Lower 9 School Development Group [L9SDG]. (2011, August 8). Lower Ninth Ward School Development Group victorious in pressuring RSD to build high school in the Lower Ninth Ward [Press release]. New Orleans, LA: Author.

Lubienski, C. A., & Weitzel, P. C. (Eds.). (2010). *The charter school experiment: Expectations, evidence, and implications*. Cambridge, MA: Harvard Education Press.

Martin, N. (2010, September 17). President Lobo meets with Cowen, mayor, Lobo looks to New Orleans as model for rebuilding. *The Hullabaloo*. Available: http://thehullabaloo.com/2010/09/17/president-lobo-meets-with-cowen-mayor/

Maxwell, L. A. (2007, December 13). Foundations donate millions to help New Orleans schools' recovery. *Education Week*. Available: www.edweek.org

Meese, E., Butler, S. M., & Holmes, K. R. (2005, September 12). *From tragedy to triumph: Principled solutions for rebuilding lives and communities.* Washington, DC: Heritage Foundation.

Mind Trust. (2011). *Creating opportunity schools: A bold plan to transform Indianapolis public schools* [Report prepared by Public Impact]. Indianapolis, IN: Mind Trust. Available: www.themindtrust.org/files/file/opp-schools-full-report.pdf

Miron, G. (2010). Performance of charter schools and implications for policy makers. In C. A. Lubienski & P. C. Weitzel (Eds.), *The charter school experiment: Expectations, evidence, and implications* (pp. 73–92). Cambridge, MA: Harvard Education Press.

Nelson, F. H. (2010, September). Teacher quality and distribution in post-Katrina New Orleans [Brief]. Washington, DC: American Federation of Teachers.

Nelson, F. H. (2013). *Value-added measures of school effectiveness in New Orleans: Reassessing the miracle of the state takeover* [Report]. Washington, DC: American Federation of Teachers.

New Orleans Independent Media Center. (2009, July 20). Behind the curtain of the Louisiana charter school experiment [Article]. Available: http://neworleans.indymedia.org/print.php?id=14120

New Schools for New Orleans [NSNO]. (2008a). Lead [Web page]. Retrieved from http://newschoolsforneworleans.org/

New Schools for New Orleans [NSNO]. (2008b). Serve [Web page]. Retrieved from http://newschoolsforneworleans.org/

New Schools for New Orleans [NSNO]. (2008c). Start [Web page]. Retrieved from http://newschoolsforneworleans.org/

New Schools for New Orleans [NSNO]. (2010). Our impact [Web page]. Retrieved from http://newschoolsforneworleans.org/

New School for New Orleans [NSNO]. (2011). *Putting student achievement first: Annual update* [Report]. New Orleans, LA: Author.

New Schools for New Orleans [NSNO]. (2012a). Charter school investments [Web page]. Available: www.newschoolsforneworleans.org/charter-school-investments

New Schools for New Orleans [NSNO]. (2012b). National influence [Web page]. Available: www.newschoolsforneworleans.org/national-influence

New Schools for New Orleans. (2012c). Our donors [Web page]. Available: http:newschoolsforneworleans.org/

New Teacher Project. (2010). About us: Our business model [Web page]. Available: www.tntp.org

Osborne, D. (2012). Born on the bayou: A new model for American education. Washington, DC: Third Way.

Pedroni, T. C. (2011). Urban shrinkage as a performance of whiteness: Neoliberal urban restructuring, education, and racial containment in the postindustrial global niche city. *Discourse, 32*(2), 203–215.

Picard, N. (2013, April 26). Louisiana's great education giveaway [Guest blog]. Louisiana Voice. Available: http://louisianavoice.com/2013/04/26/guest-column-metairie-attorney-dissects-the-post-katrina-politicalization-patronage-of-louisiana-public-education/

Picower, B. (2013). Education should be free! Occupy the DOE!: Teacher activists involved in the Occupy Wall Street movement. *Critical Studies in Education, 54*(1), 44–56.

Pocan, M. (2011, October). Inside the ALEC dating service: How corporations hook up with your state legislators. *The Progressive, 75*(10), 19–21.

Ravitch, D. (2013a). *Reign of error: The hoax of the privatization movement and the danger to America's public schools.* New York, NY: Knopf.

Ravitch, D. (2013b, January 25). When students awaken, everything will change [Blog post]. *Diane Ravitch's Blog.* Available: http://dianeravitch.net/2013/01/25/when-students-awaken-everything-will-change-2/

Recovery School District [RSD] & New Orleans Public Schools. (2008, August). School facilities master plan for Orleans Parish [Public document]. New Orleans, LA: Authors.

Rocketship Education. (2011, August). Charter school application to the Louisiana Department of Education. Available: www.louisianaschools.net/lde/uploads/charter apps_f2011/Rocketship.pdf

Saltman, K. J. (2010). *The gift of education: Public education and venture philanthropy.* New York, NY: Palgrave Macmillan.

Scott, J. T. (2013). Rosa Parks moment? School choice and the marketization of civil rights. *Critical Studies in Education, 54*(1), 45–58.

Simon, S. (2012, August 16). Teach for America alumni at the head of the class. *Reuters.* Available: www.reuters.com/assets/print?aid=USBRE87F05S20120816

Smith, N. (2012, January). The Louisiana Recovery School District: Lessons for the Buck-eye State. Washington, DC: Thomas B. Fordham Institute. Available: www.edexcellence.net/publications/the-louisiana-recovery-school-district.html.

Solórzano, D. G., & Yosso, T. J. (2009). Critical race methodology: Counter-storytelling as an analytical framework for educational research. In E. Taylor, D. Gillborn, & G. Ladson-Billings (Eds.), *Foundations of critical race theory in education* (pp. 131–147). New York, NY: Routledge.

Southern Poverty Law Center. (2010a). *P.B. et al. v. Pastorek.* [Complaint]. Available: http://cdna.splcenter.org/sites/default/files/downloads/case/pb_v_pastorek.pdf

Southern Poverty Law Center. (2010b). Special education in New Orleans public schools. Available: www.splc.org/access-denied/special-education-in-new-orleans-public-schools

Southern Poverty Law Center. (2013, August 2). Memorandum of law in support of plain-tiffs' renewed motion for class certification. Available: http://bit.ly/19n3H6U

Stovall, D. (2013). Against the politics of desperation: Educational justice, critical race the-ory, and Chicago school reform. *Critical Studies in Education, 54*(1), 33–43.

Underwood, J., & Mead, J. F. (2012). A smart ALEC threatens public education. *Phi Delta Kappan, 93*(6), 51–55.

United Teachers of New Orleans [UTNO]. (2010, March). *The New Orleans model: Short-changing poor and minority students by over-relying on new teachers* [Report]. New Orleans, LA: Author.

United Teachers of New Orleans [UTNO]. (2011, July). Update on student achievement trends in New Orleans: Unprecedented growth or unprecedented hyperbole? [Brief]. New Orleans, LA: Author.

United Teachers of New Orleans [UTNO], Louisiana Federation of Teachers [LFT], & American Federation of Teachers [AFT]. (2006, November). "National model" or flawed approach? The post-Katrina New Orleans Public Schools [Report]. New Orleans, LA: Author.

United Teachers of New Orleans [UTNO], Louisiana Federation of Teachers [LFT], & American Federation of Teachers [AFT]. (2007, June). No experience necessary: How the New Orleans school takeover experiment devalues experienced teachers [Report]. New Orleans, LA: Author.

Usdin, S. N. (2012). Meet Sarah [Orleans school board campaign material]. Available: www.sarahusdin.com/meetsarah/

Vanacore, A. (2012a, October 26). New Orleans Mayor Mitch Landrieu endorses Usdin, Koppel and Marshall for school board. *Times-Picayune.* Available: www.nola.com

Vanacore, A. (2012b, October 9). Sarah Usdin draws $110,000 haul in Orleans Parish school board race. *Times-Picayune.* Available: www.nola.com

Veltri, B. T. (2010). *Learning on other people's kids: Becoming a Teach for America teacher.* Charlotte, NC: Information Age.

Walter Cohen High School Students, (2012, October 5). List of demands for Recovery School District Superintendent Patrick Dobard. New Orleans, LA: Author.

WDSU-News. (2013, November 15). High school students protest teacher's firing [Broadcast transcript]. Available: www.wdsu.com/news/local-news/new-orleans/high-school-students-protest-teachers-firing/-/9853400/22980804/-/8h5lpn/-/index.html

Weaver-Hightower, M. (2008). An ecology metaphor for educational policy analysis: A call to complexity. *Educational Researcher, 37*(3), 153–167.

Welner, K. G., & Howe, K. R. (2005). Steering toward separation: The policy and legal implications of "counseling" special education students away from charter schools. In J. T. Scott (Ed.). *School choice and diversity: What the evidence says* (pp. 93–111). New York: Teachers College Press.

Wilson, S. (Ed.). (2009, November). Teacher quality [Education policy white paper]. Washington, DC: National Academy of Education.

Woods, C. (2009). Upholding community traditions: An interview with Cherice Harrison Nelson. *American Quarterly, 61*(3), 639–648.

WWL-TV. (2013, November 20). Carver Collegiate students protest school conditions, discipline [Broadcast transcript]. Available: www.wwltv.com/video?id=232692271&sec=554637&ref=rcvidmod

APPENDIX

Methodology

As a New Orleans native, I have been involved in educational activism in the city for over two decades. Since 2005, I have conducted research focused on newly instituted education reforms, including charter school and human capital development, the political dynamics of policy formation, and effects on working-class communities of color (e.g., see Buras 2005, 2007, 2009, 2011a, 2011b, 2012a, 2012b, 2013a, 2013b; Buras, Randels, Salaam, & Students at the Center, 2010; Buras & Urban South Grassroots Research Collective, 2013). I travel to New Orleans at least once quarterly and generally stay for seven to ten days, working with educational and community organizations; meeting with teachers, grassroots activists, and other stakeholders; and collecting relevant documents. I am committed to this work because of the rich and complex cultural history of New Orleans as well as my enduring belief that the South remains an understudied yet crucial context for understanding black education and the politics of racial and economic power. Current educational reforms in New Orleans, and the struggles surrounding them, provide an important window onto these issues and also illuminate the implications of market-based education reform nationally.

In this book, I focus on data related to the recent history of educational policy formation and implementation with respect to charter schools and the racial, economic, and spatial dynamics shaping the reconstruction of New Orleans. The evidence used to inform my arguments is taken from historical, documentary, geographic, interview, and participant observation data. An archive of photos taken in New Orleans since 2005 also supports my analysis. Table A.1 provides a list of selected data sources and methods of data collection organized by institution.

I consulted primary and secondary historical sources, school district policies and documents, state data and reports, news articles from local and national sources, and organizations' literature, including their websites. With key documents, I performed several readings and made careful notations on content pertaining to race; political economy; past (pre-2005) and present (post-2005) educational assets and challenges; and perspectives on current school reform. In addition, I wrote informal memos and created sketches that charted confluent perspectives and linkages between policy actors at different geographic scales (local, state, and national), which required indexing and cross-referencing the content of documents. My procedure included network ethnography, which Ball and Junemann (2012) define as a method consisting of extensive Internet searches around particular edu-businesses and philanthropies; interviews with key edu-business people (and attendance at related meetings); and the use of these searches and interviews to construct policy networks (pp. 12–13). This was especially relevant to chapters 2 and 6. Further, Geographic Information System (GIS) technology was used to generate the racial demography map and school locations map in chapters 1 and 2, respectively. I am indebted to Jack Reed in the Department of Geosciences at Georgia State University for his technical expertise and assistance. Archives on Francis T. Nicholls High School (later Frederick Douglass High School) and United Teachers of New Orleans, both at the University of New Orleans, were pivotal to chapters 4 and 5, respectively. Teacher, administrator, alumni, and community interviews, documents from Students at the Center and Mos Chukma Institute, classroom-school observations, and public meeting observations and fieldnotes contributed to the case studies in chapters 3 and 4. For the case study on Martin Luther King Elementary in chapter 3, interviewees were given pseudonyms. Finally, the majority of photos included in this book are part of a visual archive that I have built to document the reconstruction of place and space in New Orleans since 2005.

I have interviewed a broad range of more than 50 education stakeholders. I conducted semi-structured life-world interviews (Kvale, 1996), typically lasting one to two hours. I interviewed organizers affiliated with a range of parent, teacher, school, and community reform organizations, including representatives of the state and local teacher unions and veteran teachers. I identify these latter two sets of interviewees by referring to them as either "representatives" of one of the teacher unions or "affiliates" (that is, veteran teachers). I transcribed each interview and coded for recurrent themes, made notations on the patterns observed, and authored analytic memos. I also took fieldnotes in multiple venues, such as classrooms, public meetings, and community spaces, and during ongoing informal exchanges with stakeholders.

Refrences

Ball, S. J., & Junemann, C. (2012). *Networks, new governance, and education.* Bristol, UK: The Policy Press.

Buras, K. L. (2005). Katrina's early landfall: Exclusionary politics behind the restoration of New Orleans. *Z Magazine, 18*(12), 26–31.

Buras, K. L. (2009). "We have to tell our story": Neo-Griots, racial resistance, and schooling in the other South. *Race Ethnicity and Education, 12*(4), 427–453.

Buras, K. L. (2011a). Challenging the master's plan for the Lower Ninth Ward of New Orleans. *Z Magazine, 24*(5), 19–22.

Buras, K. L. (2011b). Race, charter schools, and conscious capitalism: On the spatial politics of whiteness as property (and the unconscionable assault on black New Orleans). *Harvard Educational Review, 81*(2), 296–330.

Buras, K. L. (2012a). "It's all about the dollars": Charter schools, educational policy, and the racial market in New Orleans. In W. H. Watkins (Ed.), *The assault on public education: Confronting the politics of corporate school reform* (pp. 160–188). New York, NY: Teachers College Press.

Buras, K. L. (2012b, March). Review of "The Louisiana Recovery School District: Lessons for the Buckeye State." Boulder, CO: National Education Policy Center.

Buras, K. L. (2013a). Let's be for real: Critical race theory, racial realism, and education policy analysis (Toward a new paradigm). In M. Lynn & A.D. Dixson (Eds.), *Handbook of critical race theory in education* (pp. 216–231). New York, NY: Routledge.

Buras, K. L. (2013b). "We're not going nowhere": Race, urban space, and the struggle for King Elementary School in New Orleans. *Critical Studies in Education, 54*(1), 19–32.

Buras, K. L., Randels, J., Salaam, K. Y., & Students at the Center. (2010). *Pedagogy, policy, and the privatized city: Stories of dispossession and defiance from New Orleans.* New York, NY: Teachers College Press.

Buras, K. L., & Urban South Grassroots Research Collective. (2013). New Orleans education reform: A guide for cities or a warning for communities? (Grassroots lessons learned, 2005–2012) [Afterword by A. D. Dixson, A. Bigard, and Students of Walter Cohen High School Students]. *Berkeley Review of Education, 4*(1), 123–160.

Kvale, S. (1996). *Interviews: An introduction to qualitative research interviewing.* Thousand Oaks, CA: Sage.

TABLE A.1 Selected Data Sources and Methods, 2005–2013

Entity, Organization, or Field Site	Methods of Data Collection
State Government	
Louisiana State Legislature: governor, senators, and representatives who pass and administer laws in Louisiana and mediate between government authorities at local and federal levels	Documents (e.g., state constitution, education laws, Minimum Foundation Program, news articles)
Louisiana Board of Elementary and Secondary Education (BESE): state-level body that makes policy for public schools in Louisiana and governs Recovery School District	Fieldnotes; public hearing transcripts; documents (e.g., reports, news articles)
Recovery School District (RSD): state-governed school district, under authority of Louisiana state superintendent of education and BESE, that took over "failing" public schools in New Orleans	Public meeting observations; fieldnotes; documents (e.g., school district data, reports, School Facilities Master Plan, news articles)
Local Government	
Bring New Orleans Back Commission (BNOB): commission established by mayor to formulate plans for city's reconstruction	Documents (e.g., online materials, committee reports)
Orleans Parish School Board (OPSB) and New Orleans Public Schools (NOPS): locally governed school district under authority of locally elected OPSB	Documents (e.g., online materials, school district data, reports, news articles)
Nonstate Actors	
Cowen Institute for Public Education Initiatives: action-oriented think tank at Tulane University	Interviews; fieldnotes; documents (e.g., annual reports, surveys, white papers, newsletter)
New Schools for New Orleans (NSNO): charter school incubator	Fieldnotes; documents (e.g., organizational pamphlets, online materials, news articles, Parents' Guide to Public Schools)
teachNOLA–Teach For America–New Teacher Project: alternative teacher recruitment triad affiliated with Recovery School District	
New Leaders for New Schools (NLNS): school leader and charter school board member recruitment and training initiative	
New Orleans Parent Organizing Network: parent organizing partner associated with above organizations	
Louisiana Federation of Teachers (LFT): state affiliate of American Federation of Teachers	Interview; documents (e.g., letters to state officials, legislative briefs, broadsides)
United Teachers of New Orleans (UTNO): local affiliate of American Federation of Teachers	Group interviews; fieldnotes; documents (e.g., policy briefs, reports, video)
Veteran teachers: native-born teachers who have taught in NOPS for 10–35 years	Individual and group interviews

(Continued)

Entity, Organization, or Field Site	Methods of Data Collection
Martin Luther King Elementary School: longstanding open-access public elementary school in Lower 9th Ward	Oral histories; school–community event observations; fieldnotes; documents (e.g., newsletters, school program materials); school–neighborhood photos
Mos Chukma Institute: indigenous healing-arts program at King Elementary school	Documents (e.g., program materials, audio-visual materials, class projects); fieldnotes
Lower 9 School Development Group (L9SDG): community-based organization focused on School Facilities Master Plan and rebuilding of schools in Lower 9th Ward	Interviews; fieldnotes; documents (e.g., demographic survey, architectural plans, call for Congressional investigation)
Frederick Douglass High School: longstanding open-access public high school in Upper 9th Ward	Public meeting observation; fieldnotes; alumni and community interviews; Douglass Community Coalition documents (e.g. mission statement, correspondence); school–neighborhood photos
Students at the Center (SAC): writing and digital media program partly housed at Douglass High School	Teacher interviews; documents (e.g., SAC books and digital media materials); classroom observations at Douglass; participant observation in SAC story circles
Guardians Institute: school and community-based youth program that upholds New Orleans' cultural and indigenous arts traditions	Documents (program materials; books; audio-visual materials); published interview; curriculum materials; participant observation at community events; fieldnotes; photos
Save Our Schools–New Orleans, Louisiana (SOSNOLA): grassroots parent organization focused on equity and school reform	Interview; documents (e.g., petition, online materials)

Archives

Orleans Parish School Board Collection, Francis T. Nicholls Series: archive at Earl K. Long Library of University of New Orleans	*The Rebel Yell* student newspaper; school yearbooks; documents; photos
United Teacher of New Orleans, Local 527 Collection: archive at Earl K. Long Library of University of New Orleans	Oral history interviews; newspaper clippings; documents (e.g., staff writings, memos)
Primary and Secondary Historical Writings	Historical literature (e.g., reports, journal articles, books) was consulted on New Orleans public schools, black veteran teachers in New Orleans, and black teacher associations in Louisiana

INDEX

Note: 'n' after a page number indicates a note; 'f' indicates a figure; 't' indicates a table.

Made in the USA
Columbia, SC
30 August 2019